MUSIC, ART, CULTURE,
AND POLITICS FROM
AROUND THE WORLD

GIRL FRIDAY BOOKS

Published by Girl Friday Books™, Seattle
www.girlfridaybooks.com

Produced by Indelible Editions

INDELIBLE
EDITIONS

Design: Andrea Duarte

Cover credits: Volodymyr Tverdokhlib/Shutterstock.com,
Ian Littlewood/Alamy Stock Photo
Interior credits begin on page 271.

ISBN (hardcover): 978-1-954854-73-4
ISBN (e-book): 978-1-954854-85-7

Library of Congress info:
2022908050

First edition

BELLS

MUSIC, ART, CULTURE, AND POLITICS FROM AROUND THE WORLD

JAAN WHITEHEAD

IN HONOR OF MY GREAT-GRANDMOTHER
NANNIE SPELMAN MELVILLE

AND WITH LOVE FOR MY DAUGHTER,
SARAH

The Great Bell Chant

May the sound of this bell penetrate deep into the cosmos
Even in the darkest spots living beings are able to hear it clearly
So that all suffering in them ceases
Understanding comes to their heart
And they transcend the path of sorrow and death.

The universal dharma door is already open
The sound of the rising tide is heard clearly
The miracle happens: a beautiful child appears in the heart
Of a lotus flower.

One single drop of this compassionate water is enough
To bring back the refreshing spring to our mountains and rivers.

Listening to the bell I feel the afflictions in me begin to dissolve
My mind calm, my body relaxed
A smile is born on my lips
Following the sound of the bell
My breath brings me back to the safe island of mindfulness
In the garden of my heart, the flowers of peace bloom
Beautifully.

—THICH NHAT HANH, ZEN BUDDHIST MONK

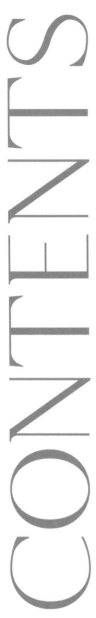

INTRODUCTION

I n the early evening of April 15, 2020, the deep tolling of "Emmanuel," the largest and oldest bell at Notre-Dame Cathedral, rang out over Paris to mark the anniversary of the great fire that had destroyed so much of the cathedral one year earlier. As the world watched in horror, the roof of the cathedral went up in flames and its steeple collapsed. The fire came within a half hour of reaching the Gothic towers that housed the cathedral bells before it was stopped, saving the bells.

One of those bells was "Emmanuel," cast in 1681 at the behest of King Louis XIV and rung for France's most historic occasions. Choosing to toll "Emmanuel" as the sole commemoration of this anniversary was a stirring tribute to the resiliency of the cathedral, the bells, and the French people.

"Emmanuel" is one of many remarkable bells in the world. The Yongle Bell in Beijing is twenty feet tall and covered with 130,000 characters of Buddhist teachings, which flow out into the air when it is rung. The Tsar Kolokol in Moscow is so large that the area inside the bell was consecrated and used as a chapel. The Chion-in Bell in Kyoto takes seventeen people to ring and leads the ringing of all the Kyoto bells on New Year's Eve. And the Bell for the Fallen in Rovereto, Italy, cast from the metal of weapons used in World War I, rings every evening in remembrance of soldiers lost in war.

Besides these grand bells, there are many bells that are remarkable in less spectacular and quieter ways: the charm of wind chimes in the breeze, the tinkle of a baby's rattle, the echo of a ship's bell across the water, or the somber ringing of the death bell tolling out the years. There are musical bells like the glorious Chinese chimes and startlingly beautiful bells like the Byodo-in Bell in Japan. And there are bells that surprise us like the bell on the International Space Station 230 miles above the Earth.

All of these bells are part of a fascinating story that reaches back to the earliest days of mankind, for bells are one of the great artifacts of history. Spanning time and space, they have appeared in every society in every time period and played a wealth of roles in these societies. Many cultures have attributed sacred power to bells, their sound being the "voice" of God in Christianity, the "voice" of the Buddha in

"Emmanuel," the largest bell at Notre-Dame Cathedral, is rung for France's most important occasions. Cast 350 years ago, it weighs thirteen tons and is considered one of the finest bells in Europe.

Buddhism, and the "voice" of supplication to ancestors in other religions. Often, bells were believed to have magical powers. Warriors wore them around their necks or on their clothing to protect them in battle or used them to put curses on their enemies. Sailors long thought that ship's bells could protect them from the dangers of the sea, and early Christian monks carried bells to ward off evil spirits. And, in all cultures, bells have played more prosaic roles: the clocks, school bells, fire bells, and telephone bells of daily life.

The stories gathered here explore this world of bells; their magic and mysticism, their political and religious power, their wide-ranging musicality, and their familiarity in our everyday lives. But there is another story behind these stories about the origins of the book and the journeys that created it, journeys I took in the footsteps of my great-grandmother.

This story begins in 1924 when my great-grandmother, Nannie Spelman Melville, sailed out of New York Harbor for a three-year trip around the world. On this trip, she collected small handbells, which my mother inherited and which were in a corner cupboard in our dining room when I was growing up. There were elephant bells from India, a bronze bell in the shape of a fish from China, a water buffalo bell from Java, two English altar bells carved with images of the four Apostles, and many small bronze bells shaped like Dutch boys and girls with pantaloons, mop caps, and wooden shoes. Fascinated by these bells, I would sit in front of the cupboard and imagine the stories each bell had to tell.

It wasn't until many years later, when my mother sent me the bells while I was setting up a new apartment in New York, that I learned Nannie's story. Born in 1855, shortly before the Civil War, Nannie grew up in Baltimore and married a man named James Moore Melville. They lived in Baltimore for many years and had nine children, two of whom died young. In 1891, the family moved to Chicago for Jim's

Nannie as a young woman in Baltimore.

work and bought a rambling house just north of the city near Lake Michigan, where their last child was born. These were happy years. Nannie entertained, joined clubs, did social work, and witnessed the marriages of many of her children.

child to child. As soon as she arrived at Carey's, she went to a travel office and booked a ticket on the *President Garfield*, one of the Dollar ships leaving New York the next week. Without any other preparation, she took the train to New York, boarded her ship, and

The stories gathered here explore this world of bells; their magic and mysticism, their political and religious power, their wide-ranging musicality, and their familiarity in our everyday lives.

This world started to slip away from her in 1911 when she was diagnosed with cancer, had extensive surgery, and was an invalid for more than a year. Under the stress, Jim started having attacks of angina that became more and more severe until he died in 1914 at age sixty-one. With Jim's death, Nannie's financial situation became precarious. She didn't have enough money to maintain the life she had been leading and had to sell her house, using the proceeds to live on. Without a home, she started living with her children a few months at a time. Eventually she tired of this and imagined she could live abroad more cheaply than at home, while also having the adventure of travel. She began reading about the Dollar Steamship Lines and their around-the-world trips where you could pay one fee and get on and off their ships at different ports, depending on your schedule. On her way to another extended stay with her son Carey in Massachusetts, she realized how weary she was of going from

sailed out of the harbor on October 2, 1924. Almost seventy years old and traveling alone with limited funds, it was a remarkable undertaking for a woman in that era.

Nannie sailed down the East Coast to Cuba, through the Panama Canal and up the West Coast to San Francisco, the home port of the Dollar Lines. In San Francisco, the ship provisioned before going on to Honolulu. Nannie stayed in Honolulu for a year with her son Malcolm, who was stationed in the navy there, and took courses in Chinese literature and art at the University of Hawaii.

When Malcolm was posted home, Nannie continued on her trip around the world. She had remarkable adventures: encountering civil war in China, riding a camel in Egypt, being in Bethlehem for Christmas Eve, attending a grand procession at the Vatican and the opera at La Scala, experiencing a mutiny on one ship and an outbreak of smallpox on another. She traveled to Japan, China, the Philippines,

Nannie collected these small Dutch bells in 1926 and 1927 while she was traveling in Europe. The two tall bells, the lady carrying an umbrella (left) and the monk-like man with a book (right), came from Belgium. The smaller bells were collected in the Netherlands and show the "mop" caps and wide pantaloons typical of the era.

Nannie in later life when she was living in North Carolina.

Burma, and Ceylon before spending a month in Palestine and Egypt and then going on to Europe. While in Italy, she began what became one of the great joys of her trip, seeing the famous paintings she had read about or seen photos of all her life. In the Uffizi and later in the Louvre, the Tate, and the Antwerp Royal Gallery of Art, she stood in front of paintings for hours, savoring their beauty. In Belgium, she fell in love with the medieval town of Bruges, which she used as a base for exploring the rest of Europe. It was during the many stops on this long trip that Nannie collected her bells.

Finally, it was time to go home, and she sailed out of Genoa on October 4, 1927, again on the *Garfield*. She had been away for three years. There had been times during her journey when she got discouraged; when she suffered from heat or, one time, had the flu, or the weather was rough at sea or rainy on land, or, more often, when her mail didn't catch up with her for a long time and she had no word from home, making her feel "dreadfully alone," as she put it in her memoir. But no matter how down she felt, her spirits always picked up when a new interest captured her imagination or she met new friends to share her adventures. She had great emotional and physical resiliency, and any times of doubt were outweighed by the excitement of her travels.

After arriving home, Nannie lived with her children again until she finally found a good home for her later years with Emma, her son Donald's widow, in North Carolina. During this period of her life, she wrote her memoir and started giving talks about her bells to women's groups. Nannie died in 1940

NANNIE'S MEMOIR
MAY 1926

During the years I lived abroad, I paid many visits to the old city of Bruges in Belgium. It is such an historic city; the residents are past-masters at getting up parades and pageants, both religious and historic. The bell concerts in the "Grand Palace," as they call the market square, were delightful. Sometimes the St. Cecilia chorus was in one of the lower galleries of the Belfry and sang to the music of the bells. We always engaged a table at one of the eating and drinking places opposite the Belfry and sat there during the concert. No vehicles were allowed in the square, and busses brought hundreds of tourists from Ghent, Ostend, and Brussels. It was very gay and delightful.

Chinese Mandarin hat button bells have colorful enamel bases covered with spiritual symbols, such as bats and plum blossoms. Their handles are imitations of the jewels worn on the hats of high-ranking Chinese officials.

at the age of eighty-five and is buried in Chicago next to her husband.

With Nannie's story in my head and her bells on my bookshelves, I found myself drawn more and more into the world of bells. I started collecting bells of my own and meeting other bell collectors through the American Bell Association. I even hosted a meeting of the New York chapter of the association at my apartment, where I told Nannie's story and showed her bells. She would have smiled if she had known that, three generations later, her bells were again being talked about and admired.

I also started gathering everything I could find on the history and lore of bells. There were so many different kinds of bells. There were tiny bells, less than an inch high, and giant bells over twenty feet tall. There were plain bells and harmonious ones. There were round, square, and rectangular bells and ones made of metal, porcelain, and glass. There were bells for everyday use and for special occasions, bells that created wonderful music, and deeply sacred bells that expressed a society's relationship with its gods and ancestors. Bells were musical, political, religious, artistic, economic, and cultural. And, like Nannie's bells, each had a story to tell.

My fascination with bells then took a new path. As I became more attuned to the world of bells, I started noticing them in the world around me, and every once in a while a bell seemed to speak to me. The first was a bell hanging in a tall, elegant frame in Temple Square in Salt Lake City, Utah, which turned

As I continued my journey into the world of bells, I reached farther out into the world, exploring stories of pyramid bells in West Africa, reindeer bells in Arctic Norway, Buddhist temple bells in Japan, and a stunning set of bronze chimes from ancient China.

out to be the Nauvoo Bell commemorating the pioneer trek to Salt Lake made by the Mormons in the 1840s. That bell led me to many more, and I started collecting the stories of these special bells—the bells on the Ringling Bros. Bell Wagon in the Circus World Museum in Baraboo, Wisconsin; the bell brought up from the wreck of the *Edmund Fitzgerald* to serve as a memorial for its lost crew; and the wonderful peal of bells at the church of St. Mary-le-Bow in London, a center for the English practice of change ringing.

As I continued my journey into the world of bells, I reached farther out into the world, exploring stories of pyramid bells in West Africa, reindeer bells in Arctic Norway, Buddhist temple bells in Japan, and a stunning set of bronze chimes from ancient China. There were also early Christian bells on the lovely Scottish island of Iona, Russian chime bells, sacred Tibetan handbells, early Belgian carillons, and the bell on the International Space Station.

Over the next twenty years, I traveled to China, Japan, Norway, England, Scotland, and Canada, as well as many places in the United States, in search of these stories. All of these journeys were surrounded by periods of research and reading that were almost as much fun as the trips themselves. At one point in Nannie's memoir, she says that, when in the midst of a particularly exciting experience, she often felt that she was just "bubbling over." I felt that way many times over these years.

The stories in this book are a legacy of Nannie and a tribute to her spirit of adventure. The stories begin in ancient China, range through Japan, Tibet, and Africa, move on to Europe, Russia, and the United States, and end on the International Space Station. Because the stories are so diverse, I have prefaced them with two background chapters, one on the history and culture of bells and one on bells and their music.

Nannie's bells are still sitting on the bookshelves in my apartment in New York. They kept me company while I was writing these stories. Now they are joined by other bells I collected during these years—tall glass English wedding bells in jewel colors of red, blue, and green; ornate porcelain bells from Meissen in Germany; fanciful green flint glass bells with coordinated clappers and handles from France; enamel bells with highly colored patterns and handles shaped like the eight Taoist Immortals; Chinese hat button bells using the hierarchy of colored jewels used on Mandarin hats as handles; a Tibetan ritual bell; a unique silver bell of a woman with raised arms designed by Salvador Dalí; and many more. Although many of these bells are grander and more colorful than Nannie's bells, her bells remain the heart of the collection, always reminding me of her remarkable adventures.

Author with the bell at Hoko-ji Temple in Kyoto.

PART I

THE WO
BELL

RLD OF
S

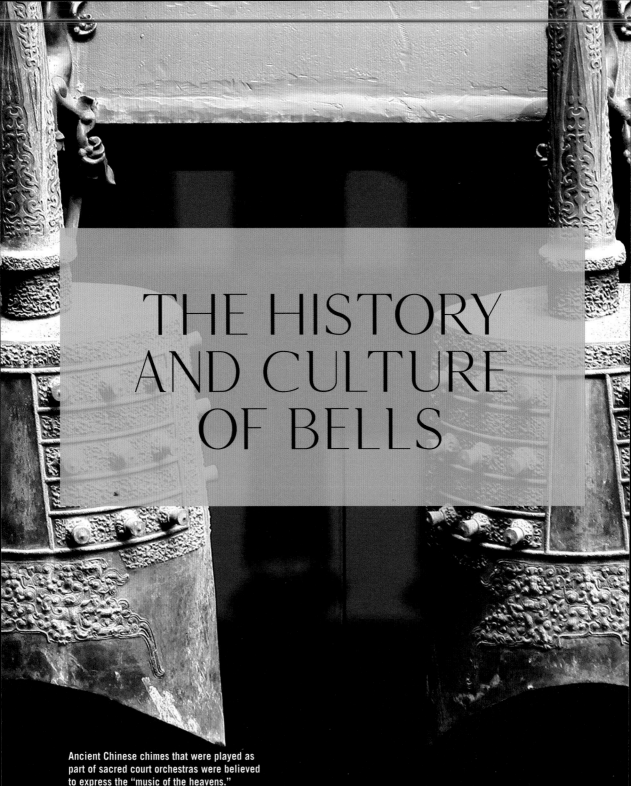

THE HISTORY AND CULTURE OF BELLS

Ancient Chinese chimes that were played as
part of sacred court orchestras were believed
to express the "music of the heavens."

The HISTORY *of* BELLS

Although bells are prevalent in cultures across the world, the most important distinction in their historical development is between Eastern bells and Western bells. As with many technological advances, bells in the East developed much earlier than bells in the West, creating two distinct historical lineages. The bells of these lineages also evolved with different shapes, sizes, and appearances.

BELLS OF THE EAST

In almost all societies, bells first appeared in the form of what today we call crotals, which are tiny, round objects with a small opening holding a pellet that makes a noise when shaken. All early tribes, whether in America or Africa or the Far East, developed some form of sound instruments from natural materials, and one of the most common was the crotal. Although different materials were used over time—the most stunning being the gold crotals of the Incas and Aztecs—their basic form and use have changed little. Today, crotals are still used throughout the world in rituals and as ornaments on clothing and, more familiarly, as sleigh bells.

The more sophisticated history of bells began with the development of metal. The sound of bells comes from the vibrations in the material they are made of, and metal vibrates more clearly and has richer tones and aftertones than other materials. The earliest metal bells, probably made of copper, were hand-forged by hammering pieces of metal flat and then folding them over and attaching the sides to form a rectangular-shaped bell. Either hit from the outside with a stick or hammer or from the inside by a small clapper, these early bells had a dull, flat sound.

When it was discovered that mixing a small amount of tin with copper created a far superior metal, bronze alloy became the dominant form of metal, ushering in the Bronze Age around 3000 BCE. Bells made of bronze were found to have a finer tone, particularly after casting replaced hand-forging as a way to make bells. When bells are cast by pouring molten metal into a mold and allowing it to cool, a smoother surface is created that does not have the indentations and roughness common to hand-forged bells. Casting also allowed bells to be made in a variety of shapes, and it was soon discovered that the rounder the bell, the more even the vibrations and the purer the note.

Because Eastern societies were so much more developed than Western societies at the time of the Bronze Age, the East took the lead in the development of bells. From archeological evidence, we know that China has one of the oldest bell cultures. Besides crotals, small bells called ling were in use by 2000 BCE. Crude bells made by hand, first in pottery, then in metal, they had an unusual almond- or fish-mouth-shaped rim with a clapper inside. Ling were probably used on animals to signal their presence.

By 1500 BCE, a more sophisticated bell had developed called a nao. Now cast in bronze, these bells were much larger and had a shape feet, were hung on chime racks and played as part of sacred court orchestras. The bells covered many octaves, and each bell could produce two different notes, depending on whether it was struck on the front or the side of the bell, a remarkable achievement. These bells dominated Chinese society for a millennium, holding great spiritual, political, and social power. Their complex musicality was one of the

---

The bells covered many octaves, and each bell could produce two different notes, depending on whether it was struck on the front or the side of the bell, a remarkable achievement. These bells dominated Chinese society for a millennium, holding great spiritual, political, and social power. Their complex musicality was one of the highest accomplishments of the Bronze Age.

---

like a truncated grain scoop with a shank handle. Struck from the outside with a mallet or stick, they continued the early almond- or fish-mouth-shaped rim and were decorated with animal and other motifs. Often grouped together in threes and attached to a base, they were played musically, one of the first instances we know of musical bells.

With time, the nao became larger and more resonant, evolving into magnificent bell chimes. By 500 BCE, these bells, now known as yongzhong or bianzhong (zhong meaning bell), became some of the most beautiful and technically sophisticated bells the world has ever known. Sets of up to sixty-five bells, ranging in size from a few inches to almost four

highest accomplishments of the Bronze Age.

After the unification of China in 221 BCE, these beautiful chime bells fell out of favor and were gradually replaced in importance by large Buddhist temple bells that had straight or sloped sides and long waists with rounded shoulders and rounded mouths. Hung from ornate frames, these temple bells were struck from the outside by a large mallet, emitting a deep, sonorous boom. As temple bells became larger and larger, often over ten feet tall, they became the largest hanging bells in the world, like the Hoko-ji Temple bell on page 24. Because of their size, it often took several men to ring the bells by striking them with large, swinging logs. In monasteries, such bells were

A Nao bell, one of the earliest-known bronze bells that developed in China, was one of the first examples of bells being played musically.

The temple bell at Hoko-ji Temple in Kyoto is one of many monumental Buddhist temple bells found throughout the world.

often paired with large drums, each in its own housing, the drum being sounded in the morning and the bell at evening time.

The look of the temple bells varied from country to country in the East; sometimes the mouth of the bell was a plain circle and sometimes a scalloped one, sometimes the bells were elaborately decorated, and sometimes they were quite plain. Wonderful examples of these huge bells can be seen at the Great Bell Museum in Beijing, where two large rooms are filled with rows and rows of them, overwhelming in their presence. Also in the Great Bell Museum is the famous twenty-foot-high Yongle Bell, a stunning bell to see. Many other magnificent temple bells can be seen throughout the East, particularly in Cambodia, Myanmar, and Japan.

Confucian and Taoist temples also used large temple bells, and an additional attraction of Confucian temples was the special use of pien chung and pien ching. Pien chung are racks of small bell chimes similar to the early Chinese chimes. Pien ching are racks of stone slabs that resonate like bells. In Confucian temples, the two sets of musical instruments were played off against each other, first the bell chimes and then the echo of the stone chimes.

Throughout the East, bells proliferated through history, becoming a rich part of each country's culture. In addition to large temple bells, there were many smaller bells used in ritual ceremonies, as well as tiny wind chimes tinkling under the eaves of pagodas and other buildings. All of these bells can still be found in most Eastern countries today.

BELLS OF THE WEST

While China was creating magnificent sets of chimes, Western societies were still using primitive, hand-forged bells. Casting did not become common in Europe until the sixth and seventh centuries CE, and the knowledge of how to successfully tune bells did not come until much later, in the seventeenth century. The carillon, the Western descendent of the Chinese chimes, was not developed for another 2,000 years.

With time, the West acquired the knowledge to make and tune fine bells, but the bells created in the West had different shapes, sizes, and decorations than Eastern bells. In the West, bells have a conical shape, with rounded shoulders, an inward curving waist, and a flared lip. In contrast, in the East, bells are either straight-sided or have slightly rounded sides. Also, Eastern bells are rung by being struck on the outside by a stick or mallet, rather than from the inside with a clapper, and many are very large, even monumental, in size compared to the smaller bells in the West. Eastern bells also tend to be more ornate than Western bells, often featuring elaborate symbols and decorations.

Western bells developed with the development of Christianity. The earliest Christian

Throughout the East, bells proliferated through history, becoming a rich part of each country's culture. In addition to large temple bells, there were many smaller bells used in ritual ceremonies, as well as tiny wind chimes tinkling under the eaves of pagodas and other buildings.

The mission bells at San Juan Capistrano are typical of the bells the Spanish brought to the California missions in the eighteenth and nineteenth centuries. Many still ring today.

bells were simple handbells carried by hermits and monks to announce their presence and protect them from evil spirits. They were hand-forged, often of iron, and had a tinny sound. As monasteries were formed, larger bells were made that were hung on the walls of the monasteries to call the community together and regulate the time. By the sixth and seventh centuries CE, bronze casting developed in Europe, particularly in Italy, and larger, more ornate bells were made and started being adopted in churches, as well as monasteries. In order for the sound of the bells to go out over a larger area, the bells were made even larger and hung in towers, bell towers becoming a distinctive part of Christian architecture.

Western bells evolved as people learned what gave a bell a melodic sound. First, the crude, rectangular shape of the early bells was made rounder, which improved the tone, then the lip was flared to give the clapper a longer arc of motion, and the waist was narrowed, yielding the bell shape familiar to us today. But it wasn't until the sixteenth and seventeenth centuries that an understanding of the tonality of bells developed in Europe, and Western bells could be played musically.

Today, both Eastern and Western countries have wonderful bells that enrich their societies in many ways, but a traveler moving from East to West will still be surprised by the differences in the bells of Eastern and Western countries.

The CULTURE *of* BELLS

Although Eastern and Western bells have different histories, the roles they play in society are remarkably similar across cultures. The most important distinction in the culture of bells is the distinction between sacred and secular bells and the profound importance this has in understanding the power that bells have held in many societies. Because we live today in such a secularized world, it is easy to forget that, for most of history, the sacred worlds of religion and myth dominated societies. Only over time did these sacred worlds become diminished in favor of the secular worlds of man and science. The further you go back in history, the more sacred and complex bells become.

SACRED BELLS

Throughout human history, people have reached out to find something greater than themselves, something to aspire to, to relieve their suffering, and to give greater meaning to their lives. Underlying these efforts has been the assumption that there is a world beyond what humans can see and experience, a world that is inherently good and harmonious. This is the mysterious realm of the sacred, the world of gods, natural spirits, and ancestors who have the power to intervene in the human world and provide the means for its protection. The role of most religions is to provide a connection to this sacred world, a framework

of belief and a set of rituals that can bridge the divide between the human and sacred worlds. Bells are an important part of these rituals. These are the sacred bells of history.

In ancient China, rulers believed that the music of bells, if properly rung, replicated the ideal harmony between heaven and earth, and was the model for human behavior. This music was also the center of important rituals used to appeal to the ancestors for their blessings on the empire. Such bells became one of the ruler's most jealously guarded possessions.

In Buddhism, the sound of bells has always been the "voice" of the Buddha calling people to enlightenment. This "voice" comes not only from the great temple bells but from small Buddhist bells, such as the beautiful handbells of Tibet, which are some of the most spiritually powerful bells in the world.

In Christianity, bells were believed to have magical powers. The bell's metal was believed to carry the power to repel evil, while the prayers and warnings inscribed on bells were considered to be prophetic. But, most of all, it was the mysterious, lingering sounds of bells that made them seem magical. In many Christian churches, bells were treated almost like people; they were baptized to give them names and set apart for sacred use; the clapper was called a tongue; and each bell was believed to have its own unique "voice." Many of the inscriptions on bells used the personal pronoun

The handles of the Taoist Immortal bells depict the Eight Immortals. The Immortals carry something symbolic that reflects their distinctive personality, such as a musical instrument or a magic fan.

"I," referring to the bell. One such inscription found on an old English bell stated:

I praise the true God, I summon the people, I assemble the clergy, I mourn the dead, I put plague to flight, I grace the feast, I wail at the funeral, I abate the lightning, I proclaim the Sabbath, I arouse the lazy, I scatter the winds, I soften the cruel.

Many other parts of the world also created notable sacred bells. There were beautiful Indian handbells with handles depicting Hindu deities and equally beautiful Taoist handbells whose handles depicted the Eight Immortals. In Africa, many bells were used. A double bell—two bells attached by a common handle—called a ngonge was found in many areas of Africa. Whole bells were cast in the shapes of animals or human heads, and many bells had handles depicting humans or deities. Africa is also the home of the famous quadrangular bells of Benin. Egypt, Turkey, the Middle East, and most other areas also had a wide variety of sacred bells. The only countries where sacred bells are not found are Islamic countries. Islam is the one religion that does not use bells because they are believed to disturb the currents in the atmosphere that are reserved for departed souls and the daily calls to prayer, both central to Islamic practice.

Sacred bells have played powerful roles in the spiritual life of societies throughout history, carrying in them a mystery that often feels strange today. The stories of history's sacred bells put us back in touch with the awe and beauty of these bells and remind us that sacred bells continue to play powerful roles in many cultures today.

SECULAR BELLS

Secular bells are the bells of our everyday lives: the school bells and bicycle bells that are so familiar to us that we often are not even aware of them. These bells have always co-existed with sacred bells and are found extensively in all societies. And, like sacred bells, they have important cultural roles to play, the most universal being to help people communicate with one another.

In 2001, an extraordinary event took place when thirty-three-year-old Erik Weihenmayer succeeded in climbing Mount Everest. What made it so extraordinary was that Erik is blind; he has been blind since age thirteen as a result of a rare disease. He was able to reach the summit of Everest, in part, because the climber ahead of him had a bell attached to his backpack, and Erik could follow the sound of the bell as he moved up the icy slopes.

Erik's journey is a unique instance of a bell being used to communicate, but there are many more. Before the development of

electricity, the sound of bells permeated daily life. In the early morning, the town bell rang in the municipal tower to signal the opening of the town gates. In the evening, it rang to signal their closing. The bell rang to tell people when to start and stop work, and it rang for curfew, warning people that it was time for them to be in their homes and cover their fires for the night. The town crier walked the streets, stopping at different corners where he rang his bell to gather people to hear the news. The night watchman rang his bell as he did his rounds to let people know all was well, while the muffin man, the pancake man, and the scissors grinder rang their bells to let people know they were coming. In medieval times, convicts carried bells on their way to execution to warn people that their evil spirits were near. The same was true of lepers. In times of plague, bells were hung on carts to let people know when it was time to bring out their dead. And, in times of danger, bells were rung to warn people of storms, fire, and enemy attacks.

In more modern times, bells have been used as warning devices on moving vehicles. Starting with horse carriages and sleighs, bells were used to alert people that a vehicle was approaching. Then trains, fire engines, streetcars, cable cars, and almost all moving vehicles had some form of warning bell. Many of these were beautifully made and are collector's items today.

Bells are also a familiar part of life at sea. Ships have bells, both as warning signals and to regulate the rhythm of the day. Lighthouses also have bells, often placed on the ground near the lighthouse and used when fog is so

This lovely hand-painted porcelain table bell made in Meissen, Germany, in the eighteenth century is one of the earliest porcelain bells made in Europe.

dense the light in the tower cannot be seen by ships offshore. And bells are the haunting sound heard from buoys suspended in the water that warn ships of danger.

Other bells that help us communicate are doorbells, animal bells, and tap or counter bells

ceremony was held in lower Manhattan at the site of the destruction of the World Trade Center eight months earlier. The ceremony was to mark the completion of the clearing of the site and the removal of the last debris, making it ready for restoration. It was also to

---

A second, although less well known, role secular bells play in our lives is in ceremonies of celebration and commemoration. The deep tones and lingering resonance of a bell make it particularly attractive for such ceremonies, touching our hearts and drawing us into the emotion of the occasion.

---

in hotels and shops. There are also unique bells like the bell at the New York Stock Exchange that is rung to announce the issue of a company's first public stock. And there are lovely bells made of glass, porcelain, and silver that were used for centuries at dinner tables, such as the Meissen bell on page 30. Although technology has replaced many bells over the years and the Internet makes communication seem ubiquitous, bells remain an important part of our daily lives, as well as a rich part of our cultural heritage.

A second, although less well known, role secular bells play in our lives is in ceremonies of celebration and commemoration. The deep tones and lingering resonance of a bell make it particularly attractive for such ceremonies, touching our hearts and drawing us into the emotion of the occasion.

On the morning of May 30, 2002, a

memorialize those who lost their lives there.

The ceremony began with the tolling of a fire engine bell. The bell was tolled five times, then five times, then five times, then once more five times; 5-5-5-5 being the code used in New York City firehouses to signal a death, usually of a colleague or noted dignitary. In this case, the bell was rung to honor the firefighters who died at the twin towers. Following the ringing of the bell, an empty stretcher covered with an American flag was slowly carried up the long ramp from the bottom of the site, symbolizing all the people who died in the attack and were never found or identified. Then came rows of bagpipers and drummers and, finally, a yellow truck drawing a flatbed trailer that carried the last piece of debris from the site, a fifty-ton steel column from one of the towers covered in a black cloth. When everything was out of the site, "Taps" was played and New York Police

The Mental Health Bell, created in 1953 to commemorate the accomplishments of the Mental Health Association, provides a symbol of hope for people afflicted with mental illness.

13, 1953, it was transformed into a three-hundred-pound bell that has become a symbol of hope for all those affected by mental illness. The inscription on the bell reads:

Cast from shackles which bound them, this bell shall ring out hope for the mentally ill and victory over mental illness.

Department helicopters flew overhead.

The destruction of the twin towers evoked many commemorative events across the country, but the one this day was especially memorable for the firefighters who honored their lost comrades with their own bell.

In 1953, a different kind of commemorative bell was created by the Mental Health Association. Before reform movements in the twentieth century, mentally ill patients were often treated inhumanely, shackled or chained to walls in institutions with very little care. After years of advances in mental health reform, the association decided it wanted a symbol for its work and chose a bell. From its New York headquarters, it sent out a call to all mental hospitals and institutions in the country to send in any metal shackles and restraints they still had. The piles of metal were gathered in the building's lobby and described by one person as a "chamber of horrors." The accumulated metal was shipped to the McShane Bell Foundry in Baltimore, Maryland, and on April

Bells are also used to honor individuals. In the spring of 2020 during the COVID-19 pandemic, Heather Jean Jordan, a Canadian school teacher and bell ringer in Banff, Alberta, went every day to St. George-in-the-Pines Anglican Church to ring their nine-bell carillon. After ringing down the scale, she played a stately version of "Amazing Grace" in honor of all the people in Banff who were ill or had been lost to the virus and in honor of the many medical and other workers still serving the city. Each day, people lined up on both sides of the street to listen to the music, surrounded by the towering, snow-covered mountains of Banff.

Although these are examples from the West, secular bells are used in similar ways in other parts of the world. In 1468, a great bell was cast in Korea to bring honor to a deceased queen and hung near her tomb. In many walled cities, large bells were rung to signal the closing of the gates in the evening and the opening of them in the morning. Sometimes, these civic bells were paired with large drums, as in monasteries. In Japan, small bells were used to call guests to the tea ceremony and as part of Kabuki theater. They were also put on firewatchers' lookouts as warning bells. And, of course, a wide variety of animal bells are found throughout the world—on elephants, camels, horses, cows, sheep, and almost every animal imaginable. One of the few places that the history of Eastern and Western bells met was on the Silk Road, where camels and other animals hung with bells traveled between the two worlds.

In addition to their many cultural roles, bells have been a source of wonderful music, from the welcoming chimes of church bells on Sunday morning to the complex music of the carillon to the lovely music of the Eastern Orthodox Church called zvon.

BELLS IN THE ARTS

A special place bells are found in our lives is in the arts. Victor Hugo's *The Hunchback of Notre Dame* and Ernest Hemingway's *For Whom the Bell Tolls* are well-known novels that feature bells. The wild ringing of bells in the final part of Pyotr Ilyich Tchaikovsky's "1812 Overture" is famous, as is John Philip Sousa's "The Liberty Bell March." There is a wonderful Japanese dance-drama called "Musume Dojoji" that weaves a tale of love and revenge around a huge monastery bell, the dance-drama evolving over time from Noh drama to Kabuki theater to avant-garde theater in New York. But the art form most naturally suited to bells is poetry, where the rhythm and beat of ringing bells can be picked up in the cadence of the poem. Edgar Allan Poe's "Bells," Alfred, Lord Tennyson's "In Memoriam," Bret Harte's "Angelus," and Friedrich Schiller's "Song of the Bell" are all wonderful poems about bells.

BELLS AND THEIR MUSIC

CREATING MUSIC

Bells are some of the most complex musical instruments in the world. They have been described as "quivering" metal, which is a good description. When you strike a bell, all the metal in the bell, from lip to crown, vibrates or quivers, pulsing outward and inward in decreasing waves, which is what creates the sound. As such, bells are percussion instruments, along with drums, cymbals, triangles, and pianos, that emit sounds when struck.

When you hear a bell ring, it sounds as though you are hearing one note, but you are really hearing a chord. This chord is made up of different notes sounding at different intervals along the vertical wall of the bell. The sound of each note is determined by how fast the metal is vibrating at that point. The faster the metal vibrates, the higher the note; the slower it vibrates, the lower the note. In a bell, the fastest vibrations are near the top of the bell and the slowest near the rim.

In order for a bell to have a pleasing sound, these different notes must be in harmony with each other, which means the bell must be in tune with itself. However, not all notes are equal in their importance to the overall sound of the bell. Rather, there are five notes that dominate the sound. In a typical Western bell, the main sound you hear when a bell rings is the note that sounds just above the lip of the bell, which is called the fundamental or prime. A second, higher note, called the nominal, sounds an octave above the fundamental. Between the two are a series of partial notes, the most important being the partial third (in bells a minor third) and partial fifth. Most bells

also have a note that sounds an octave below the fundamental, which is the note that creates much of the low, often haunting hum tone we hear after a bell rings.

If the bell is well tuned, these five notes sound pleasing. For example, if you play the chord C-E♭-G-C and lower C on a piano keyboard, it sounds harmonious. But if you play the chord C-D-A-B with lower C, it will sound discordant and jarring. The bell has to be cast for the harmonious chord, which is determined by the thickness and composition of the metal, the height and diameter of the

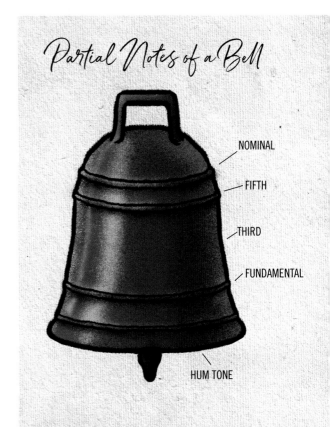

Partial Notes of a Bell

NOMINAL

FIFTH

THIRD

FUNDAMENTAL

HUM TONE

bell, and, most of all, the shape of the bell, which is called its profile.

To create music, of course, you need more than one bell. You need a set of bells, all of which have to be tuned individually and also tuned with one another. If they are not tuned with one another, it is like having an orchestra playing with different instruments all in different keys. Casting a single bell in tune with itself is difficult, but casting a whole set of bells, each bell in tune with itself and with all the other bells, is a real accomplishment. When that happens, wonderful music can be created.

Over history, there have been many forms of bell music, the most fundamental being chimes. A chime is any group of tuned bells that are played together musically; a single bell that is part of a chime is called a chime bell. Often these bells were cup-shaped, hung from a simple rack, and played by tapping them with a hammer. There are sketches of the Biblical King David playing chime bells.

More sophisticated forms of music developed in the West, starting in the sixteenth and seventeenth centuries. Carillons were developed in Europe, mainly in Belgium and the Netherlands, combining large sets of bells in tall towers that were attached to a keyboard and played by a carillonneur. Change ringing began in England about the same time—a unique form of bell music where sets of bells are played in complex and intricate patterns. Change ringing is also played on bells in tall towers.

A third form of bell music is zvon, the music of the Eastern Orthodox Church. Zvon is played on combinations of bells hung in low towers. It is a rich and spiritual form of bell music that has permeated Orthodox church services through history. Carillons, change ringing, and zvon are all explored in stories later in the book.

One other form of bell music has had an upswing in popularity in recent years: handbell ringing. Rather than the elaborate mechanisms of carillons or change ringing and zvon, handbell ringing just requires a group of ringers and a set of tuned bells. Standing in front of the bells, which rest on a flat surface, each ringer raises and lowers the bells in a steady way to ring them, each person controlling from two to several bells. With enough ringers and bells, everything from nursery

King David playing an early version of chime bells.

Handbells were originally used as practice bells for English change ringing, but developed in Europe into a form of music. The practice came to America when P. T. Barnum included a group of handbell ringers in his 1847 vaudeville tour of the country. It became more widely known in the early 1900s and is now a popular activity for church and school groups.

tunes to symphonic music can be played.

Ancient chimes, carillons, change ringing, Russian zvon, and handbell ringing all showcase the rich musicality of bells. But that musicality depends on having melodic and well-tuned bells.

MAKING BELLS

Bell making is an ancient art that has changed little over the centuries. Although bells may be made from many materials, the three most common types of bells are glass, porcelain, and metal, all of which have existed since the earliest times.

Glassmaking, ceramics, and metal working have been called the "arts of fire." For each, batches of raw material are heated to very high temperatures and thereby transformed into new substances. At 2,400 degrees F, sand, soda, and lime become glass; at 2,650 degrees F, clay and special additives become porcelain; and at 2,000 degrees F, copper and tin become bronze. If the raw materials are the right quality and mix, the heating process successful,

the new material cooled carefully, and the molds and decorations finely done, remarkable bells can be made.

The famed American glass artist Dale Chihuly called glass "the most magical of all materials," and that is certainly true of glass bells. The magic of glass bells comes in part from the beauty of their shape and sound, but even more from the beauty of light playing through them, refracting and sparkling and often creating rainbows of color. Because of their transparency and the way they interact with light, glass bells have a range of expression surpassing other bells.

One of the fundamental characteristics of glass is that it has an unusual chemical structure that allows it to be malleable for a short time after it is created in the furnace. During this time, the glassmaker can form it into many shapes by blowing, pulling, and twisting it. Glass also absorbs chemicals well, so it can be made in many colors. Adding copper, cobalt, or iron produces blue and green shades of glass, the cool end of the color

spectrum, while adding cadmium, gold, or sulfur produces the red, yellow, and orange colors of the warm end of the spectrum. The beauty of glass can be seen in the stately bell above, which is known as a wedding bell. Wedding bells were made in England from the mid-eighteenth to the mid-nineteenth century.

Porcelain is a particular kind of ceramic, one that is white, thin, hard, translucent, and resonant. Though it was produced in the Far East for centuries, the formula for porcelain was not known in Europe until it was discovered in Germany in the early eighteenth century. After its discovery, a factory was set up in Meissen, a small town outside Dresden, and the first European porcelain was produced. Over the next fifty years, Meissen developed a wide range of shapes, patterns, and colors and became the premier producer of porcelain in Europe. Eventually, the formula was stolen

by workers, and other factories were started elsewhere, particularly in Vienna and France and later England, but Meissen remained the touchstone name for fine porcelain, as seen in this lovely Meissen bell covered with delicate flowers.

Most bells, however, are made from metal. Looking at a typical metal bell today, it would seem that, given centuries of experience, bell makers could create a mold that would produce a perfect or near-perfect bell and that could be duplicated over and over again, greatly simplifying the casting of bells. However, the complex structure of metal bells suggests how many complicated variables go into casting a good bell and how many things can go wrong. The history of bells is littered with cracked and broken bells that had to be recast, including the Liberty Bell and Big Ben.

The first challenge of the bell maker is

(LEFT) Tall glass wedding bell in amber with ruffled base and elegant "steeple" handle, made in England. (THIS PAGE): Rare white Meissen table bell with colorful flowers made in Germany in the eighteenth century.

choosing the kind and composition of the metal. Most metal bells are made of bronze, which is an alloy of copper and tin. It is composed of about 80 percent copper and 20 percent tin, though the proportion can change depending on the caster and the desired properties of the bell. For instance, adding more tin makes the metal harder and more brittle, while adding less tin makes the metal softer and more malleable. Very large bells are usually cast with more copper and less tin so the bell will be less brittle, reducing the danger of cracking when it is repeatedly hit with its heavy clapper. Smaller bells tend to have more tin and less copper to make them harder and more resonant. Bell founders have to find the right balance for each bell, making it hard enough to create a rich resonance but not brittle enough to be vulnerable to cracking.

The bell maker's next important decisions are the size and weight of the bell and its profile or shape. Over the years, knowledge has accumulated on what proportions produce the best sound in bells, such as the ratio of the height of a bell to its diameter at the rim or the diameter at the top of the bell to the diameter of the rim, and bell founders have tables of these ratios to guide them. For larger bells, the width of the bell's wall also has to be determined, as it is usually thickest at the rim,

THE MYSTERY **OF PORCELAIN**

The seventeenth and eighteenth centuries were the great age of alchemy, an age of mystery and drama when early scientists were trying to understand the nature of matter and how it could be transformed from one state into another. Their great quest was to transform base metal like lead into gold. The search for ways to create gold was particularly aggressive in the areas that were later unified into Germany.

At the beginning of the eighteenth century, Augustus the Strong, the leader of Saxony, heard about a talented young alchemist named Johann Friedrich Böttger, who was boasting that he could create gold. Desperate to find new funds to finance his wars, Augustus abducted Böttger and put him in prison to force him to produce the gold he had promised he could make. Over a number of years, Böttger was moved from prison to prison, escaping more than once, but always found and returned. His physical and mental health suffered, and he became more and more frightened for his life, as Augustus threatened to have him executed if he did not create the gold. Finally, Augustus was persuaded that, rather than executing Böttger, who was still a talented chemist, he should be put under the tutorship of the master chemist Ehrenfried Walter von Tschirnhaus, who was working to find the formula for porcelain. After many years of imprisonment and just after von Tschirnhaus's death, Böttger announced that he had succeeded in discovering the formula. Böttger had not discovered the secret of gold, but he had discovered the secret of porcelain and was finally set free.

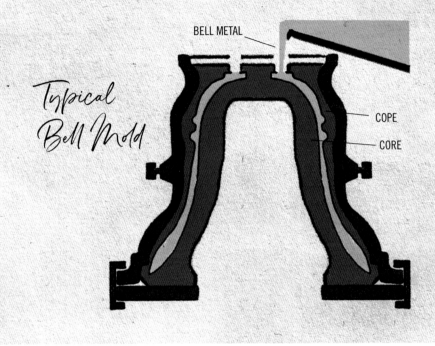

Typical Bell Mold

BELL METAL

COPE

CORE

becoming thinner toward the waist and shoulder. For many Western bells, the lip is further thickened to create what is called a sound bow, the bulge we see at the rim of many bells. The sound bow both magnifies the fundamental note and prevents the bell from cracking when it is hit too often with its clapper.

After the size and weight of the bell are determined, the caster has to decide on the profile of the bell. Creating the profile is one of the most critical decisions a caster makes, for the shape of the bell as it curves from lip to crown determines how the partial notes of the bell align with one another, its musicality. To create a harmonious sound, the key five notes —the fundamental, minor third, fifth, nominal, and hum tone—have to be aligned in the correct proportions. If the curve of the bell from crown to shoulder to waist to flared lip doesn't create this alignment, the shape has to

be adjusted or the bell recast.

After choosing the metal and determining the characteristics of the bell, the next step is creating the mold. Western bells are cast in a two-part mold, an inner mold called a core and an outer mold called a cope. Both are made in the shape of the desired bell, the outer mold being slightly larger than the inner mold. After the two molds are fitted together and clamped in place, molten metal is poured into the top of the mold until it fills the empty space. When cooled, the molds are broken off, revealing the new bell.

Usually, each bell is unique, so the molds are made new for each casting. The core, or inner mold, is built up on a steel plate using bricks and loam, loam being a mixture of clay and sand. To create the desired shape, a board called a strickle board is designed in the exact shape or profile of the inside of the desired

A worker at the Rincker Bell Foundry in Sinn, Germany, uses a strickle board to make the inner mold for a large bell.

bell. The strickle board is attached to a rod in the middle of the plate and allowed to swing free, moving around the mold to create its shape as more loam and bricks are added. When complete, the mold is dried and dusted with graphite powder, which prevents the new bell's metal from sticking to it.

The cope is made the same way, but upside down. It is built up inside a generic metal mold using a strickle board that has the same contours as the one used for the core, but is slightly larger. When finished, the cope is also dried and dusted with graphite powder. However, there is usually another step in preparing the cope, which is to imprint on the inside of the mold any wording or decorations that are desired for the outside of the new bell. Because the molds are the negatives of the new bell, the imprints on the cope have to be a reflected version of what will appear on the finished bell.

When the mold is ready, the cope is lowered onto the core so the two lips meet and are clamped together, a delicate moment since the two molds have to be perfectly aligned. If they are not, the bell will be unbalanced. The outer cope also has holes in it for gases and impurities to be released during the casting.

The mold is now ready for the pour. The bell metal is heated to around 2,000 degrees F in the furnace, and the slag of impurities coming out of the metal as it is heated are skimmed off the top. The metal is poured into a large ladle and rolled over to the mold where it is carefully poured in, the pourer pressing any remaining slag back so it will not enter the mold. If it is a very large bell, the mold is put in a pit in the ground to keep it stable.

The next step is to cool the bell. Bells have to be cooled carefully so all the metal cools at the same rate. If the metal is cooled too fast, its molecular structure can be distorted, making the bell susceptible to cracking. Or, if the metal on the outside of the bell cools faster than the metal on the inside, the metal can be stressed, making the bell weaker and eventually causing cracking. For a large bell, proper cooling takes

Pouring the molten bronze metal into the bell mold after being heated to 2,000 degrees F.

With so many variables involved in creating an appealing bell, it is not surprising that bell making is a delicate and sometimes unpredictable art. Although there are now a number of technological advances that can help the bell founder, in the end, the quality of a bell still depends, to a large extent, on the art and skill of the founder.

days, impatience causing the deaths of many bells in the history of bell founding.

After the bell cools, the molds are broken off, revealing the new bell, which is brushed clean and any roughness around its rim filed off. This is the moment of truth—how will the new bell sound? If it is well cast and has the desired sound, it is called a "maiden," but if it is a dud and has a dead sound, it is called a "kettle" and has to be recast.

The last challenge for the bell founder is to tune the bell. If the bell is a "maiden," it will not need tuning. But most bells need some tuning, so they are cast with an extra layer of thickness called the tuning reserve. To tune the bell, the bell is inverted on a revolving lathe and small amounts of metal are scraped off the inside of the bell at the locations of the key partial notes. Thinning the metal this way changes the tone of that partial so it comes into tune with the rest of the bell. Of course, when one partial note is changed, the bell's profile changes, so the other partials are also affected. The art of the tuner is to find the balance among these partials as he tunes the bell.

All of these aspects of bell founding are part of casting a well-tuned bell. However, some bells still sound better than other bells, for there are more subtle dimensions to the sound of a bell that influence how rich and pleasing it is. How sweet is the sound of the bell? How deep and full its resonance? How clear its tone? Does it have complex after tones, and how long do they linger? Does the sound of the bell seem mysterious or ethereal? Does it evoke strong emotions and move us? Does it give the musician a range and depth of sound that extends his skill and creativity as a musician? These more elusive qualities of a bell—its unique nature, what makes it different from another bell of the same pitch—are called its timbre.

Many things contribute to the timbre or quality of a bell's sound. In addition to the choice of metal, the skill in casting, and the success in cooling and tuning a bell, there are intricate aspects of how a bell rings that affect its sound. For example, in addition to the five main partial notes that define the pitch of a bell, there are many less significant partial notes that sound along the wall of a bell when it rings. These additional partials are not tuned, and, unless they can be dampened or muted, they can muddy the clarity of the bell's primary chord.

Another relevant property of bells is how their sound, starting strong, slowly fades away. This is called the decay rate of the sound, and each partial tone along the side of the bell has its own decay rate, the shortest being those of the high notes near the top of the bell and the longest being the low notes at the bottom of the bell. When a bell is rung, its sound changes in minute ways as the various partials decay at different rates, leaving the hum tone to linger the longest. How these decay rates interact is also part of the bell's unique sound.

Finally, the clapper affects the bell's sound. It has to be the right size so that, as it swings, it hits the bell cleanly on the sound bow. It also has to be the right weight; a clapper that's too light will produce a weak sound, not bringing out the full resonance of the bell, while a clapper that is too heavy will eventually damage the bell. The material of the clapper also has to fit the bell. If the clapper is too soft, it will create a dull sound; if too hard, it will create a harsh sound and also hurt the bell.

With so many variables involved in creating an appealing bell, it is not surprising that bell making is a delicate and sometimes unpredictable art. Although there are now a number of technological advances that can help the bell founder, in the end, the quality of a bell still depends, to a large extent, on the art and skill of the founder.

THE **BELL FOUNDER'S** WINDOW

The Bell Founder's Window is at York Minster in England, a medieval cathedral famous for its stained glass. Known for its beauty, the bell window has three tall panels, each showing historical, allegorical, or decorative scenes featuring bells. Depictions of bells are also along all the borders of the panels. The window was given to the cathedral by Richard Tunnoc, a goldsmith, bell founder, and one-time mayor of York, who commissioned it in the early fourteenth century. One of the scenes on the third panel shows the actual casting of a bell.

PART II

THE BELLS OF

A

AFR

SIA AND
ICA

Close-up of three tiers of the Zeng bells, with a statue of a woman helping to hold up the bell rack.

THE ZENG BELLS

By seeing the rites of a ruler, we may know the character of his government. By hearing his music, we may know the character of his virtue.

—CONFUCIAN SCHOLAR

In the fall of 2011, I sailed out of Los Angeles on the MS *Hanjin Phoenix*, a 50,000-ton South Korean freighter. It was the first step on my journey to Wuhan, China, to see the Zeng bells. Though they were created 2,500 years ago, the Zeng bells remain some of the most beautiful and technically sophisticated bells the world has ever known.

I chose to travel to China by freighter because I wanted to experience the time and distance of going there, rather than boarding an airplane and twelve hours later finding myself on the other side of the world. I needed to cross the ocean and go back many centuries if I was going to find a connection to these ancient bells. I had taken an earlier trip to Australia on a freighter and found I liked the intimate contact with the life of the ship and sea that a freighter offers. It is not luxurious travel—not nearly as comfortable and entertaining as Nannie's ships—but it was enormously peaceful and gave me time to expand my reading of Chinese history, art, and culture. I was the only passenger on board, and the captain extended the courtesy of allowing me to spend my days on the bridge, the navigational center of the ship. The crew found a chair for me and put it next to one of the panoramic windows so I could look out over the ocean as I read. By the time we sailed into the Sea of Japan after two weeks at sea, I felt I had traveled a great distance toward the world of the Zeng bells.

The Zeng bells are part of the Chinese bell tradition going back thousands of years. Ranging over many octaves, these magnificent sets of ancient bells were played as part of sacred court orchestras and had the remarkable quality of producing two different notes, but between ruler and ruled, parent and child, and even within the emotional life of each individual. If properly used, music could bring order and stability to all these dimensions of life. The Zeng bells were a central part of this ethereal relationship between music and the universe.

The Zeng bells were also part of an extraordinary archeological odyssey that took place in

---

I was fascinated with the beauty and musical qualities of these bells, but also with the remarkable role they played in ancient Chinese society. For the ancient Chinese, music was the "voice of heaven." Its inherent harmonic structure duplicated the inherent harmonic structure of the universe.

---

depending on where they were struck. This achievement was lost to history until examples of these bells were unearthed in tombs during the twentieth century. The set of sixty-five bells belonging to Marquis Yi of Zeng are the most stunning ones found so far.

I was fascinated with the beauty and musical qualities of these bells, but also with the remarkable role they played in ancient Chinese society. For the ancient Chinese, music was the "voice of heaven." Its inherent harmonic structure duplicated the inherent harmonic structure of the universe. In ideal times, music could express the desired relationship between heaven and earth and was the model for spiritual and philosophical life. It was also the model for political and social life, for harmony was needed not only between heaven and earth

China during the twentieth century. As China began to modernize in the 1920s, extensive road building and other construction projects unearthed the tombs of ancient rulers, which were filled with a wealth of artifacts. Although there had long been legends of great Bronze Age cultures, little was known about ancient China before this time. As more and more sites were excavated, the history of this ancient age began to be revealed.

This archeological odyssey took place in two parts. In the 1920s and 1930s, a number of burial sites were uncovered, the most important being at Anyang in Henan province. The rich find of inscribed artifacts from this site not only established the existence of the Bronze Age cultures but allowed researchers to classify them into three major dynasties: the early Xia dynasty from 2100 to 1600 BCE, the Shang dynasty that flourished from 1600 to 1050 BCE, and the Zhou dynasty that dominated China until it was united into an empire in 221 BCE.

After being interrupted by civil war and the Cultural Revolution, a new, even richer, period of archeological discovery began in the 1970s that more fully uncovered the extraordinary sophistication of China's Bronze Age—fabulous bronze ritual vessels, extensive orchestras of musical instruments, beautifully lacquered caskets, and ornate fittings for warriors and chariots. The technical achievement and beauty of these relics were breathtaking, including the now famous Terracotta Warriors that have traveled to museums around the world. As more and more sites were excavated, archeologists began to chart how the use and design of the various artifacts changed over time, building a picture of the political, social, and spiritual history of this ancient age.

The Zeng bells were discovered in 1977 when a group of soldiers from the People's Liberation Army was sent to level a low hill near the town of Suizhou, north of the city of Wuhan in Hubei province. As they worked, they discovered a large burial pit dug into the hill and called in archeologists to excavate it. By the late spring of 1978, the archeologists had uncovered the whole tomb, where, in a finely lacquered casket, they found the remains of a forty-five-year-old man who was identified as Marquis Yi, the head of the small state of Zeng. From inscriptions on one of the bells in the tomb, they learned that Marquis Yi had died in 433 BCE, in the second half of the Zhou dynasty.

The tomb was laid out in four chambers representing the main areas of a palace. The central and largest chamber corresponded to the public area of the palace, the ceremonial hall or courtyard. In the ceremonial hall, the set of sixty-five bronze bells was found, still hanging on its chime rack and, remarkably, still in perfect pitch. With the bells was an assemblage of other musical instruments, including drums, zithers, flutes, panpipes, mouth organs, and a set of thirty-two chime stones. Also found in the ceremonial hall were more than 100 elaborate bronze vessels, such as food containers and wine vessels, that were used in ritual ceremonies. In other chambers of the tomb, a small eight-piece musical ensemble composed of stringed instruments, mouth organs, and a drum was found, as well as an armory containing the remains of more than 4,000 bronze weapons, armor, and chariot fittings. Most of these artifacts, including the Zeng bells, are now housed in the Hubei Provincial Museum in Wuhan.

After disembarking from my freighter in Shanghai and spending a few days in Beijing, I went to Wuhan, where I had arranged for a guide-interpreter to go with me to the Provincial Museum to see the bells and speak with museum personnel. As we entered the Zeng exhibit, the first thing we saw was Marquis Yi's casket, lacquered in gold and brown and covered with intricate designs and pictographs. Surrounding the casket were many of the elaborate bronze ritual vessels found in the tomb.

When we turned the corner, there were the chimes, even more magnificent than I had imagined. The massive size of the bells combined with their beauty was overwhelming.

The magnificent Zeng bells, created 2,500 years ago in ancient China, are some of the most beautiful and technically sophisticated

Close-up of individual Zeng bells showing their intricate decoration and fish-mouth rims. It is the shape of the rims that creates the unique two-tone phenomenon of the bells.

The chime rack is eight feet tall and shaped like an L, with the long side stretching thirty-six feet. Lacquered a bright red with gold inscriptions, it is held up at each end by the raised arms of elaborately modeled human forms. The sixty-five bells hang in graduated sizes along the three tiers of the chime rack. The largest bell is almost five feet high and weighs 450 pounds. Together, the bells weigh 11,000 pounds. Between the bells and the chime rack, there are 3,755 gold-inlay characters. It is a huge, elaborate, and beautiful ensemble in perfect condition.

Looking more closely at the individual bells revealed their unique shape and decoration. Straight-sided with flat tops and long shank handles, they have sets of nine bosses or knobs repeated around the top half of the bell, all surrounded by elaborate decorations. In the middle panel of the bells is a gold-inlaid inscription that says "Marquis Yi of Zeng made this, cherish it." The most distinctive feature of the bells, though, is the shape of their rims. Pointed at each end, the rims curve up in an arc from one end to the other, forming what is described as a fish-mouth or almond-shaped rim. These unusual rims are what create the unique two-tone phenomenon of these historic bells.

Like other bells, the Zeng bells sound a series of notes at different intervals along their vertical walls. The strongest note sounds near the rim where the bell is struck, and, for most bells, this is the fundamental or pitch tone of the bell. All the other tones above it are partial or overtones ranging up the scale and up the side of the bell, the highest overtones being near the crown. To produce a clear and harmonious tone, these partial overtones must be in harmony with the fundamental.

The Zeng bells—and other two-tone bells of the Bronze Age—complicate this by producing two different fundamentals, one when you strike the lower front of the bell and the other when you strike the side. In tests done on two-tone bells, researchers found that, because of the almond or fish-mouth shape of their rims, the vibrations created by striking the bell on the front do not interfere with the vibrations created by striking the bell on the side; they are independent of each other, so each tone is complete in itself. Musically, each bell is two bells.

In Western musical terminology, there are three main scales. The chromatic scale is the largest and includes all twelve white plus black notes on a piano plus the octave note. Next is the diatonic scale, which includes only the eight white notes on a piano plus the octave note (do, re, mi, fa, so, la, ti, do). Finally, the pentatonic scale, which is the smallest, uses only five of the white notes, usually the first, second, third, fifth, and sixth, plus the octave note (do, re, mi, so, la, do).

The Zeng bells are a fully melodic instrument; they have all twelve notes of the chromatic scale over three octaves, with two more octaves having partial series of notes. Beginning two octaves below middle C, they have been described as ranging from the "lowest tones of a cello to the highest notes of a flute." Researchers believe the bells belonged to at least five different original sets of bells and were probably assembled because they were a harmonic fit. Studies so far also suggest

MUSIC'S ROSETTA STONE

Gold writing found on many of the Zeng bells came to be recognized as one of their most remarkable features. These inscriptions documented the musical theory of the age, the only inscriptions like them found so far and ones that changed our understanding of musical history. At the time these bells were made, each of the many states competing for power in China had its own pitch standard that was based on chime bells. This pitch standard was used to tune the rest of the orchestra, as well as being the basis for many nonmusical weights and measures. Setting and protecting this standard was a key role for each leader, serving as one of the ways he proclaimed his legitimacy to rule. In Western terminology, a pitch standard might be C in one state, E in another, and A in another. The Zeng inscriptions translated these various pitch standards. For example, one bell might describe itself as "do," the first tone in the key of C, the pitch standard of Zeng, but also "mi," the third tone in the key of G in another state like Chu, and "so," the fifth tone in another state like Ji. With this information, the pitch standards of the different states could be understood in terms of each other, unlocking the codes of their musical relationship, a Rosetta Stone for ancient Chinese music.

that much of the music played on the bells probably used the five notes of the pentatonic scale, the additional notes being available to fill in the music transposed to different keys. For the Zeng bells to be played as an ensemble, each bell had to be tuned with itself in two keys and then all the bells had to be tuned together, a remarkable achievement.

After we spent some time exploring the Zeng exhibit, one of the museum curators joined us. Although the original bells are protected behind glass and not allowed to be played, the curator played a keyboard he had designed that duplicated the tone of each bell. He also talked about the complex political and spiritual roles the bells played in society. Ancient China was a feudal culture whose spiritual life depended on ancestor worship and which was headed by a series of all-powerful kings. A king received the "Mandate of Heaven" or the power to rule, but he could only maintain that power if he followed the ways of good government and personal virtue. The outward manifestations of good government and personal virtue were the long-established ritual ceremonies, which, if followed meticulously, would attract the favor of the ancestors and ensure the well-being of the kingdom. Bell chimes were an essential part of these ritual ceremonies.

The ceremonies were usually carried out at elaborate feasts in which the ancestors were invited to participate through the use of proxies. Stately bronze vessels for wine and food were used for offerings at the feast, each with a carefully prescribed function. Music, particularly bell chimes, orchestrated the ceremonies, providing their structure as well as their cadence. Usually, the racks of bell chimes were placed along one or more of the walls of the temple, the stone chimes along another wall, and the string and wind instruments and their players in front. The whole orchestra was accompanied by carefully scripted song and dance.

Although we don't know all that happened in these ceremonies, some descriptions have been found in ancient collections of poetry and song, as well as in inscriptions on ritual bronzes. The ceremony started with the bells and drums calling in the ancestors. The supplicants then voiced lengthy praises of the ancestors, asking for their divine help. The ancestors replied through an oracle that the blessings would be bestowed, as long as the rituals were carefully kept. A poem in the *Shi Jing* (*Classic of Poetry*) from ancient China offers one description:

They strike the bells solemnly,
They play their se and qin zithers,
The reed-organs and the musical
* stones blend their sounds:*
Accompanied by them they perform the
* Ya and Nan (dances).*
They wield their flutes without error.

A sacred food vessel used as part of important ritual ceremonies in ancient China. The elaborate shape and decoration of the vessel show the high level of casting in China at that time.

A finely decorated sacred wine vessel used as part of ritual ceremonies.

The formal ceremony then drew to a close, again with bells and drums, and was followed by a great feast. This ceremony allowed the ancestors to be praised and feted in exchange for their blessings and help with earthly problems, all within the structure of the ritual music, liturgy, song, and dance. One of the most important roles of a ruler was to maintain these rituals in good order, for much of the well-being of the society depended on them.

Because ritual vessels and musical instruments, particularly bells, were so central to kingly power, they became potent symbols of that power. Precious resources and technology were invested in them, and they became a primary expression of status in the state. The Chinese feudal system had a rigid hierarchy of well-established ranks, with each rank being allowed a defined number of ritual vessels and bells, both in this life and in the tomb. At their peak, bells and other bronze ritual objects carried social as well as political and spiritual power. Marquis Yi was of the second rank and was thus allowed bells along two walls of his tomb.

Marquis Yi's tomb was one of the most important archeological finds of the twentieth century, not only for the wealth of musical instruments and other artifacts it contained, but because Marquis Yi lived at a pivotal time in Chinese history. He lived near the end of the great Bronze Age and the beginning of the "modern" age that succeeded it. Within a century of Marquis Yi's death, the beautiful musical chimes and ritual vessels that had dominated the culture since Shang times were no longer highly valued. The two-tone bells were lost, and the music changed from highly regulated ritual to popular entertainment, which had little use for bell chimes or court orchestras. After a thousand years of Bronze Age civilization, the extraordinary musical accomplishments of that civilization were lost until they were rediscovered in the twentieth century. The tomb of Marquis Yi and its bell chimes dramatize the high musical and artistic accomplishments reached by the fifth century BCE.

The discovery of the Zeng bells made them a living part of Chinese history. In more recent years, the bells have taken on a new life. After the bells were installed in the Hubei Museum, a group of scholars and musicians gathered, and they were able to make a replica of the bells, preserving the original. This replica became the centerpiece of the Hubei Song and Dance Ensemble, which created a program of music and dance that plays several times a day at the museum and has traveled widely outside China. The ensemble is shown on the next page.

While I was in Wuhan, I went to see the ensemble perform a number of times. After one of the performances, my interpreter and I talked with the director of the ensemble. I was particularly curious about how they had developed the music they played, since there are no historical records of what ancient music sounded like.

The director said that they had been researching and working on this for many years, and that the music evolved from a mixture of sources, such as the ancient folk music of Hubei province, classic Chinese poetry, such as the *Shi Jing* and the *Chu Ci*, and exploration of the range of the sounds of the instruments themselves. Working with all these

The Hubei Song and Dance Ensemble playing a replica of the Zeng bells. The group has toured around the world, bringing the music of the bells to many countries.

influences, the researchers created music they believe is close to the ancient music. In the concerts, the ensemble plays these ancient songs along with well-known international music, such as Beethoven's "Ode to Joy."

The grandeur and remarkable music of the bells can be seen in "Bianzhong of Marquis Yi: Traditional Chinese Bells," a YouTube video created in 2017 by the Behring Global Education Foundation. In the video, the ensemble plays a number of songs using the bells as well as replicas of other instruments found in the tomb. Three players stand behind the chime rack using mallets to strike the small- and medium-sized bells, while an additional player stands in front using a long pole to strike the larger bells. The medium-sized bells dominate the music and sound rather like a xylophone, while the largest bells come in like a soft roll of thunder. The video shows the mammoth size, vitality, and power of the bells, as well as the grace and agility of the players.

Another chapter in the new life of the bells took place when the Chinese composer Tan Dun was commissioned to create a symphony to be played at the ceremony commemorating the reunification of China with Hong Kong in 1997. In a conversation with the renowned cellist Yo-Yo Ma at Tanglewood in the United States, Yo-Yo Ma mentioned that he had long dreamed of playing his cello with the Zeng bells. As a result, Tan Dun composed his *Symphony 1997* for the Zeng bells, Yo-Yo Ma's cello, a choir of children's voices, and the Hong Kong Philharmonic.

In discussing the symphony, Tan Dun said he didn't want to recreate the past with the bells; rather, he wanted to create new music with this ancient instrument. Having collected a wide range of drumming tools, he tried them out on the bells, expanding the sounds the bells could make beyond those created by the original poles and mallets. He then paired the bells with the cello, whose tones are remarkably in harmony with the deep, sonorous tones of the bells, while also providing a bridge to the sweet voices of the youth choir. The Philharmonic filled in the rest of the musical space.

Tan Dun also said that he conceived the symphony not just for the Hong Kong reunification, but as a universal statement of harmony and peace in the world. The three movements of the symphony—"Heaven," "Earth," and "Mankind"—are the three parts of this harmony, just as they were for his ancient ancestors. The final anthem in the symphony, "Song of Peace," which was adapted from a poem by the revered Tang dynasty poet Li Po, articulates this hope.

Song of Peace

*Heaven, Earth, and all Mankind,
  Listen!
The bells which no longer sound
  "farewell" knock at spring's door,
The wind of winter past blows the
  bugle of jubilation,
The drum, no longer announcing
  war, plays with everlasting harmony,
The mother, no longer crying, sings
  of joyous peace,
Ah! Heaven, Earth, and Mankind
  are symbiotic,
Everything in the world is one.*

My guide, Kiyoji Tsuji, standing under the huge temple bell at Manpuku-ji Temple in Kyoto.

THE TEMPLE BELLS OF KYOTO

To strike a temple bell is to bring out the gentle mind of Buddha.

—DOGENZENSHI, *FOUNDER OF EIHEIJI TEMPLE*

Once you experience the ringing of a monumental Buddhist temple bell, you are unlikely to forget it. Eight to ten feet tall and hung just off the ground, these bells are rung by swinging a large, suspended beam against the outside of the bell. When the beam hits the bell, there is a deep *BOOM*, a heavy strike tone, low in pitch. The boom then becomes a rumble as the sound reverberates out into the air. Finally, the rumble fades away as the vibrations cease, which can take up to a full minute. The larger the bell, the more powerful the sound, and the farther it carries.

Very large bells can be heard miles away.

One of the best places to see these monumental bells is in the Japanese city of Kyoto, a city rich with Buddhist temples. In the fall of 2017, I visited Kyoto. After taking the high-speed train from Tokyo, I was met at the station by Kiyoji Tsuji, an art professor who would be my guide and interpreter. Over tea at my hotel, we discussed our schedule. Although we would visit as many temples as possible, we decided to concentrate our interest on five temples: Tofuku-ji Temple to introduce me to temple life; Chion-in, which has the largest bell; Mii-dera, with the sweetest sounding bell; Byodo-in, the most beautiful bell; and Myoshin-ji, home of the oldest bell. He also

The massive sanmon gate at the entrance to the Tofuku-ji Buddhist Temple in Kyoto. The pond in front of the gate is filled with lotus plants, a symbol of purity and rebirth in Buddhism.

showed me a rare journal he had found in a used bookstore about the history of temple bells, which gave me fascinating information I had not been able to find elsewhere.

The next day, we started with our visit to Tofuku-ji Temple. As we came into the temple grounds, the first thing we saw was a large pond filled with lotus plants, a symbol of purity and rebirth in Buddhism. The pond marked off the sacred space of the temple from the outside world.

As we walked over the bridge that spanned the pond, we were faced with a giant gate called the sanmon, the official entrance to the inner space of the temple. The sanmon was two stories tall with large roofs of black tiles arching gracefully out from the sides. Most of the other buildings in the temple had similar roofs, creating the appearance of waves of these roofs flowing across the temple grounds.

Within the temple grounds, we saw the Buddha Hall, which houses the shrine of the Buddha and is used for ceremonial chanting, worship, and special occasions. Then we saw the hatto, where the Dharma, or teachings of the Buddha, are passed on to the students. The hatto is usually the largest building in a Buddhist temple and almost always has a powerful painting of dragons on its ceiling, since dragons are believed to be protectors of the temple. To the side of the hatto was the zendo, a long hall where the monks meditated, the central practice of Buddhism and the main focus of temple life.

The other important building on the temple grounds was the hojo, or abbot's quarters, which included both living space and space to receive and entertain important visitors. Many lovely temple gardens are created around the hojos as quiet places of meditation. The hojo at Tofuku-ji is surrounded by four of these gardens. The largest one, a dry-stone garden on the west side, is particularly lovely, with tall stones representing mountains or islands placed strategically in a large bed of sand, which represents the ocean and is raked into circular patterns or waves. The garden represents a miniature of the vast physical and spiritual world of Buddhism.

A much smaller building on the temple grounds is the shoro, or bell tower, which houses the bonsho, the temple's largest bell. There are many bells in Buddhist life, such as the medium-sized temple bells used to call the community to meals, worship, and meditation, handbells used to start and end meditation sessions, and lovely wind-bells hanging under the eaves of buildings. However, the most important bell, the bell that identifies the temple, is the bonsho.

Shoros have different shapes at different temples, but most are simple roofed structures held up with massive timbers. Unlike most large Christian bells, which are hung in high towers and rarely seen by anyone except their ringers, large Japanese bells are hung close to the ground and open to the air, so you can see these massive bells and feel their powerful vibrations.

Suspended next to the bell is the wooden beam used to strike it, the size of the beam depending on the size of the bell. Attached to the beam are the ropes used to pull it back and forth. There is usually only one rope and one ringer, but very large bells may require a number of ringers to sound them, each pulling on their rope to get the beam swinging back and forth. The shoro is one of the smallest buildings on the temple grounds, quite plain in comparison to the elegance of the other

A lovely dry-stone garden at Tofuku-ji Temple. It is a miniature representation of the all-encompassing physical and spiritual world of Buddhism. The tall stones represent mountains or islands, while the raked sand represents the patterns of the ocean.

The bell tower or shoro at Hoko-ji Temple in Kyoto, showing both the massive bell and the long, heavy wooden beam used to strike it.

became the country's centers of learning and art and, over the centuries, helped created a unique culture in Japan, inspiring the gardens, poetry, tea ceremonies, paintings, ceramics, and calligraphy that flourish today.

The first large temple bells were brought to Japan from China and Korea. Then, in the seventh century, Korean bell founders started coming to the southern Japanese island of Kyushu to cast bells. Soon, Japanese casters took over, and Kyushu became the main source of early Japanese temple bells. Over time, family lineages of bell founders grew and existed for generations. Bell founding also expanded to different geographical locations, often depending on the political situation and who was commissioning the bells. The bells themselves, however, changed remarkably little from the seventh century to the twenty-first century, over 1,400 years.

When you look closely at one of these temple bells, like the bell from Eikan-do Temple, you can see their origin in ancient Chinese chimes: the bosses that surround the upper part of the bell; the mark, usually in the shape of a lotus on Buddhist bells, indicating where the bell should be struck; the panels separated by raised lines where there might be designs or writing dedicating the bell or describing its meaning; and the elaborately decorated handle. Unlike Chinese chimes,

buildings, but, as the home of the bonsho, it is central to temple life.

Buddhism came to Japan around 550 CE, more than 1,000 years after its founding in northern India. In the eighth and ninth centuries, when Japan was unified under an emperor and ruling aristocracy who built strong political ties with Buddhist sects, Buddhism became influential. The greatest flowering, however, began in the twelfth century when the military class replaced the aristocracy as rulers of the country and, along with a growing merchant class, became patrons of Buddhism. Large temple complexes were built, particularly in Kyoto, which was then the capital of the country. Although primarily monastic homes and schools, these temples these bells are round, rather than angular, have sloping sides, and are rung as solitary bells, rather than as an ensemble. The most striking difference, however, is their size; they are monumental and weigh many tons. Truly magnificent, they are some of the most distinctive and beautiful bells in the history of the world.

The day after we went to Tofuku-ji, we went to Chion-in, a temple in the foothills on the east side of the city. Kyoto is in a basin, almost completely surrounded by low mountains, which is part of what makes it so lovely. After

climbing the long steps up to the temple, one can see a wonderful view across the city.

Chion-in Temple is famous for its bell, the heaviest in Japan and one of the heaviest in the world. Cast in 1636, the bell is over ten feet tall, measures nine feet in diameter, and weighs seventy-four tons. To reach the bell, you have to climb farther up the hill to where it hangs in its bell tower on a knoll. It is a massive bell, simple in its design, but imposing in its bulk. In a collection of articles on Buddhist temple bells in Kyoto written in the 1920s and 1930s, Beatrice Lane Suzuki describes the Chion-in Bell:

It does not ring often, but those who have heard it never forget its great rolling boom that deepens all over the city and dies away in waving whispers. Whenever I listen to it, I feel as if the whole spirit of Buddhism breathes through it. As long as this bell rings out its philosophy of life, Buddhism will never vanish from the soul of the Orient.

The bell at Eikan-do Temple shows the influence of earlier Chinese bells.

Ringing the Chion-in Bell, which is one of the largest bells in the world and needs seventeen people to ring. When families gather to celebrate New Year's Eve, it leads the ringing of bells throughout the city of Kyoto.

The Chion-in Bell is particularly important on New Year's Eve, a time when families gather for feasts and celebrations. At midnight, all the temple bells in the city ring 108 times, representing the number of worldly temptations we are subject to in our lives. Each stroke of a bell purifies us of one of these temptations, leaving us cleansed to start the new year. Because of the size of the Chion-in Bell, its sound is the strongest in the chorus of temple bells ringing in the new year in Kyoto.

The Chion-in Bell takes seventeen people to ring. The seventeen ropes are attached near the front of the swinging beam. Sixteen ringers each take a rope and fan out in an arc around the beam, while a shorter rope is taken by the leader, who stands in front of the bell. At his direction, the ringers pull on their ropes to get the beam swinging. When enough momentum is gathered, the leader signals that it is time to hit the bell. He puts one foot on the edge of the platform under the bell, and, as the beam comes toward him, he throws himself back off the ground, using all his weight to pull the beam into the side of the bell, rolling on his back as he does so. As the resounding boom fills the air, he lets the beam pull him back up, and the process starts over again. Because the sound of the large bells takes so long to diminish, ringers have to check the beam just short of the bell for a couple of strokes until the air is clear and another full strike can be made. Otherwise, the sounds of successive strikes would be muddied.

The temples are the physical settings for these remarkable bells. More importantly, they are the spiritual settings for the bells. All through history, the sound of a bell has been considered its "voice." The temple bells are the "voice" of the Buddha. The name Buddha comes from the Sanskrit root that means both to wake up and to know, so Buddha means the awakened or enlightened one, and it is the historical Buddha's process of enlightenment that founded one of the great religions/ philosophies of the world. The bell is a symbol of that enlightenment, and its voice is the call of the Buddha to summon people to their own awakening. The larger the bell, the more powerful the voice, and the further that call goes out into the world.

The Buddha taught for almost fifty years across northern India before his death. His teachings, however, were not written down until much later, and, over the years, he taught many things in many ways. With time, disagreements in interpretation arose, and, eventually, different schools of Buddhism emerged. One of these schools traveled from India to the countries of Southeast Asia—Sri Lanka, Myanmar, Thailand, Laos, and Cambodia—while a second school traveled to Northeast Asia—to China via the Middle East and the Silk Road and from there to Korea and Japan. A third school found its fullest expression in Tibet. Each of these schools formed many sects and also adopted a pantheon of past and future Buddhas, celestial figures, elaborate rituals, and rich statuary. The two sects that became most popular in Japan were Zen Buddhism and Pure Land Buddhism. About half the temples we visited were Zen and half Pure Land.

On the day after our visit to Chion-in, we

THE **BUDDHA'S STORY**

The historical Buddha, Siddhartha Guatama, was born in the sixth century BCE in Nepal near the northern Indian border. He was the son of a feudal lord and was raised in great wealth and ease. He led a contented life until he became overwhelmed by the suffering he saw in the world, particularly the suffering from disease, old age, and death. At age twenty-nine, he set out in secret, leaving his father's house and his young wife and son, to go to the forest, a traditional place of spiritual retreat in India. There he sought to understand the suffering of life, first by studying with famous Indian yogis or teachers and then by joining a small group of ascetics who believed that a severely austere life would bring salvation. Neither experience brought him the enlightenment he was seeking, so he set off on his own to find another way.

One day, when he was in Bodh Gaya in northeast India, he resolved that he would sit under a nearby fig tree and meditate until he found enlightenment. After a long night of seeking, he finally broke through and gained insight into the pain and suffering of life. He rose and went to a deer park near Sarnath, where he gave his first sermon, "Setting in Motion the Wheel of the Dharma," to the five ascetics who abandoned him when he rejected their way but now became his first followers.

In the sermon, he explained that our suffering comes from something fundamentally wrong or dislocated in the way we see life. Like a wheel with a crooked axel, we attach our idea of happiness to the attainment of worldly things. We constantly crave happiness and cannot let go of the desires we believe create happiness. To overcome this, we need to understand that all life is impermanent, that all things are constantly changing, and that our ideas of happiness are illusionary. In order to see the true nature of life, we need to let go of these illusions. The Buddha said we can do this by following a path of radical change, which he sorted into eight steps of meditation and self-understanding that would winnow away our wrong habits and lead us to enlightenment. He then set out on a lifelong journey of pilgrimage to bring his wisdom to others.

took a half-hour train ride to Otsu on the outskirts of Kyoto to visit Mii-dera, a temple on the hills overlooking a lovely lake. Because Mii-dera is out of the city and rarely visited by tourists, the temple did not have the strict regulations for visitors that the temples in the city did. My guide had been in touch with the officials at the temple and arranged for me to ring their bell.

Housed in a lovely old shoro, the bell was large and imposing, a replica of an older bell that had cracked in 1814 and was now preserved in one of the temple buildings. Taking up the rope attached to the wooden beam, it took five swings to gather enough momentum for the beam to strike the bell, which shocked me with the power of its reverberations. I rang it a number of times, getting a little better with

When reflected in the water at Byodo-in Temple, the Phoenix Hall looks like a graceful bird taking flight. On the roof of the hall are two golden phoenix statues.

each strike. I felt it was a great privilege to ring the Mii-dera Bell, often considered the sweetest sounding bell in Kyoto.

After ringing the bell, we walked through the temple grounds. Mii-dera is an old temple, destroyed and rebuilt many times. Silent and a bit dusty the day we visited, it felt almost deserted, although an active community of monks lives there. We sat for a long time on a bench near the bell tower absorbing the temple's ancient peace.

The next morning, we set out to see one of the most beautiful bells in Kyoto in the striking Byodo-in Temple located at the southern edge of the city in the town of Uji. Founded in the middle of the eleventh century, its main building stretches along the shores of a pond, which is part of the temple's gardens. The central part of the building, with its high, tiled roof, is flanked by two long wings and is known as the Phoenix Hall, both because it looks like a bird with outstretched wings and because it has two golden phoenix statues on its roof. When the hall is reflected in the pond, it looks as though it is starting to take flight.

The famous Byodo-in Bell is in the temple museum. Believed to have been cast in the twelfth century, almost a thousand years ago, the bell is covered in rich decoration, reflecting the influence of Korea on Japanese bell founding. Korean bells are more elaborately decorated than Japanese bells, both with inscriptions and with lovely images of the Buddha, graceful Buddhist spirits called devas, and cosmological symbols. The influence of Korean bells on Japanese bell founding waxed and waned over the centuries, but the Byodo-in Bell is one of the finest examples of that influence, with its flying devas in the middle panels, lions around the lower panels, and

The beautiful Byodo-in Temple
Bell reflects Korean influence on
Japanese bell making. Cast almost
a thousand years ago, the original
bell is in the temple museum, while a
reproduction rings in the bell tower.

intricate designs in the vertical spaces. With its graceful shape and elaborate dragon handle, it is remarkably beautiful.

The next day, we went to see the most spectacular temple in Kyoto, the Kinkaku-ji Temple or Temple of the Golden Pavilion. I wanted to see this temple more for its history than its bell. In 1950, a young monk who had come to hate the beauty of the temple burned it down. A few years later, Yukio Mishima, one of Japan's most famous writers, wrote a haunting novel, *The Temple of the Golden Pavilion*, in which he explored the possible psychology of this monk and how he could have done such a shocking thing. Having read the book, I was fascinated by the story and wanted to see this remarkable temple. Rebuilt to its former glory, it was as ethereal as I imagined.

On one of my last days in Kyoto, we went to see what is considered to be the oldest bell in Japan at Myoshin-ji Temple, located in the northwest part of the city. Known as the Ojikicho Bell, it was cast in 698 at Kyushu, the date being marked on the bell as the "twenty-third day of the fourth month, 698." A few other bells have been discovered from around this period but without such a clear attribution, so the Ojikicho Bell is considered the oldest bell in Japan.

The Ojikicho Bell is no longer rung because

The original Temple of the Golden Pavilion was burned down by a disgruntled young monk in 1950 and has since been rebuilt. The incident is the subject of a famous novel by Yukio Mishima.

The Ojikicho Bell at Myoshin-ji Temple was cast in 698 and is the oldest bell in Japan.

it is cracked—not surprising after 1,300 years. In 1974, the Iwasawa Bell Company, after prolonged study of the tones of different bells, cast a replica of the bell. The first casting was unsuccessful because the tone of the new bell was poor, so a second casting was made, which was successful, and that bell now hangs in the Myoshin bell tower. The original can still be seen where it is preserved in the temple's grand hatto. Classified as a national treasure, it has a wonderful worn look and the elegant simplicity characteristic of Japanese temple bells.

Monumental Buddhist temple bells are a powerful aesthetic melding of vision and sound and are some of the finest bells in the world. Although written for a Pure Land Temple, a poem by Beatrice Lane Suzuki captures the spirit of all of these bells.*

In the vast temple shadows are falling.
Priests' voices rise in an anthem of prayer.
Incense is floating, candle-lights gleaming,
Pious hearts beating, hands clasped
  with beads.
Namu-amida is heard on all lips.
Praise be to Buddha! Praise be to Shinran!
See! Through the temple shadows are
  gathering,
Voices are praising, heads they are bent.
Praise be to Buddha!
Praise be to Shinran!
Hark! Hear the bell!
Hark! Hear the bell!

* *Shinran was one of the leaders of Pure Land Buddhism, and Namu-amida was one form of its mantra.*

In Tibetan Buddhism, the bell represents wisdom and the vajra scepter represents compassion. When brought together, they represent enlightenment, the Buddhist union of wisdom and compassion.

BUDDHISM
IN TIBET

The vajra and bell are not two cold metallic objects, but symbols that reach to the very heart of our potential as human beings.

—VESSANTARA

One of the most powerful bells in history is the lovely handbell shown on page 76. Called a dribu in Tibetan and a ghanta in Sanskrit, it is central to the practice of Tibetan Buddhism. The two foundations of Buddhism are wisdom and compassion. The bell represents wisdom and is usually paired with the scepter, or vajra, also shown on page 76, which represents compassion. In Tibetan practice, the bell is held in the left or female hand, while the scepter is held in the right or male hand. When these two symbols are brought together—as when the hands holding them are raised and crossed over the heart—they represent enlightenment, the union of wisdom and compassion, the ultimate attainment of Buddhism.

I had always wanted to go to Tibet and hoped to travel there on my trip to China. However, I am susceptible to altitude sickness, and, though I was able to go up 9,000 feet in Western China, I could not attempt the 12,000 feet of Lhasa in Tibet. Fortunately, my daughter is a Tibetan Buddhist. She studied at Naropa, the Buddhist university in Boulder, Colorado, and has practiced and taught Buddhism and Tibetan Buddhist meditation for many years. With her help, I was able to gain insight into this complex body

A close-up of the vajra scepter, which symbolizes indestructible power.

of thought and the role of the bell in it.

Tibet is a unique country, particularly in its remoteness and beauty. Often called the "roof of the world" and the "land of the snows," it is a high plateau towered over by majestic mountains. Although at one time it was a warrior nation that dominated much of central Asia, for most of its history Tibet's dramatic geography isolated it from the surrounding world. This isolation fostered an insulated culture that survived for centuries until the Chinese invasion in the 1950s.

The heart of this culture is Tibetan Buddhism, which permeates all aspects of Tibetan life and society. Tibetan Buddhism is the third line of Buddhism that developed from the Buddha's original teachings. Its unique quality is how it dramatizes the process of enlightenment—the

transformation of the ordinary world into the sacred world—through the active use of ritual that includes physical movement and sound, as well as the power of the mind. The bell and vajra are two of the most potent symbols of this ritual, each of them opening up whole realms of Tibetan thought and practice.

Both the bell and the vajra came to Tibet from India beginning in the seventh century CE. The vajra symbolizes the diamond thunderbolt, the weapon of Indra, the Hindu God of Atmosphere. Diamonds are the hardest known substance and are indestructible, while the thunderbolt has always been a symbol of divine power, so the vajra symbolizes indestructible power. A founding legend of Tibetan Buddhism is that the Buddha had a great battle with Indra and wrested the thunderbolt from him, transforming it into a central symbol of Buddhism. While Indra's vajra had open prongs symbolizing aggressive power, Buddhism closed the prongs, making them a symbol of peace.

Also from India, the Tibetan bell is a descendent of Hindu handbells. Originally known as lotus bells, these Hindu bells were shaped in three parts: the circular handle represented the universe, the upper hemisphere of the bell represented the purity of the universe, and the lower, flared part of the bell represented the lotus. Over time, these bells took on deeper meaning when their handles were transformed into representations of different Hindu gods. The photo on page 81 shows a Hindu bell with Nandi, the sacred bull mount of the god Shiva, on the top of the handle. Shiva is one of the three principal gods of Hinduism. Held in the hand of a priest, these Hindu bells became holy instruments.

In Tibetan Buddhism, the bell took on a new form. The body of the bell was covered with a carefully prescribed set of ritual symbols, while the handle was replaced with half a vajra, also covered with ritual symbols like the bell on page 76. With this new iconography, the bell became a carrier of powerful ritual meaning. Usually paired with the vajra, the bell was held in the hands of monks during ritual chanting and seen on visual representations of Tibetan deities.

Today, Tibetan Buddhism is distinguished by three primary characteristics. The first is that it is founded on lineages of teachers, or lamas, who transmit the scriptures and practices to pupils over many generations. To enter into

An early Hindu bell called a lotus bell.

the study of Buddhism, pupils must work with a lama and be part of a lineage because the work is powerful and can be easily misunderstood or misused by novices. Some lineages may be oriented to a particular monastery, set of texts, or certain meditation practices, but they all share the basic precepts of Tibetan Buddhism. These long lineages called schools, now spanning hundreds of years, are what give the teachings their authenticity and authority.

The second distinguishing characteristic of Tibetan Buddhism is the institution of the Dalai Lama. Both Buddhism and Hinduism accept reincarnation, the belief that we live many lives over eons of time, each new life depending on how well we lived our previous life. Our goal is to live better and better lives, renouncing earthly desires until we reach enlightenment or Nirvana and are freed from samsara, the endless cycle of birth and death. Central to Tibetan Buddhism is the ideal of the Bodhisattva, a being who reaches the brink of Nirvana but then turns back and re-enters the cycle of rebirth in order to help others

BUDDHISM **COMES TO TIBET**

Buddhism came to Tibet in two waves called the First and Second Propagation of the Dharma, or teaching. The first wave began around 600 CE at a time when Tibet was a fractured group of warrior principalities. A powerful king named Songtsen Gampo succeeded in unifying these principalities into one political unit. Looking at the nations surrounding him, particularly China and India, he saw that they were Buddhist and seemed to have a higher level of culture than Tibet. He decided to bring Buddhism to Tibet, both as a unifying force and a way to advance Tibetan culture.

Over the next two centuries, Buddhism flourished. Great Buddhist teachers came to Tibet from India. Monasteries were built and monks ordained, rituals were established, and the great body of Sanskrit Buddhist scriptures was translated into the Tibetan language. With time, much of the resistance from the native Bon religion was also overcome. But near the end of the ninth century, a leader came to power who wanted to destroy Buddhism, razing monasteries and temples, killing or banning monks, and removing texts. Following this destruction, Buddhism was almost lost in Tibet for two centuries.

The Second Propagation of the Dharma began near the beginning of the eleventh century and was again led by a powerful king, Yeshe Ö, who reigned in the western part of Tibet. Yeshe Ö decided to invite Atisha, a famous teacher from India, to come to Tibet. Though it took many years for this to happen, Atisha did come and succeeded in reforming the dark practices that had infiltrated the Buddhism that still survived in the country, providing the foundation for a renewal of Buddhist institutions and practices. A number of other noted Indian teachers came to Tibet, and many Tibetan students went to India. As a result, there was a great revival of Buddhism in Tibet that has now lasted for a thousand years.

Many sacred Indian bells have handles representing Hindu deities. This one shows Nandi, the sacred bull mount of the god Shiva, one of the three principal gods of Hinduism.

move forward. Tibetan Buddhists believe that these special beings live among us, and that the Dalai Lama is one of them. The Dalai Lama we know today is the fourteenth Dalai Lama and, although formally the head of one of the schools of Buddhism, he is the spiritual leader became particularly important when, in the eleventh and twelfth centuries, Muslim forces invaded India and destroyed these great monasteries, along with their teachings and practices. After over 1,500 years, much of Buddhism was erased in the country of its

---

In Tibetan Buddhism, the mandala is a sacred space, the home of one or more of the deities, and a template for visualizing these deities and the qualities they personify. When we enter a mandala in our minds, we are entering on the journey toward enlightenment. The mandala organizes our energies and guides us in that journey.

---

of all Tibetan Buddhists and their representative in the world.

The third—and by far the most important—distinguishing feature of Tibetan Buddhism is tantric ritual, the heart of Tibetan Buddhism and the setting for the vajra and bell. Around the seventh or eighth century CE, a group of writings was discovered in India. Although the origin of these writings is disputed, they advocated an advanced set of ideas and rituals that could accelerate the path to enlightenment. Called tantras—which means to weave—these new writings were incorporated into the teachings of the large monastic universities in northern India that were the seats of Buddhist learning. The great teachers, such as Atisha, brought these teachings to Tibet, and they became the founding doctrines of Tibetan Buddhism, which became known as Tantric Buddhism. This development

birth. Tibet became the purest repository of the Tantric form of those teachings and the vehicle for carrying them forward.

By the time Tantric Buddhism reached Tibet, a remarkable pantheon of deities had emerged in Buddhist thought. As the embodiment of enlightenment, the Buddha encompasses many qualities, such as wisdom, compassion, peace, and generosity. As Buddhism developed, advanced meditators began to visualize personifications of these qualities, and new Buddhist deities emerged with separate identities. Although many were adapted from Hindu deities, these new deities were not considered gods; rather, they were embodiments of universal or higher truths.

Meditation has always been the central practice of Buddhism and the path to enlightenment. Before Tantric Buddhism, meditation was primarily a practice of contemplation,

A stunning mandala painted on the ceiling of a Buddhist shrine near the Potala Palace in Lhasa. Within it, the mandala contains all of the journey to enlightenment, the highest attainment of Tibetan Buddhism.

working through the energies of the mind to achieve the transformation of the ordinary world to the sacred world and our consciousness to enlightenment. With Tantric Buddhism, meditation took on a new dimension in which the quest for enlightenment was acted out in compelling rituals using tantric symbols and visualizations. It became an active practice, drawing on all the energies of the mind, body, and voice to aid in this quest. When properly used, the rituals could accelerate understanding of universal truths personified by the deities, helping practitioners on their Buddhist path.

There are many important ritual symbols in Tantric practice, but the most important is the mandala. Mandala means circle or world and

is a symbol found in many cultures, such as Native American sand paintings. In Tibetan Buddhism, the mandala is a sacred space, the home of one or more of the deities and a template for visualizing these deities, and the qualities they personify. When we enter a mandala in our minds, we are entering on the journey toward enlightenment. The mandala organizes our energies and guides us in that journey. One of the remarkable things about the Tibetan bell is that, in addition to being a ritual object, it is also a mandala. Exploring how a mandala works sets the stage for exploring how the bell acts as a mandala.

The mandala above is painted on the ceiling of a stupa or Buddhist shrine near the Potala Palace in Lhasa. Like all mandalas, it is a

The base of the Tibetan bell represents the outer walls, the inner court, and the elaborate decorations on the walls of the Bodhisattva Prajnaparamita's palace.

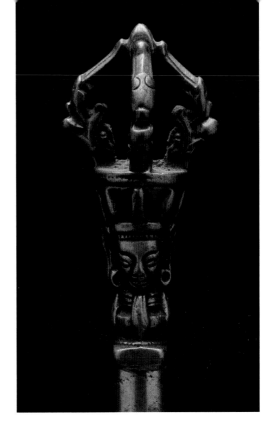

The handle of the bell shows Prajnaparemita looking out with a loving expression.

geometric marvel, a series of circles that enclose squares that in turn enclose more circles. The outer rim of the mandala has three special circles, which represent the walls protecting the inner, sacred space of the palace of the deity. To enter the mandala, you must open your mind and heart to overcome the barrier of these walls.

The outer wall, shown in alternating stripes of colors, is a wall of flames. Fire changes the nature of things—ice to water to steam—so to pass through the wall of flames, you must be willing to undergo the transformation from your old world to a new, sacred world.

The next wall is a narrow black circle that has golden vajras spaced around it. The vajra is indestructible, and to pass this wall you must have an unshakable commitment to enter the sacred space. The third wall is a circle of lotus petals, the ultimate symbol of purity and rebirth in Buddhism. To pass through this last barrier, you must be ready to experience this rebirth.

Having successfully passed through the three barriers, you are now in the sacred space of the mandala. Before you is the magnificent palace of the deity, decorated with jeweled garlands and other elaborate and beautiful decorations. The palace is square and may have one or two or more levels. There are four entrances at the four cardinal points, each with a large gate. As you pass through one of these gates, you enter the abode of the deity, who is

usually surrounded by other deities and attendants, each with their own colors and symbols. It is a place of beauty and deep peace, and each step you take forward takes you farther into that beauty and peace. You may make this journey many times, each time experiencing a deeper understanding of it. The Tibetan bell duplicates this journey.

The Tibetan bell is the mandala or home of the revered Bodhisattva Prajnaparamita, who embodies the "Perfection of Wisdom" literature, one of the most foundational teachings of Buddhism. To enter her home, you start at the lower rim of the base of the bell, which is a plain space representing the outer world in which the mandala is created. Moving upward, there is a row of vertical vajras between two rows of beads. These represent the three outer walls of the mandala: the wall of fire, the wall of vajras, and the wall of lotus petals. Having

Looking from the top, the bell looks like a mandala, with the palace at the center and the walls surrounding it.

passed through these barrier walls, you move up the side of the bell to an elaborate set of decorations. Although hard to see, there are eight makaras around the bell. Makaras are composite creatures from ancient Indian iconography that here most resemble the powerful jaws of a crocodile, symbolizing the tenacity needed to follow the path to enlightenment. Out of the mouths of the makaras flow garlands of jewels, and between each garland is a single vajra. These are the beautiful decorations on the outside of the palace. Still

higher up, there is a row of horizontal vajras just under the rim of the bell representing the actual wall of the palace.

As you move over the rim and on to the sloping shoulder of the bell, you have entered the palace, where you find eight lotus petals, the dais of the deity. Rising from the dais is the handle of the bell as pictured on page 85, which shows Prajnaparamita sitting on her throne and looking out at you with a loving expression. She wears a crown on her head with five jewels that merge into the half vajra that forms the upper part of the handle of the bell. The prongs of the vajra arch outward and then come together at the tip of the handle, completing the bell.

Viewed from the side, the levels of the bell's mandala travel up from the bottom of the bell to the top. However, if you look at the bell from the top, you can see the mandala in a more traditional two-dimensional form, the outer rim forming the circle around the deity's throne. As a mandala, the bell represents the journey toward wisdom, a remarkable role for a bell.

If you now turn the bell on its side, you can see a further manifestation of the symbolism of the bell. One of the necessary characteristics of a bell is that it is hollow inside; without this hollow space, the bell could not ring. When you look at the hollow space in the bell, it appears empty, except for the clapper. This "emptiness" represents one of the most difficult and profound concepts in Buddhism.

In writing and speaking we have only words, so we attribute words to concepts that can't truly be contained in words. "Emptiness" is one of these. The more you try to penetrate it, the more complex and opaque it becomes. Only the most advanced practitioners can approach comprehension of it, and then not through words but through experience. The rest of us can have only an intuitive glimpse of it.

The Buddha's ultimate insight at his enlightenment was that the suffering we experience in life comes from our attachment to worldly things and our belief that these things are real and can bring us happiness. As we start to follow the Buddha's path, we begin to realize that this is a false view of reality. The more we look at our lives, the more we understand that things are constantly

As we start to follow the Buddha's path, we begin to realize that this is a false view of reality. The more we look at our lives, the more we understand that things are constantly changing, life is impermanent, and our ideas of happiness are illusions. It is only when we release these false illusions that we can comprehend the true nature of reality and the meaning of a joyous life.

changing, life is impermanent, and our ideas of happiness are illusions. It is only when we release these false illusions that we can comprehend the true nature of reality and the meaning of a joyous life. At its simplest, "emptiness" symbolizes the absence of these transitory and false beliefs and our eventual and overwhelming comprehension that the phenomena of this world have no inherent existence and no true reality. Wisdom is the conscious recognition of this "emptiness."

In meditation, "emptiness" is usually visualized as a lovely, limitless, blue sky. As we visualize this sky, deities, mandalas, and other Buddhist symbols emerge from it and become the focus of our meditation. Eventually, they fade away, leaving us again with the blue sky, which also fades away. The limitless blue sky is one intuitive understanding of emptiness. The bell is another. The hollow of the bell symbolizes the dome of such a sky. As a mandala, the outside of the bell represents the journey to wisdom, while as a symbol of "emptiness" the inside of the bell represents wisdom itself. Within what at first seems a relatively simple, although beautifully adorned, bell, there are worlds of profound Tibetan thought and practice.

In 1737, the school of Tibetan Buddhism headed by the Dalai Lama had 3,477 monasteries and 316,230 monks in Tibet, and that was only one of the schools. For centuries, Buddhist life was rich and dense. When the Chinese invaded Tibet in 1950, they started to destroy the monasteries and kill or exile the monks in an effort to diminish Buddhist culture. In 1959, during an uprising in Lhasa to protest Chinese rule, the situation became so dangerous that the Dalai Lama was advised to leave. Only twenty-three years old at the time, he made the treacherous crossing of the Himalayas to northern India. Here he established a government in exile in Dharamsala, where he still lives and teaches today. With him went thousands of Tibetans who formed the beginning of a large diaspora that seeded Tibetan Buddhist communities all around the world.

In recent years, some of the monasteries in Tibet have been restored or rebuilt, and more monks are allowed to practice. But ongoing importation of Chinese nationals into the country continues to dilute the culture, particularly as new generations come of age. It is not possible to know what will happen in the future, particularly when the Dalai Lama dies and the issue of succession for Tibetan leadership has to be faced. But two things seem certain: Tibetan Buddhism has put down strong enough roots around the world that it will survive, and the Tibetan bell will continue to play its extraordinary role as a symbol of the Buddhist journey to wisdom.

When you look at the hollow space in the bell, it appears empty, except for the clapper. This "emptiness" represents one of the most difficult and profound concepts in Buddhism.

A highly decorated quadrangular or pyramid bell from Benin, with a man's face on the front surrounded by royal symbols, including leopards and ceremonial swords.

THE BELLS
OF BENIN

*Art forms can serve as means of formulating new ways to view the
political process, and, most especially, political legitimacy.*

—**PAULA BEN-AMOS,** *ART, INNOVATION, AND POLITICS*

In the winter of 2000, I went to see "Art and Oracle: African Art and the Rituals of Divination," a special exhibit at the Metropolitan Museum of Art in New York City. This was in the early days of my bell explorations, and I hoped the exhibit might tell me something about African bells.

It was an exquisite exhibit, and although it did not feature bells specifically, it did give me a context for seeing how ritual objects were used in different African cultures to reach beyond the human world and attract the attention and help of the gods, ancestors, and spirits of the divine world. It also showed how the aesthetic power of these objects, the art of the objects, enhanced their ritual power. The skill of the artist, joined with the skill of the ritual practitioner, raised the ritual objects into sacred symbols.

The objects in the exhibit took many forms, including sculptural figures, musical devices, masks, and jewelry. They were all engaging, but there was one object near the end of the exhibit that particularly caught my attention. It was a striking brass plaque about eighteen inches tall and thirteen inches wide that showed three warriors, each holding a cylindrical gong with a highly stylized bird on its top. Two of the warriors are striking their gongs with a metal rod. The plaque was powerful, the figures standing out in bold relief and the details of their dress and expressions finely drawn. The signage near the plaque identified

The bird of prophecy plaque symbolizes the power of the Oba and shows warriors striking cylindrical gongs with birds of prophecy on the tops.

it as part of the famous brass art of the ancient Kingdom of Benin in West Africa.

The plaque was a depiction of a pivotal event in the history of Benin when, in the sixteenth century, the reigning king was faced with an invading army from a neighboring kingdom. Before this time, the bird portrayed on the plaque, known as the "bird of prophecy," was believed to be a harbinger of disaster. When the king was leaving the city to meet the invading force, the bird appeared to the troops. Instead of heeding the warning and turning back, the king advanced, destroyed the enemy, and expanded his kingdom. The victory was portrayed as showing that the king had the power to change history. To reinforce this understanding, the king commanded the royal brass casters to create images of the bird of prophecy on plaques and other art objects and to use it as the central image in an important ceremony that celebrated the power of the kings of Benin. Continually reminding people of this victory reinforced their belief in the power of the king to overcome the forces that threatened the kingdom.

Although I was intrigued with the beauty of the plaque, I was more intrigued by how the plaque had been used to enhance the legitimacy of the ruling king, effectively transforming art into political power. The permanent galleries of African art in the museum contained more examples of Benin art, including many more plaques depicting historical and symbolic scenes, powerful ceremonial heads, and altar centerpieces with beautifully molded human and animal forms. More important, I found bells there—unique, four-sided or quadrangular bells that looked like truncated pyramids—that were part of this art. Over the next few years, I saw more examples of these unusual bells in collections of Benin art in the Museum of African Art in Washington, DC, and the British Museum in London. Different from any bells I had seen, I decided to look more deeply into their history and the role they played in Benin society.

In post-colonial Africa, the name Benin has become confusing because it is now the name of a separate nation near Nigeria, formerly known as Dahomey. But the name originally referred to the kingdom of the Edo-speaking people located just west of the Niger delta that was, and still is, centered on Benin City in Nigeria. Although the origins of the kingdom have been obscured by time, in Benin tradition, it is believed to have been founded at the beginning of the tenth century by a series of powerful kings, the Osigo, or "kings of the sky." This first dynasty lasted a few hundred years until abuses of power led to the overthrowing of the last king. During this first dynasty, the contours of the political and social structure of the kingdom were set, as were many early artistic traditions.

After an unsuccessful attempt at republican rule, a second dynasty of kings was established in the late thirteenth century. In order to find a new ruler, the elders of the kingdom sent to the Yoruba city of Ife, the most important spiritual center in the region, and asked the Yoruba king to send a new ruler. The king sent his son, and, although the son stayed only a short time in Benin, he married an Edo woman and fathered a son. This son, Eweka,

became the first oba or king of the new dynasty. That dynasty still exists today, more than 700 years later.

The history of Benin is the history of her obas, for the political, economic, and spiritual life of the Edo people was directly tied to the oba: he owned most of the economic resources; he held the legislative, executive, and judicial powers; and he was the spiritual leader of the kingdom, believed to be a divine intermediary between the human and spiritual worlds. With so much power, the oba's well-being became synonymous with the well-being of the kingdom. His wisdom, skills, and military courage determined the extent of the kingdom's territory and riches, while his personal strength determined how well he could intercede in the spiritual world for the kingdom's benefit.

To protect these powers, the oba needed to be constantly vigilant in maintaining and enhancing belief in his legitimacy. Danger could come from rivals within the kingdom or from warring armies outside the kingdom. In the face of such potential dangers, it was important not only to tell the stories of the oba's accomplishments but to craft these stories with an eye toward reinforcing the oba's power. In this context, Benin art evolved to be intimately interwoven with the political life of the kingdom.

In societies without a written history, storytelling, imagery, ritual, and ceremony become their historical memory. In Benin, many stories and images were represented on ritual art objects. Travelers tell of entering the courts of the palace and finding hundreds of brass plaques mounted vertically on carved wooden pillars, each representing a historical story or a ceremony that symbolized that story. These plaques were the equivalent of today's photographs, both recording and commemorating events. Images of power were also found on ancestral altars, a central part of Edo spiritual life, and on items of personal dress. All of the art—developed over centuries and, in altered form, still being produced today—provided a rich array of symbols and stories that not only helped people remember their history but helped form that history.

Used this way, art becomes part of the process of shaping history, celebrating what the Benin art scholar Paula Ben-Amos calls the "construction of social memory" that presents the "winning" version of history. She illuminates this point by showing how the Edo expression for casting a plaque, *sa-e y'ama*, has different levels of meaning. At its simplest, it means the actual process of pouring metal into a mold. But it also means making something permanent, which is what happens when the metal hardens. And, at the most general level, the phrase means to establish a tradition, which is what happens when a story told on a plaque becomes part of a society's heritage. When the story of the oba's victory was told on the bird of prophecy plaque, it became part of tradition, ritualized in a ceremony that was repeated over time, reinforcing the legitimacy of the oba's power. Art becomes the aesthetic face of power, carrying within it a deep and complex interplay of meanings that compel respect and obedience.

The quadrangular bells were an important part of this aesthetic transformation and of the brass art that so distinguished Benin society. The original brass casters probably came from Ife during the fifteenth and sixteenth centuries when, with the beginning of trade with the West, Benin was able to greatly increase its supply of brass. The first of these was a famous brass caster named Igueghae who, after his death, became the equivalent of the patron saint of the brass casters guild. Located in Egun Street, where it still exists today, the guild developed into ten hierarchal sections, each headed by a hereditary chief and each responsible for a particular form of brass art. The fourth level was responsible for casting bells. Almost all of the brass work was commissioned by the oba, who also supplied the metal for the work; it was art for the court, not for the people.

This very stylized royal art depicts what we would call ideal forms, rather than individualized people or animals. Although there are differences due to different artists and changes over time, generally an oba's face is representative of all obas' faces, a leopard of all leopards, a warrior of all warriors. This stylization was based on a uniform set of images that were passed down from generation to generation within the guild and were considered to be the guild's property. In creating his work, the artist visualized these forms in his head and, when the image was complete, quickly executed it on the mold. During this process, the artist was mentally and spiritually removed from the material world, allowing the power of his creativity to emerge from these mental images. It was a spiritual process deeply embedded in Edo sensibility.

Although there are many variations, a

THE CIRE-PERDUE **METHOD OF CASTING**

The form of casting the Edo people used in their brass work is the intricate and demanding ancient form of casting known as the lost wax, or cire-perdue, method. In this process, a core of clay is formed in the general shape of the head, plaque, bell, or other object to be cast. A layer of beeswax is then applied to this core and molded by hand into the detailed shape desired. Over the wax form, a thin layer of smooth clay called slip is applied, which locks in and preserves the fine detailing in the wax. Layers of rougher clay are then applied until the form is firmly encased in clay, the artist often using metal bands to hold the wax and clay in place.

After the form has air-dried, it is heated until the wax melts, runs out, and is "lost," while the clay is baked hard enough to withstand the molten metal. The brass is melted in crucibles over a hot fire and poured into the hollow space left by the lost wax. After the metal is cool, the form is broken open and the clay layers knocked off, leaving the brass art, which is filed and polished into a smooth, finished piece. Although used by many cultures through history, the Edo people took this form of casting to its highest level, modeling the wax with exquisite detail, creating powerful three-dimensional images like those in the warrior plaque above.

typical Benin pyramidal bell was six to ten inches tall and had a crosshatched or similar geometric background design upon which a small head was molded in relief on the front side of the bell—an Edo head or, sometimes, a more abstract spiral design indicating a head. Around the head and on the sides of the bell were symbolic designs, such as ceremonial

---

The bells indicated a warrior's rank and could be used to announce victories. The bells were also considered a powerful medium for protecting the warriors. As in many cultures, the sound of bells was thought to be potent for warding off evil spirits.

A pyramid bell with a face on a front panel of open lattice-work.

swords, leopards, pythons, crocodiles, mud-fish, or other Edo symbols, all part of the vocabulary of Edo culture. The handle of the bell was a wide loop, usually cast with the bell. There are other Benin bells that have round shapes and different designs, but it is the quadrangular bell that is the most prominent and the most deeply identified with the Kingdom of Benin.

Although the royal brass art was found throughout Benin life, there are two particular places the quadrangular bells were found. One was on the battle dress of warriors. As seen on many of the historical plaques, a small version of the quadrangular bells hung around a warrior's neck, usually from a necklace of leopard's teeth. The bells indicated a warrior's rank and could be used to announce victories. The bells were also considered a powerful medium for protecting the warriors. As in

Bells worn by Benin warriors protected them in battle and warded off evil spirits.

Pyramid bell with a crosshatch pattern on the front and an abstract symbol representing a man's head.

and anger. The spirit of Ogun in the metal, along with its endurance and beauty, gave the bells their special power to repel evil.

The other important place the quadrangular bells were found was on ancestral altars, where they were placed near the front of the altar and rung at the beginning of ceremonies to call the attention of ancestral spirits to people's supplications and sacrifices. In Edo mythology, there are two co-existing worlds, the visible world of everyday life and the invisible spirit world inhabited by greater and lesser gods, hero deities, and ancestral spirits. The creator god, Osanobua, rules the spirit world, like the oba rules the visible world, but he is so supreme that people do not feel a strong sense of intimacy with him. Instead, his oldest son Olokum, the god of water and of health and fertility, is considered more accessible and became the god worshiped most often. There are also a host of lesser gods, such as Ogun, the god of metal so important to brass casters and warriors, as well as numerous spirits, some good and some evil. Also, in the spirit world are the special spirits of people's ancestors who are venerated and worshiped, the most important being the ancestors of the oba.

The spirit world is a living reality to Benin people because the boundaries between the spirit and visible worlds are not inviolate. Gods and spirits reach into the visible world and affect people's lives on a daily basis, while

many cultures, the sound of bells was thought to be potent for warding off evil spirits. For the Edo people, the material the bells were made of added to their power. Brass endures; it is not destroyed by time, so it represents the continuity of the Edo kingdom. Brass is also shiny, a quality considered beautiful in the Edo aesthetic. And brass is an alloy of copper and zinc and is reddish in color. For the Edo people, red is a color of power and is the color of Ogun, the god of metal, who represents fire certain individuals, such as the oba, can draw divine power from the spirit world. Because of this ever-present potential for interaction between the worlds and because the spirit world is so much more powerful than the visible world, people must continually appeal to and appease the gods and spirits. They also need to do all they can to strengthen the divine powers of the oba, who is the only person who can partially balance the power imbalance between the two worlds. The vital impact the spirit world can have on everyday life creates the dynamic of Edo religion as represented on ancestral altars, for it is here that praise, supplication, and sacrifices to the gods and spirits take place.

Ancestral altars are central to the life of the family and the life of the state. When an oba dies, the first responsibility of the eldest son is to set up an altar for him. The altar becomes the place to commemorate and honor the deceased, the place to communicate with him and to ask help for those still living. Around the front of the altar are the many bells that are rung to call the ancestor to the ceremonies. As in many cultures, in Benin, bells are the "voice" that connects the human world with the spirit world.

In addition to the bells, the altars hold many beautiful examples of Benin art. A person's rank in society determines what can be placed on his ancestral altar. Common people have the plainest altars, which include specially carved staffs, simple bells, and ceremonial swords. A chief's altar is more elaborate, with additional ceremonial objects and bells and a carved wooden head commemorating the ancestor. The oba's ceremonial altar is by far the most elaborate with lovely bells and a beautifully cast centerpiece that has a detailed brass figure of the deceased king in full ceremonial regalia surrounded by attendants and other special symbols, such as the kingly leopards. Flanking the centerpiece or behind it is one or more magnificent brass heads. Only the oba and the queen mother can have a head

Stately head of an oba with a high collar of coral beads found on ancestral altars.

cast in brass on their altars. The heads are strong and regal, with large almond-shaped eyes, finely chiseled lips, and the exceptionally high collar and woven cap of coral beads that represents kingly power in Benin. The center-pieces, heads, staffs, and bells all personify the sanctity and power of the ancestors in Benin life.

Ancestral altars are one essential medium for drawing the favor of the deities to the people; the other is the royal ceremonies carried out throughout the year. Many of these ceremonies center on the oba, either honoring his ancestors or strengthening his powers, but there is one ceremony, Igue, that inadvertently played a crucial role in the destruction of the kingdom in the late 1800s.

Igue is the festival of the yam, yams being Benin's staple crop. Celebrated in four stages over the course of the agricultural cycle, the festival was an appeal for blessings on the crop, but, at a deeper level, it was an appeal for blessings on the land, to keep it sanctified and free from evil. During the harvest stage of this celebration, the festival became most potent. At this time, the oba and a few select chiefs went into seclusion for a period of ritual fasting. During this time, the oba could not have contact with the outside world. A violation of this period of fasting by the British in 1897 was the immediate cause of the end of Benin as an independent kingdom.

After flourishing in the fifteenth and sixteenth centuries, Benin fell into a period of civil strife that eventually was succeeded by another golden era in the eighteenth century. By the middle of the nineteenth century, however, the kingdom had again weakened. By

this time, the English were the main colonial power in the region. The English were particularly interested in gaining control of the rubber and other valuable resources in the interior of the area, as well as the trade routes that connected these resources to the coast. Trade treaties had been signed between the British and the oba, but there were misunderstandings on both sides, which angered the British.

In January of 1897, James Phillips, a young acting consul general of the British forces on the coast, decided to proceed to Benin City without the authority of the Foreign Office to force decisions on trade and other matters. Upon receiving word of his intentions, the oba requested that he postpone the visit, since the oba would be in the midst of the yam ceremony and could not receive visitors. Local chiefs also told the acting consul that it was not possible for him to go to Benin City at this time. However, Phillips rejected the advice and proceeded on his way.

When the oba heard the English were still coming, he felt he had to acknowledge them in some way, so he sent a small group of chiefs to escort them, strongly admonishing the chiefs that no harm was to come to the group. However, the chiefs, incensed by the violation of their religion and other British demands, attacked the convoy and killed all but two of the Englishmen and most of their African escorts. The English used this attack to quickly mount a "punitive expedition" that overran and destroyed the kingdom, including Benin City. Much of the city was burned, including the oba's palace, the oba was sent into exile, and many chiefs either killed themselves to avoid being captured or were executed by the British. The British looted the royal palace, removing thousands of plaques, brass heads, bells, and other ceremonial and religious

artists back to the city, starting training programs for new artists and rebuilding many of the artistic guilds.

However, there were significant differences for the brass workers under Eweke II's reign, as

During the siege, most of the artists fled the city to outlying villages. With the patronage of the oba gone, their art taken to Europe, and their guild dispersed, the brass workers could no longer function as they had. It was not until 1914, when the British partially reinstated the senior son of the banished oba, that art began to revive.

objects that they took back to England, where most of them were sold, forming the basis for the important collections of Benin art found in European and American museums today. In taking over the kingdom's resources and trade routes, the British also robbed the kingdom of much of its artistic, political, and religious heritage.

During the siege, most of the artists fled the city to outlying villages. With the patronage of the oba gone, their art taken to Europe, and their guild dispersed, the brass workers could no longer function as they had. It was not until 1914, when the British partially reinstated the senior son of the banished oba, that art began to revive. The new oba, Eweka II, named after the dynasty's founding oba to reinforce his legitimacy, rebuilt the palace and altars and needed replacements for the lost art. He was a caster and carver himself, and he gathered

there were for all artists. The oba no longer supplied the raw materials, so the brass casters had to acquire their own brass. The oba also only supplied some orders, so artists needed to find a wider market, eventually developing commercial and tourist markets for their work, which changed how they worked. Without enough good examples of their former art, they had to develop their own forms, as well as respond to European and American tastes, working much faster to turn out enough pieces to support themselves. The work, although good, no longer reached the aesthetic heights of the artistic tradition that was its heritage. Although a large part of the work remained part of Edo life and religion, the spiritual sanctity and political power of the art was diminished.

In the 1960s, a new burst of artistic activity occurred among the Edo people. Artists began

British soldiers with the looted treasures they took from Benin that later became the foundation of museum holdings of Benin art in Europe and the United States.

to build a contemporary body of brass and ivory work that reclaimed a part of the dignity and quality of the precolonial legacy. There was also a movement, particularly on the part of university-trained artists, to work in new media, such as paint, and to explore new subject matter, such as twentieth-century history and Christianity. Benin art began to evolve as an independent art form, separate from the oba and traditional culture. Ceremonial heads, plaques, staffs, and bells were still needed for ancestral altars and for commemo-

rating special events, and the hereditary guilds were still responsible for a large part of the work, but the new art also reflected the influences of international art trends, commodity markets, and individualist perspectives.

Since that time, Benin artists have continued to expand their repertoire, but with increasing attention to how their art contributes to a renewal of Edo culture and identity. Rather than being judged on its precolonial heritage, the artists want their work to be judged on its own merits and on its contribution to contemporary Edo life. As a result, a dialogue has now developed between Nigeria and European and American museums that aims to increase Western understanding that Benin art is more than beautiful art; it is a vital part of Nigeria's heritage. There are now increasing calls to return at least part of the art that currently resides in these museums to Nigeria.

In response to these calls, a commitment was made in 2018 to build a museum in Benin that would house exhibits of Benin art lent by the major European museums on a rotating basis. During the fall of 2020, the plans for this museum, the Edo Museum of West African Art, were presented by its architect David Adjaye. In an interview with *The New York Times*, Adjaye said that he saw the museum not as a place of the past but as a living space for people to reconnect with their cultural heritage. He designed the museum building as an abstract representation of the precolonial palace, so that the building, as well as the exhibits of art, would become the footprints of that heritage. At the same time, the museum would be a community center and a showcase for contemporary artists. A number of Western museums are now in the process of returning part of their collections to the new museum.

Also in 2020, a major initiative was announced by Hamburg's Museum Am Rothenbaum called "Digital Benin," which will bring the collections in European and American museums online, along with cultural information and images from Benin. "Digital Benin" will be a valuable resource for the museum. Both of these initiatives are steps forward in restoring the cultural integrity of Benin art.

The bells of Benin are distinguished by their unusual quadrangular shape and by the powerful role they have played in Benin society. As more attention is given to Benin art and culture, hopefully, these unusual bells will become better known, taking a more prominent place in the world of bells.

PART III

THE B

OF BRI

ELLS
TAIN!

The Iona Abbey, a large medieval abbey on the Scottish island of Iona, features a Celtic cross that is approximately a thousand years old and is a reminder of earlier times when St. Columba first brought Christianity to the island.

SCOTLAND'S "SACRED ISLE"

It is but a small isle, fashioned of a little sand, a few grasses salt with the spray of an ever-restless wave, a few rocks that wade in heather, and upon whose brows the sea-wind weaves the yellow lichen. But since the remotest days, sacrosanct men have bowed here in worship.

—FIONA MACLEOD

I first heard about Iona from an Episcopal minister in Washington, DC. He described it as one of the most sacred places he had ever been —a small island off the west coast of Scotland filled with grace and natural peace that encapsulated the development of Christianity in the West. He said the island was often covered with gray mist, but, when the skies cleared, it glowed with the ethereal light of the Scottish Highlands. The island then became a place of white beaches, blue water, green pastures, and golden flowers, a place for walking, meditation, and prayer.

Inspired by this conversation, I started reading about the island and found both further testimony as to its sacred nature and a fascinating story that crystalized both the history of Western Christianity and the history of Western bells. I decided to visit the island, both to experience being there and to learn more about this surprising history.

To get to Iona, you take Scottish Rail from Glasgow up the west coast of Scotland to the town of Oban. From there, you take a ferry to the island of Mull, a fairly large island, and then a bus across Mull to its western end. There, you take another ferry to Iona, which is only three miles long and a mile wide. Landing at the small village on the protected east side of the island, you can walk along the only street to the Argyll Hotel, where I stayed. Much of the rest of the island is fields and craggy hills where sheep roam and a battered west coast open to the winds and waves of the Atlantic Ocean. Dominating the landscape is a massive, restored medieval abbey, a short walk north of the village.

I spent almost a week on the island, much of it in a small library high up in the abbey that had a window looking out to the sea. The library had many of the books I had seen referenced but could not find at home, so I did most of my research there, quickly finding that the history of Christianity and bells on Iona was even richer than I had imagined.

Over a period of 1,500 years, three distinct waves of Christianity came to Iona. In the sixth century, St. Columba came from Ireland and founded a monastery that became a center of learning and civilization for three centuries during the Dark Ages. From Iona, St. Columba spread Christianity to much of Scotland, helping to create the powerful and unusual monastic movement of Celtic Christianity.

In the twelfth century, a second wave of Christianity came to the island. During this medieval period, Iona became an important site of Catholic Christianity when the Benedictines built the large abbey there, while an Augustinian nunnery was built just down the road. Together they brought more than 300 years of new Christian presence to the island.

After the Protestant Reformation expelled Catholicism from Scotland in the sixteenth century, the abbey and nunnery were abandoned and fell into ruins. However, in the twentieth century, a third wave of Christianity came to the island in the form of the Iona Community, an ecumenical group of socially oriented Protestants and Catholics who helped restore the abbey complex and today use it as a place of spiritual retreat and outreach.

What is so intriguing about Iona is not only that such a tiny and remote island carries so much Christian history but that each succeeding wave of Christianity illuminates a different stage in the development of Western bells. Bells have always been part of the ceremony and symbolism of the Christian Church, and, just as the spread of Buddhism was so influential in the development of Eastern bells, the evolution and spread of Christianity greatly influenced the development of Western bells.

In St. Columba's time, bells were simple handbells, first carried by individual missionaries and then used in monasteries to call people to worship and meals. They were the clocks of the early monasteries and, over time, became a more and more sacred part of monastic life.

By the Middle Ages, these small handbells had been augmented by much larger hanging bells as bell towers were developed and ways found to hang and ring larger and larger bells. The medieval bells still played most of the same roles in the practices of monastic life as they had in early times, but they were no longer the humble, personal bells of the early Celtic missionaries; they were the majestic institutional bells of the Roman Catholic Church.

When Protestantism banned Catholic rituals and destroyed many Catholic symbols in Scotland, bells lost many of their sacred roles, held suspect because they were closely associated with the mystery and magic of early Christianity, as well as the later practices of Roman Catholicism. As a result, bells became more secular. During the 1,500 years of

poetry and nature, of prophecy and miracles, has become a personification of the mystical imagination and faith that seem to set the island apart and make it holy.

We know a great deal about Columba's world because Adamnan, a later abbot and a relative of Columba's, wrote a history of Columba's life that remains one of the finest

---

What is so intriguing about Iona is not only that such a tiny and remote island carries so much Christian history but that each succeeding wave of Christianity illuminates a different stage in the development of Western bells.

Christian history on Iona, bells developed from simple to sacred to secular, following the evolution of Christianity on the island from Celtic to Roman Catholic to Protestant.

However, even now, after so many centuries, it is the story of St. Columba that most defines the island. Not only was St. Columba a deeply engaging historical figure, but the Christianity he brought to the island was the fullest expression of the island's own inherent spirituality. Iona has been described as a place where there is an unusual closeness between heaven and earth and between man and God. It has never been the things man built on the island, the things we see with our "outward" eye, that have been important; it is what we see with our "inward" eye, the spiritual grace that seems to emanate from the island's own rocks, wind, and water. St. Columba, a man of

sources of information about this early Christian era. From Adamnan's descriptions, we know that the monastery St. Columba built was made of simple wooden buildings plastered with mud. There was an oratory, or chapel, a communal sleeping room, and a refectory, which probably also served as a scriptorium or writing room. St. Columba had a separate sleeping cell and his own writing hut on a hill near the chapel.

The sound of bells punctuated the life of the monastery. The day started at dawn as a monastery bell called the community to the first of many services held during the day and night, the longest service being during the night with the full liturgy of psalms, hymns, scripture, and prayer. The services were conducted in Latin, although Gaelic was used for everyday speech. Since there were no

An early bell called a clagan or clocca carried by Christian monks and used to punctuate the different parts of the daily services. Usually handmade of iron and quite crude, these bells were used for years in Ireland and Scotland.

being carried. Sometimes, these rough iron bells were dipped in bronze, which filled in the cracks and gave a more solid and even surface to the bell. However, even covered with bronze, they had a flat, tinny sound.

The services were the public devotion of the monastery, designed to keep God's presence continually with the monks throughout the day and night. The monks were also expected to spend considerable time in private prayer and meditation, and they spent time in the everyday work of the monastery, such as growing crops and tending stock, maintaining the buildings, cooking and cleaning, and ensuring the monastery remained self-sufficient. While some worked in the fields or around the buildings, others worked in the scriptorium, copying manuscripts, such as Bibles, lives of the saints, and other books, such as St. Augustine's *City of God*. Since there were no printing presses at that time, all books and liturgical documents had to be copied by hand. From this simple life on Iona, St. Columba founded the large family of monasteries in Scotland and Ireland that created much of the spiritual, intellectual, and artistic legacy that defined Celtic Christianity.

That one man on such a small island could have so much influence is due both to the circumstances of the time and the rare nature of the man. When St. Columba landed on Iona in 563, the Holy Roman Empire had fallen. Rome was occupied by Germanic tribes, Europe was in upheaval, and Saxon tribes were invading Britain. It was a time of chaos

musical instruments, the monks' voices took their place, chanting the plainsong of the liturgy, sometimes with two choirs echoing each other across the chapel.

The bell calling people to services was only one of the bells in the monastery. St. Columba had his own personal bell, and there would have been bells belonging to other noted monks, as well as other communal bells. These early bells, known in Ireland as clagan or clocca, were small and crudely forged out of sheets of iron by folding over the two ends of the sheet and riveting them together with flat nails to form a trapezoid-shaped bell, much like paper doll clothes are cut out and folded over with tabs to put on paper dolls. A clapper was attached inside and a handle on the top so that the bell could be shaken or rung while and destruction. The Romans had ruled Europe and Britain for hundreds of years, and the indigenous cultures of these areas had long been displaced by Roman culture. The period we call the Dark Ages descended, and learning, progress, and culture were increasingly extinguished. Books were destroyed, much of the Christianity that had spread during Roman times was fractured, and art and intellectual work was displaced.

Ireland and Scotland, as well as Wales and other small parts of England, remained outside these powerful historical forces. In the thousand years before Christ, northern Europe and the British Isles were inhabited by the Celts, an ancient race of people. As the Romans expanded their empire, the Celtic people were pushed first out of Europe to England and then out of most of England to Scotland and Ireland. But the Roman Empire stopped at England; the Romans never conquered or occupied Scotland or Ireland. Where Roman culture had replaced Celtic culture in the rest of Europe, it continued to flourish uninterrupted in these Western outposts. The melding of Christianity with this enduring Celtic culture created the unusual Christianity St. Columba brought to Iona.

One of the most distinctive things about this new Celtic Christianity was that it took its organizational form from the early monasticism of the deserts, rather than from the established Roman Church that dominated the rest of Europe. In the second and third centuries, many Christians who wanted to find a place of refuge from urban life became hermits in the deserts of Egypt and Syria, living lives of ascetic isolation in these empty spaces. Over

time, some of these hermits banded together in small communities. As the groups grew in size and complexity, they developed rules to bring order and harmony to their communal life, eventually evolving into monastic communities. Wherever these early hermits and monastics went, they carried bells to scare off demons and evil spirits, for, like religious people in other cultures, they believed bells had magical powers that could protect them from harm. These monastics were some of the first Christians to make bells talismans for their religious life.

As the monasticism of the Eastern deserts spread to the West, it took two different paths, one in Roman Europe and one in Celtic Ireland. In Europe, monasticism was absorbed into the already existing structures and doctrines of the Roman Church. When Christianity became the official religion of the Roman Empire, it was organized along the same lines as Roman civil society, with a hierarchal structure of authority headed by the pope, whose religious power flowed down through archbishops, bishops, and priests, just as civil power flowed down from the emperor to senators to citizens. Also, like civil authority, religious authority was centered in Rome, radiating out from there to the rest of the empire. Monasteries became an auxiliary part of this structure, developing into formalized monastic orders under the sophisticated rule of such inspired leaders as St. Benedict. As the missionary arm of the Church, these monastic orders became the primary means for spreading Roman Christianity abroad. In Europe, what began as the importation of the ideals of ascetic

Celtic Christianity was able to integrate many Druidic beliefs about nature into its theology and religious practices, and, in places like Iona, the hills, water, birds, and animals of the island became part of daily religious life.

individualism emerged as the fully developed Roman Catholic orders. However, monasticism was always a secondary part of Roman Christianity, a complementary form of religious practice.

In Celtic Ireland, things were different. Here monasticism became the primary organizing force of Christianity, and monasteries became the center of religious practice. When St. Patrick and other early missionaries first brought Christianity to Ireland early in the fifth century, they encountered a culture at odds with the Roman culture of Europe. Celtic Ireland was distinguished by its tribal structure, mystical Druid religion, and strong artistic sensibilities. Rather than cities, Ireland had territories controlled by different, often competing tribes. Tribal membership was the organizing principle of society, and much of tribal culture centered on warrior heroes and on oral sagas that were the carriers of tribal history and identity.

The form of Christianity that St. Patrick brought, based as it was on an urban structure of religious authority with the pope, bishops, and priests centered in faraway Rome, had a hard time taking root in this decentralized, tribal society. However, when the monastic form of Christianity arrived in Ireland later in the century, it found more fertile ground. Monasticism did have much in common with Irish society. Monasteries were decentralized and rural, rather than urban and hierarchal. Their structure—with an abbot at the head and an extended family of monks and lay members—was similar to tribal structures, where a chief had authority over an extended family. Although bishops and priests still existed, they became supplemental to the monasteries, performing only some rites and rituals. The monasteries were the central force in Irish Christianity, and the abbots had the power.

Because it was a more personal and rural form of Christianity, monasticism was also able to accommodate itself to the ancient Druidic religion in Ireland more easily than the Roman Church. For any new religion to take hold in a country in an enduring way, it must absorb some of that country's existing religious customs and beliefs. Celtic Christianity was able to integrate many Druidic beliefs about nature into its theology and religious practices, and, in places like Iona, the hills, water, birds, and animals of the island became part of daily religious life. Monasticism also accommodated the Druid past by allowing some residual beliefs in the older deities to remain part of the culture in a lessened role as the fairies and unseen beings of Irish mythology. By the beginning of the sixth century, the Roman Christianity of St. Patrick had been superseded by this new, monastic Christianity. A simpler, more populist, less formally organized Christianity, it put a direct relationship with God, rather than with priests, at the center of worship and authority.

The new monasteries also became the source of a great blossoming of Celtic art, as the remarkable artistic abilities of the Celtic people were inspired by the new religion. Books were transformed into illuminated manuscripts, and monumental stone crosses and intricate metalwork were created, becoming some of the great artworks of the Christian church. At its peak in the eighth and ninth centuries, Celtic Christianity created an artistic legacy that is still revered today.

In this time and place, the remarkable abilities of St. Columba became a catalyst to bring Celtic Christianity to its full flowering. St. Columba possessed a set of qualities that set him apart from other men. His deep spirituality and formidable intellect made him a revered monastic leader and an important writer and interpreter of the scriptures. His love of nature and understanding of men made him a sensitive poet and a humble brother to his fellow monks. And the intensity with which he could enter into prayer and meditation revealed a gift of second sight, or "quickened inward vision," that made him renowned for his prophecies and visions. These were the qualities that distinguished St. Columba's life within the monastery. But the internal life of the monastery was only half of his life. He also was an extraordinarily able administrator, a talented diplomat with powerful political connections, and had the driving force and energy needed for missionary work. It was these qualities he took abroad on his many travels that enabled him to convert much of Scotland to Christianity. His was a vigorous monasticism, as he combined the traits of churchman, nobleman, diplomat, scholar, mystic, and poet.

The glory of Celtic Christianity on Iona came to an end in the ninth and tenth centuries when the Vikings raided the island. In 797, Iona was sacked; in 802, it was burned; and in 806, eighty-six monks were killed on a small beach just south of the present village. The raids continued for another 200 years, with the ownership of the Scottish Isles going back and forth between Scotland and Norway until they were finally ceded to Scotland. Although abbots remained on the island until the early eleventh century, the relics, library, and headship of the Columban family were moved first to the monastery at Kells in Ireland and then to mainland Scotland for safety.

The second wave of Christianity came to Iona in the twelfth century when a Benedictine abbey was built on the site of the earlier monastic ruins. By this time, the ever-growing conflict between Celtic and Roman Christianity

St. Patrick's bell shrine is now in the
National Museum of Ireland in Dublin.

BELLS OF **THE SAINTS**

As Celtic Christianity matured, many of the early founders like Columba were acclaimed saints, becoming the new warriors and heroes of Celtic society. Believed to be personifications of the sanctity and power of God, the saints became channels for prayer and intercession with the spiritual world. Bells now took on a new role as one of the sacred relics associated with saints, the sacred relics being personal things that belonged to a saint, which were believed to have taken on some of that saint's powers. The primary and most sacred relics were the actual bones of a saint, while the secondary relics were physical belongings, such as bells, staffs, books, and clothing. Of the secondary relics, the bells and staffs were most important, being the insignia most often depicted as symbols of the saints.

The saints' relics were closely guarded, for they were the most precious posses-sions of monks and monasteries and considered to have the power to protect warriors in battle, to bind oaths, to heal disease, and to drive away the plague and other disasters. Many of these relics were destroyed in the Protestant Reformation, but a few survived, including a bell believed to have belonged to St. Patrick that is enclosed in a lovely bell case covered in gold and silver filigree, now in the National Museum of Ireland in Dublin.

had come to a head and been won by the more organized and powerful Roman Church. As Roman Christianity pushed farther and farther west into the British Isles, the Celtic monasteries were too scattered and decentralized to maintain their independence. With the political winds shifting to Rome, much of the spirit and practice of Celtic Christianity came to an end.

This change can be seen quite visually on Iona. In contrast to St. Columba's plain wooden buildings, the abbey the Benedictine Order built on the island was a massive Romanesque structure of elaborate arches and imposing rooms. The Benedictines did take advantage of St. Columba's legacy by building the new abbey near the tall stone cross that still stood on the site of the original monastery, and they incorporated within their design a small stone shrine to St. Columba from the ninth or tenth century, which was the last Celtic building remaining on the island. Adopting some of the relics of St. Columba helped the Benedictines, one of the most powerful European medieval orders, gain acceptance in the Scottish Isles.

By the time Christianity returned to Iona in the twelfth century, major changes had taken place in Europe in how bells were made and used, so the bells brought by the Benedictines were very different from the simple bells of St. Columba. As medieval monasteries became larger, bigger bells were needed to call people together. However, as bells got bigger and heavier, they could no longer be carried by a person; they had to be hung on something. First, they were hung on nails on the monastery walls and rung with a rope tied to the clapper.

As they got bigger, a loop was attached to the bell in place of a handle and a log or something else strong and straight was passed through the loop, allowing the bell to swing as it was rung. Over time, the logs turned into yokes that could turn in a wider and wider leaning tower of Pisa in Italy, but, eventually, most towers were incorporated into the design of the church.

By this time, bells were being cast in bronze rather than made by hand, which made their tones much sweeter. Bell casting had developed

The sound of these bells accompanied people throughout their lives. They were used to call people to services, to be the clocks of the community, to mark special events, and to warn the community of dangers, such as fire or floods. Believed to have spiritual powers, they were usually blessed, baptized, and given names.

circle, and the short rope attached to the clapper was replaced with a long rope attached to the yoke. Now bells could be raised higher while still being rung from the ground, and a number of bells could be rung together. As the sound of the bells carried farther across the countryside, bells became the clocks for the surrounding communities, just as they were for the monasteries. Bells were now part of the institutional property of the Church, a corporate symbol, rather than the personal property and symbol of an individual monk.

As bells got heavier and were hung higher, a special structure was needed to house them, a structure that was strong enough to hold the weight of the bells and withstand their lateral thrust as they swung from side to side. Bell towers became the homes for these new bells. At first, bell towers were separate structures, like the famous round towers of Ireland or the

in Europe in the sixth and seventh centuries and was fully developed by the tenth century when even small, rural churches had cast bells. The first foundries were run by the monks, but as communities turned into cities, private foundries emerged to cast bells and other metal objects, such as armaments. Bells were now an important form of communication, not just for monasteries but for all Christians living near a church.

The shape of bells also changed as efforts were made to make bells more melodious. Some of the earliest cast bells found in Western Europe were small, cup-shaped bells. The next shape that emerged was known as the beehive, which was still rather squat, but had broad, rounded shoulders and a shallow, convex shape. Next came the sugarloaf, tall and slender, with narrow, rounded shoulders and a concave shape. On the sugarloaf, the simple handle was replaced with sturdy metal

The Development of Western Bell Shapes

Cup

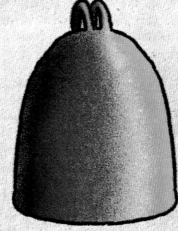

Beehive

Sugarloaf

Modern

This large, elaborately decorated Pelican Bell, showing the birds back to back, is used in Christian worship services. The bell sits on its own dish and is quite large for a handbell.

loops for hanging called cannons. Finally, through trial and error, today's familiar bell shape emerged, which had slightly rounded shoulders, a more pronounced concave side, and was between the beehive and sugarloaf in height. The new shape created a better sound, although the full knowledge of tuning bells did not develop in Europe for several more centuries.

The sound of these bells accompanied people throughout their lives. They were used to call people to services, to be the clocks of the community, to mark special events, and to warn the community of dangers, such as fire or floods. Believed to have spiritual powers, they were usually blessed, baptized, and given names. They were also often inscribed with statements of their ability to drive away danger and evil spirits. Belief in the magical powers of Christian bells endured for many centuries and is still acknowledged in some parts of the world today.

The bells were also tied deeply into a person's personal life. They were rung for confirmation, when a person officially joined the church, and for marriages, the most joyful occasion. They also accompanied a person through the many stages of death: first the Passing Bell was rung when a person was dying, then the Death Knell when a person died, then the Lych Bell when the person was carried to the cemetery (usually through a lych gate), and finally the Burial Bell when the person was laid to rest in the grave. The sound of the bells was believed to clear the air of demons and other dangers as a person's soul passed into eternity.

In addition to tower bells, small handbells were an important part of Christianity. They were used throughout the Christian service to announce to the congregation when the different parts of the liturgy would occur, particularly the celebration of the Eucharist, the center-piece of Catholic worship. The Pelican Bell is a lovely example of a Christian handbell.

The Roman Christianity of the Benedictine

The sound of the bells was believed to clear the air of demons and other dangers as a person's soul passed into eternity.

---

abbey endured on Iona for three centuries. In the fifteenth century, a major expansion and rebuilding of the abbey took place, which included the square bell tower, still a prominent part of the abbey today. However, as a result of the Reformation that challenged the Catholic Church in the mid-1500s, Scotland became Protestant, and the monastery was abandoned, eventually deteriorating into ruins.

After the Protestant Reformation, most of the Catholic monasteries in Scotland were stripped of bells and other important artifacts that either had monetary value or were symbols of Catholicism. As a result, bells lost the central roles they had played in the Celtic and Catholic Churches, including the belief in their power to ward off evil or bring blessings to people. The strict Protestantism of Scotland removed as much of the mystery from religion

The restored cloister at Iona Abbey, a peaceful place for meditation where you can hear the soft sounds of the birds and sheep of the island.

as possible, and bells were no longer sacrosanct. Bells still hung in churches and were rung to call people to services and for special occasions, but they were now an accompaniment to religion, rather than an essential part of it. Although beautiful to look at and lovely to hear, they were now more secular than sacred.

There were occasional efforts to restore the medieval monastery, but it was not until the late 1800s that the Duke of Argyll, who then owned the island, created the Iona Cathedral Trust and turned the ruins over to the trust with the understanding that they would be rebuilt. The abbey church was rebuilt by 1910, but not the rest of the abbey. Then the third wave of spiritual energy came to the island in the form of Reverend Dr. George MacLeod, a Presbyterian minister from Glasgow who, during the Depression of the 1930s, came to believe that the Christian church was too

removed from the people it was supposed to serve. He developed a communal approach to Christianity that stressed the need to bring simple physical labor together with prayer. MacLeod came to the island in 1938 with a half-dozen craftsmen and a number of young ministers to restore the cloister and the rest of the monastery. The community MacLeod established was eventually formalized as the Iona Community. The community now runs the day-to-day life of the restored abbey, drawing people of all faiths to Iona for spiritual retreat and renewal, as well as sending community members out on missions of peace and global understanding.

In my days on Iona, when I wasn't in the library, I spent most of my time walking the island or sitting in the inner cloister of the abbey, a peaceful place surrounded by the buildings that make up the abbey community.

Sitting in the cloister during the day, I could hear the distant sounds of sheep bleating and the cries of birds. Toward evening, I would hear the abbey bell ringing in the tower to call people to worship, for the abbey is still a working church. This is not the original abbey bell, but a more modern one cast in 1931 by John Taylor of Loughborough, a historically important English bell foundry.

One day near the end of my visit, Gilbert Mullen, one of the abbey staff, took me up to see the bell. We climbed the steep, circular stone steps to the ringing chamber and from there continued up a wooden ladder to the actual bell chamber. Stepping into the bell chamber, I was surprised by how large the bell was. About five feet tall and four feet wide at the bottom, it commemorates St. Columba. The bell has a rounded lip that you see as it hangs in its stock in a large, red, metal frame. There is a traditional rope around its wheel that goes down into the ringing chamber one floor below. There is also a gong attached to a second rope that goes all the way down into the church. For daily services, the gong is used to sound the bell, but for Christmas, Easter, and other special occasions, the bell is rung by a ringer in the ringing chamber. There is also a smaller bell attached to one wall of the cloister, a sixteenth-century Flemish bell brought to the abbey in the 1940s that is used as a daily signal to call people to meals and meetings. But it is the tower bell or "big bell," as it is known on the island, that most distinguishes the abbey.

After seeing the tower bell, Gilbert took me up another staircase to a narrow balustrade on the outside of the tower. From there, we had wonderful views of Iona, Mull, and the nearby islands. When I looked down, I could see the fourteen-foot St. Martin's cross, still standing after more than 1,000 years, a gentle reminder of the time St. Columba brought his spiritual and intellectual light to this small island and transformed it into a Christian icon.

The Iona Abbey bell in the abbey tower was cast in 1931 by John Taylor of Loughborough and still rings every day to call the people of the island to services.

The St. Mary-le-Bow bell tower in London, a center for English change ringing and a cultural and historic part of English history.

ST. MARY-LE-BOW

Bell ringing is the poetry of steeples.

—BEN JONSON

Belfries, pubs; sallies, stays; full peals, touches; Grandshire Major, Treble Bob Minor—this is the world of the English bell ringer. Often following in the footsteps of parents and grandparents, young ringers start at age thirteen or fourteen to learn the proper techniques of bell ringing. When they become proficient, most go on to learn the fascinating art of change ringing. This particular method of ringing developed in England in the mid-1600s and, while dominating the history of English bell ringing, has remained peculiarly English. Only a few other countries—notably English-speaking countries such as the United States and Australia—have any history of change ringing, and it is a minor part of their history compared to England.

Most English churches have three to twelve bells hung in a bell chamber high in the bell tower or belfry. Each bell is held in a yoke called a headstock, which is attached to a wheel. A rope goes around the wheel and through a hole in the floor of the bell chamber to the ringing room below. As the ringer pulls the rope, the wheel turns, which swings the bell so that the clapper strikes against its inside surface, producing the ringing sound.

A few feet from the end or tail of the rope is a padded area of colored wool called the sally.

Quite long, it is usually striped in bright, primary colors, such as red and blue. Giving good purchase to the ringer's hands, the sally also helps the ringer watch the movements of the other ropes so he can time his or her own ringing.

The new ringer learns to stand straight with weight over slightly parted feet. From the down position, the bells are "rung up" until they are perched upside down in the bell tower. This is done by increasing the swing of each bell until it reaches the top, like pushing a child higher and higher on a swing. Then the real ringing begins.

Reaching up with both hands for the tail of the rope hanging overhead, the ringer pulls straight down without shifting posture or bending the back. As the sally comes down, the ringer shifts his or her hands up to it, pulling it farther down in a smooth motion. The bell has now swung around in a full circle, the clapper striking the inside of the bell when the bell stops at the top of its swing.

In the second part of the ring, both hands bring the sally all the way down as far as the arms can go while still standing straight. The bell swings back in a full circle, ending upside down on the side where it started. The clapper again swings across and the second "ring" of the bell sounds. As the rope rises with the second swing, the ringer reverses the earlier process, shifting the hands back from the sally

Change ringers at St. Mary's Church, Rotherhithe, getting ready to pull down on the striped sallies during the two-part process of bell ringing.

to the tail end of the rope until the rope is again over the ringer's head. The bell is now at the top of its ring again, and the process is repeated. The ringer must learn to perform this two-part pull in a smooth, continuous motion so that the intervals between the sounds of the bells are even; this is "good striking." In an experienced ringer, you can see the grace and rhythm of the pull down and up and down and up again. There are many wonderful YouTube videos of change ringing where you can watch ringers in action.

After mastering the motion of the pull, the ringer has to learn to work together with other ringers. The bells are hung in different directions in the bell tower so as to reduce the stress on the tower, and so the bell ropes fall in a circle in the ringing chamber below. The ringers stand in this circle under the ropes for their particular bells. In this way, they can see one another and coordinate their motions. By watching one another carefully, they are able to time their ringing, which creates the intricate patterns of change ringing.

Change ringing developed as a result of new advances in how bells were hung. Before the early 1600s, the wheel attached to the bells could only go a quarter or a half of the way around, so the bells swung only partway up and back on each side. They could be rung in succession, but there was no way to control the timing. This was fine for calling people to church, announcing the time, tolling the dead, and warning people of danger; none of these activities required great precision.

In the early 1600s, a new kind of wheel came into use, which was a full wheel that had a stay and slider apparatus. The bell rope was still attached to the wheel, but now the wheel could go full circle. Attached to the headstock was a rectangular piece of wood called a stay, which in turn was attached to a metal slider. When the bell was rung hard enough to bring it all the way upside down, the slider hit the end of its slide, which caused the stay to stop, also stopping the bell so it could not go over the top. The bell rested in an inverted position, just past the top of the circle. When the bell swung up the other side, the slider moved to its opposite end, stopping the stay on that side and again holding the bell in an inverted position just past the top in the other direction.

With this invention, it became possible to control the timing and thus the rhythm of the bells. As each bell swung up and back, it could be checked and even held at the top before coming down again. At first, ringers performed simple rounds—ringing the bells at a regular pace in ascending or descending order. Since the smallest bell has the highest pitch and the largest the lowest, ringing "down the scale" means ringing from the highest- to the lowest-pitched bell, the usual form of a round. For six bells, this is noted as 1 2 3 4 5 6, the smallest bell being 1 and the largest 6. When you hear bell ringing in a steeple, you often hear the rippling sound of the bells rung "down the scale" from high to low before and after the main program.

With time, however, ringing simple rounds became uninteresting. In the mid-1660s, Fabian Stedman began to experiment with ringing bells in different patterns. With the full wheel, it was possible for a ringer to retard or hasten the swing of a bell to the extent that two bells could change places in the order of the round. You could check your bell just short of its full swing and ring ahead of another bell. Or you could let your bell pause at the top of its swing so that another bell could ring ahead of you. As a result, after ringing 1 2 3 4 on four bells, you could ring 2 1 3 4, with the first pair reversing their internal order, or 1 2 4 3, with the second pair reversing their order, all while maintaining the even flow of the ringing, the interval between each ring remaining steady.

With this new flexibility, Stedman realized that you could make predictable patterns in the music by switching the order of the bells in a methodical way. As he worked on this, he recognized its similarity to the mathematical concept of combinations and permutations. For any group of numbers, there is a particular set of ways the numbers can be combined without repeating a sequence. For instance, the numbers 1 2 3 can be combined in six ways.

| 123 | 213 | 321 |
| 132 | 231 | 312 |

If you imagine these numbers to be three notes on a piano, such as A, B, and C, you can play the six combinations of the notes to see how this works. Then, imagine them to be three bells ringing in sequence. In both cases, the sequences follow three strict rules: that each bell must sound once in each sequence, that each bell can only change one place in a sequence, and that no sequence can be repeated. Following these rules, Stedman translated mathematics into music.

This discovery opened up a host of ways of ringing bells that became known as change ringing, after the "changes" that take place between the bells. In 1668, Stedman published a book called *Tintinnalogia: or, the Art of Ringing*, written by Richard Duckworth, setting out the basic principles of change ringing. This was followed in 1677 by Stedman's own book *Campanalogia: or, the Art of Ringing Improved*. The types and complexities of the methods were expanded in this second book, but Stedman also began to create the terminology and language of change ringing. Each type of ring had a double name, the first proclaiming the method of the ring and the second the number of bells in the ring. The methods were given specific names, often in honor of the place the method was first rung or in honor of notable ringers. Frequently rung methods are Grandshire, Plain Bob, Double Norwich, Treble Bob, and—not surprisingly—Stedman. Other names were used to designate the number of bells in the peal. Even numbers of bells are named Minimus (four bells), Minor (six bells), Major (eight bells), Royal (ten bells), and Maximus (twelve bells). Odd numbers of bells are named Doubles (five bells), Triples (seven bells), Caters (nine bells), and Cinques (eleven bells). So typical rings would be Grandshire Cinque—the Grandshire method on eleven bells—or Stedman Caters—the Stedman method on nine bells.

As the various methods were developed, it quickly became apparent that the number of possible sequences increases exponentially as the number of bells increases. For example, for the following number of bells, the number of possible sequences is:

NUMBER OF BELLS	NUMBER OF SEQUENCES
3	6
4	24
6	720
7	5,040
8	40,320

Obviously, to ring the sequences would take longer and longer for each increase in the number of bells.

Ringing a group of bells is often called a peal, a general term for bell ringing. In change ringing, the term takes on special meaning; it refers to specific ways the bells are rung. For example, it became the custom that a true "peal" was the 5,040 sequences on seven bells. For other numbers of bells, a "peal" had to be more than 5,000 sequences. Less than a peal was called a "touch." For a true peal, the ringing had to be continuous, with the same ringers for each bell, although sometimes more than one ringer was allowed for the heavy tenor bell. Also, the sequences had to be memorized, called a "method" peal, rather than having a leader calling them, a "called" peal. When notable peals were rung, a plaque was hung in the church ringing chamber where the peal took place, noting the kind of peal, the date, the church, and the names of the ringers.

At first, the music of change ringing can be difficult to understand and appreciate. Although the bells are tuned, their music is not songs. What might be considered their "melody" is constrained by the rules of change ringing, particularly that each bell can only change

one place in each row. For the mathematician, change ringing is beautifully abstract and precise. For the musician, it is challenging and has its own satisfying musicality. For the ringer, it is a demanding physical sport, a team activity, and a social occasion. Some have called it "ordered confusion," but the North American Guild of Change Ringers calls it "cascading sequences of sounds." Like an orchestra, these sounds are integrated into one instrument, working with intelligent accord.

One of the most interesting places to hear change ringing is at St. Mary-le-Bow, a famous London church and a historic center for change ringing. In the summer of 2001, I visited St. Mary's at the invitation of Mark Regan, then the church's steeplekeeper and head of its ringing society. The church is entered off Cheapside directly into the bottom of the bell tower. I was to meet Mark and the bell ringers at six-thirty on a Thursday evening when they were having a practice session. Although I was a little early, two of the ringers were already there and more came soon. We waited in the entry until everyone had arrived, fourteen ringers that night, thirteen men and one woman. Mark unlocked the door to the tower stairs, our entrance was noted on the log on the door, and we climbed the narrow steps of the circular stairway to the ringing chamber.

The ringing chamber is a beige, octagonal room with two sets of doors a few steps up on the north and south ends of the room. The north doors go out to a balcony looking over Cheapside, and the south doors to a small rector's roof garden. Hung around the room are numerous plaques commemorating notable

THE **NINE TAILORS**

A vivid description of change ringing can be found in Dorothy Sayers's mystery novel *The Nine Tailors*. In small English towns, it is usually the practice that, when someone dies, the tenor or largest bell is tolled for them. The bell is tolled nine times for a man, six times for a woman, and three times for a child. Often the bell then tolls the number of years of the person's life. Because the tolling "tells" the people of the town the sex and age of the person who has died, the notes of the bell were often called "tellers," which was commonly corrupted to "tailors." So, the "nine tailors" in the title of Sayers's book means tolling the death of a man. In the book, Sayers weaves a complex tale of murder around the performance of a nine-hour peal on New Year's Eve at a church in a small town in East Anglia. The murder victim dies during the peal, which is a 15,840 Kent Treble Bob Major or 15,840 sequences of the Kent Treble Bob method on eight bells. Although the book is fiction, the descriptions of the process and culture of change ringing are wonderfully accurate.

peals that took place at St. Mary's, photos of significant events, such as the casting of the present bells at Whitechapel, and copies of the inscriptions and pitches of each of the twelve Bow bells.

High up in the center of the room is the spider, a wooden hanger that holds the ends of the bell ropes when they are not in use. A couple of the ringers pulled the spider down and freed the ropes. Each rope fell to a place around the room indicating the location of the bell above. The rope for the smallest and highest-pitched bell, the 1 bell, was just inside the entry door. Then, going clockwise in a circle around the room, the ropes hung from the larger and larger bells, with the last rope for the tenor, or 12 bell, just to the right of the 1 bell.

The ringers took their places with the two extra ringers sitting on the stairs to the rector's garden, while I sat on the stairs going out to the Cheapside balcony. Mark signaled for the ringers to "ring up" the bells. This was done in order from the smallest to the largest, with each bell being raised higher and higher on successive pulls until it rested upside down. After the traditional opening round, ringing the bells one after the other down the scale, a Cambridge Surprise Maximus was rung, which included changes on all twelve bells. This was followed by a Stedman Cinques that had changes on eleven bells, with the tenor ringing behind. During the second peal, Mark took me up to the bell chamber and, with large ear mufflers, I watched the grand bells swinging back and forth. We also went up the inner stairway of the steeple to the upper balcony and stepped out to hear the ringing.

Three members of the St. Mary-le-Bow ringing society pulling down the "spider" to release the bell ropes.

Following these two "method" peals, Mark called three peals before the bells were rung down a few at a time, ending with the heavy tenor, which took two men with their legs dangling off the floor to stop it. The ropes were then replaced on the spider, and the spider pulled up, the practice complete except for the traditional retreat to the neighborhood pub.

That evening at the pub, I had the opportunity to visit with the ringers informally. In talking with Mark, it was clear he shared my love of bells and generously offered to show me more bells if I was in London another time. A few years later, he took me on a tour of Whitechapel Bell Foundry, one of the historic British bell foundries where the Liberty Bell, Big Ben, and the bells of St. Mary's were cast. On a later

trip with my daughter, he took us up into the tower of St. Paul's to see Great Paul, the mammoth bell in the church's southwest tower. The heaviest bell ever cast in Britain, at sixteen-and-a-half tons, it is overwhelming when you stand next to it. Over the years, I also entertained Mark and his family in New York. As I found on all my journeys, friendships with "bell people" are rich and rewarding ones.

While talking in the pub with the bell ringers, I also learned that St. Mary's was famous for more than its role in change ringing. It was also an important part of the history and folklore of London, as well as being one of the most famous of the Wren churches.

In the Middle Ages, St. Mary's was one of only four churches assigned to ring the evening curfew. Since the church's bells were also rung in the morning, they were a living presence in the city, and it became a commonplace saying that to be a true "cockney" or Londoner, one had to be born within hearing of the Bow bells.

Also, in the Middle Ages, much of the center part of London was a commercial market, with streets such as Bread Street and Honey Lane being reminders of that time. There were so many churches in the area, with their bells sounding out over the streets and shops, that a nursery rhyme was written about what the various church bells were saying. Called "Oranges and Lemons," the nursery rhyme is still known to English children. The lines about St. Mary's are:

You owe me ten shillings
Say the bells of St. Helen's.
Poker and tongs
Say the bells of St. John's
Kettles and pans
Say the bells of St. Anne's
When will you pay me?
Say the bells of Old Bailey.
When I grow rich
Say the bells of Shoreditch.
Pray, when will that be?
Say the bells of Stepney.
I'm sure I don't know
Say the great bells of Bow.

In more recent times, the Bow bells have contributed to new London legends. During World War II, the BBC broadcast a recording of the bells as a symbol of hope and freedom to people under Nazi rule. Today, there is a plaque in the chapel on the left side of the sanctuary dedicated to the memory of Norwegians who died in the resistance. The plaque was given by the people of Norway to thank St. Mary's for providing this symbol of hope during their occupation.

St. Mary's is also one of the most famous of the Wren churches dating from the Great Fire of London in 1666, when eighty-six parish churches as well at St. Paul's Cathedral, the center of the Anglican Church in England, were destroyed. As London began to recover

The beautiful steeple of St. Mary-le-Bow, one of the first created by Christopher Wren when he started to rebuild the London churches after the devastating fire of 1666. The St. Mary's steeple became a model for many later steeples.

from the fire, considerable thought was given to how to rebuild the churches. New taxes were imposed and regulatory organizations established, but, most important, when a commission was appointed to oversee the rebuilding, they chose a young scientist and architect, thirty-four-year-old Christopher Wren, to lead this effort. Over the next forty-seven years, Wren and his associates rebuilt fifty-one of the parish churches, along with St. Paul's, creating one of England's greatest architectural legacies.

St. Mary's was one of the first churches Wren rebuilt. The most exciting part of the new church, and one of Wren's most notable achievements, was the graceful steeple rising 224 feet above the bell tower. This beautiful steeple became the inspiration for many later church steeples.

The Great Fire of 1666 was not the only time St. Mary's suffered damage. It was also badly damaged during the Blitz in World War II. In May 1941, bombs destroyed much of the church. By morning, only parts of the church's tower, steeple, crypt, and outer walls remained, most badly charred by the fires ignited by the bombs. The inner parts of the church— the sanctuary, chapels, and other places of worship—were gone, leaving only an empty shell. Lying in cracked pieces on the floor of this shell were nine of the twelve famous Bow bells, fallen 100 feet from their perch in the bell tower after their wooden frames burned. The remaining three bells were caught precariously on steel girders under the bell frames.

It took years to restore the church, but, fortunately, the key Wren designs, the bell tower and steeple, were able to be preserved. Only the inside had to be rebuilt. And, of course, a new set of bells was needed. A peal of twelve bells was cast by Whitechapel in 1957 that included metal from the bells damaged in the war. The names of the bells were inscribed on them—Katherine, Fabian, Christopher, Margaret, Mildred, Faith, Augustine, John, Timothy, Pancras, and Cuthbert, with the large tenor being named Bow.

St. Mary's has always had a strong history of change ringing. She is mentioned as a "ringing" church in the early and mid-1600s, the time when change ringing was first developing, and, having twelve bells, she has always been a challenging place for advanced ringers and the site of memorable rings. Even amidst the hustle and bustle of the modern city of London, listening to the cascading sounds of St. Mary's bells is deeply rewarding, a living embodiment of the British bell ringing tradition that has flourished for more than 400 years.

The Elizabeth Tower at the Houses of Parliament holds Big Ben in its bell chamber, just above the clock face.

BIG BEN

All through this hour
Lord be my Guide
That by Thy Power
No foot shall slide

—MEMBERS' PRAYER IN PARLIAMENT, SET TO THE BELL
MUSIC OF WESTMINSTER QUARTERS

The name Big Ben is officially the name of the hour bell for the Great Clock in the Elizabeth Tower, the northernmost of the three towers that frame the Houses of Parliament in Westminster Palace in London. However, it has affectionately come to refer to the tower, the clock, and the bell together. The story of Big Ben is the story of the bell, but it is also the story of how the bell, clock, and tower were created and became one of the most remarkable achievements of Victorian England.

Today, the tower is an architectural masterpiece that soars more than 200 feet into the air and is topped with one of the most beautiful four-sided clocks in the world. There are five bells in the tower attached to the clock; the large bell that strikes the hour and four smaller bells, known as quarter bells, that chime on the quarter hours. The sound of the bells has been broadcast on the radio since the 1920s and is known all over the world. The tower itself has become one of the best known images of Britain, appearing in movies, television, advertisements, and souvenirs.

The site of Big Ben has a rich history. In 960, an abbey was founded there on the banks of the Thames. Originally called West Minster, because it was west of St. Paul's, the main cathedral, or minster, in London, it became known as Westminster Abbey and is where many notable people are buried and important British ceremonies held. In 1040, the king and court moved there, creating Westminster Palace. Other government organizations, such as the Courts of Law, also moved there, and, in 1265, it became the meeting place for Parliament. Eventually the court and many government functions moved to other locations, but Parliament remained in the palace,

135

now also known as the Houses of Parliament.

In 1834, a massive fire destroyed most of the palace. Rather than try to rebuild what was left of the buildings, the decision was made to raze the area and build a new palace and clock tower that would incorporate the most advanced technology available at the time. It was an ambitious project with three parts: first was designing and building the new palace buildings; second was designing and constructing a clock that was to be the most accurate ever produced in England; and third was designing and casting the bells, the hour bell to be the largest bell ever cast in England. Achieving these goals took many years and involved a group of talented men with strong personalities who often clashed in temperament and ambition. As a result, the project was fraught with continual bickering, conflict, and even lawsuits. Although the final achievement stands above these conflicts, the dramas at the

Creating the clock was the second challenge. The most difficult specification for the clock was that the first strike for each hour had to be accurate to within a second of time.

time were avidly followed by the press and the people of London.

In 1835, the project began with a competition to choose the designer for the new buildings. There were almost 100 entries, and the competition was won by Charles Barry, a noted architect who had the vision to create the architectural masterpiece we have today. To assist with the design, Barry brought in Augustus Pugin, who was a talented artist and

The magnificent Houses of Parliament built in the mid-1800s after a fire destroyed the old palace. Designed by Charles Barry, the new buildings housed the most accurate clocks ever constructed and Big Ben, the heaviest bell ever cast in England at that time.

architect and is responsible for much of the elaborate Gothic detail on the buildings, as well as the graceful proportions of the bell tower. Because of the magnitude of the project, many people were interested in it, from the members of Parliament to the commissioner of public works, all of whom wanted their opinions heard. This caused delays, but the cornerstone was finally laid in 1840 and construction began.

Creating the clock was the second challenge. The most difficult specification for the clock was that the first strike for each hour had to be accurate to within a second of time. No tower clock had ever achieved that level of accuracy, and most contemporary clockmakers thought it was impossible. After eight years of debate, Edmund Beckett Denison, a politician, entrepreneur, and controversial personality was given the contract for designing the clock, along with George Airy, the Astronomer Royal, who happened to be an expert on clocks. Edward Dent was then awarded the contract to build the clock. Both Denison and Dent had been developing new ways to improve clock mechanisms, which was one reason they were chosen. Finally, in 1854, the clock was completed, waiting to be installed when the bell tower was finished.

The third challenge was designing and casting the bells. While the tower was under construction, Barry realized that the bells had to be ordered. Denison was asked to prepare the specifications for the bells—their sizes, shapes, tones, and metal content—since he had been a bell ringer while an undergraduate at Cambridge University and knew the most about bells. Denison decided the smallest quarter bell would be one ton with a note of G♯. The next would be 1.25 tons with a note of F♯. The third would be 1.75 tons with a note of E, while the largest quarter bell would

be 3.9 tons with a note of B. The massive hour bell would be about 14 tons in the note of E, one octave below the third quarter bell.

Denison also decided that the bell metal would be twenty-two parts copper to seven parts tin, more tin than was usually used in bell metal at that time. Since tin is added to copper to make the metal harder, this meant that the bell metal would be harder and more brittle than usual. The new bells would not swing; rather, they would be struck mechanically from the outside with a hammer activated by the clock mechanism, although clappers were also made for the bells so they could be rung manually if necessary.

With these specifications in hand, three major bell foundries competed for the contract to cast the bells: Whitechapel Bell Foundry, John Warner & Sons, and John Taylor of Loughborough. Denison preferred John Warner because he had been making some improvements in the design of the core and cope of bell molds. In 1856, Warner was commissioned to cast the five bells.

First, the large hour bell was cast at a foundry in the village of Norton, near Stockton-on-Tees, since the Warner foundry in London could not handle a bell of this size. It took weeks to dig the pit and prepare the mold, and two furnaces were used to melt the metal. In the early morning of August 5, 1856, the metal was poured into the mold. After cooling for two weeks, the bell was removed from the pit and finished and polished. It turned out the bell was much heavier than expected, closer to sixteen tons than fourteen tons, but its note was E as specified. The

four quarter bells were then cast in the London foundry.

The hour bell was taken by rail to the port of West Hartlepool where it was to be shipped to London on the schooner *Wave*. But, during loading, the heavy bell fell, causing damage to the ship, so the sailing was delayed until repairs could be made. Finally, after a stormy trip, the bell arrived in London in late October to cheering crowds. Taken by horse-drawn carriage to the Palace Yard, it was hung from temporary scaffolding, since the tower was not yet finished. By this time, the bell was familiarly being called Big Ben after the new commissioner of works, Sir Benjamin Hall, whose robust size had earned him this nickname. Hall had been instrumental in getting the bell project moving and pushing it to completion.

For about a year the bell hung from the scaffolding and was rung, both to test its sound and to entertain the public. Because the bell was so much heavier than expected, Denison made the hammer used to strike it much heavier. On October 17, 1857, almost a year after it arrived in London, a huge, four-foot crack appeared up the side of the bell. Everyone was dismayed, and, not unexpectedly, recriminations followed; Warner blamed Denison for using such a heavy hammer and brittle metal, while Denison blamed Warner for faulty casting.

The commission for recasting the bell was given to Whitechapel, then under the leadership of George Mears. The cracked bell was lowered to the ground, put on its side, and, over a period of days, pulverized by repeatedly dropping a heavy iron ball on it. Whitechapel

Big Ben, which rings the hour, is surrounded by the the four bells that ring the quarter hours.

hauled the metal pieces to its foundry, and, on April 10, 1858, the new bell was cast, almost two years after the original Warner casting. The new bell weighed in at just over thirteen-and-a-half tons.

The bell was loaded on a carriage and drawn by sixteen horses through the streets of London to the Palace Yard, where it was hung from the same scaffolding as the earlier bell. It hung there for five months until the tower was finally ready to receive the bells. First the quarter bells were raised over 200 feet up through the central shaft of the tower by a series of winches and hung in the four corners of the belfry. Then Big Ben was raised by an even more complex series of winches and hung in the center. Because the central shaft of the tower was so narrow and the width of the bell

so great, Big Ben had to be turned on its side and put in a cradle to be raised. It took eight men thirty-two hours to raise it, but finally all the bells were in place and the clockworks could be installed and attached to the bells. In May 1859, the clock was started; in July, Big Ben rang; and in September, the quarter bells started ringing. The tower was complete.

The interior of the clock tower is a series of chambers. At the top is the Ayrton Light, which is lit when either House of Parliament is in session after dark. Below the light is the belfry containing the five bells. A much larger room farther down is the clock room that holds the mechanisms to run the clock, with the four clock faces mounted on the outside walls of this room. Between the clock room and the belfry is the link room, a small room where the bells are attached to the clock mechanisms.

Below these rooms, a thirteen-foot pendulum is suspended in its own casing, while the three heavy weights that drive the system hang in the central shaft that runs all the way down the tower. As the weights slowly descend under the force of gravity, they provide the power to keep the pendulum swinging and the clock and bell mechanisms moving. These mechanisms consist of three sets of great wheels called trains—one the striking train that sounds the hour bell, one the chiming train that sounds the quarter bells, and one the going train that runs the clock hands, all on a long trailer in the clock room. Each of the three weights hanging below is attached to one of the trains and is its source of power. Three times a week, these weights must be wound up so they can continue to operate. The whole system is a weight-driven system similar to that of a

The clockworks in the bell tower connect the bells to the four clock faces on the outside of the tower. An intricate series of gears are powered by a weight-driven pendulum hanging down in the interior of the tower.

WINDING UP THE CLOCK

"BIG BEN" AND THE CLOCK TOWER, WESTMINSTER PALACE

This close-up of Big Ben shows the hammer that is used to strike the bell.

grandfather clock, which was developed as a miniature replica of a tower clock.

Attached to each bell in the belfry is a hammer, one part of the hammer going over the top of the bell and down its side to be used to strike the bell, while the other part goes out from the opposite side of the bell and down to the link room to be attached to the clock. When the hammer is activated by the clock, it works like a lever, raising the striking arm slightly and then letting it fall to hit the bell. When the whole system is operating, the pendulum moves the minute hand on the clock, which in turn sets off the chiming bells at each quarter hour. When each new hour is reached on the clock, the hour hand sets off Big Ben to strike the number of hours.

In October 1859, just a few months after it started ringing, Big Ben developed an eleven-inch hairline crack up from its sound bow. People were stunned. Although much smaller than the four-foot crack in the Warner bell, no one knew what to do since it was impossible to take the bell down to be recast without first removing all the clock mechanisms under the belfry. Again, recriminations flew; the bell metal was too brittle, the hammer too heavy, or Whitechapel had done a poor job of casting.

It took almost four years for a solution to be reached, the largest quarter bell standing in as the hour bell in the meantime. Once again, the public and the press offered their opinions. A few months after the bell cracked, a parody of the nursery rhyme "Oranges and Lemons" was published in the magazine *Punch*. A few of the lines were:

---

*Big Ben looks scaly, say the
  bells of Old Baily;
His voice is quite gone, say
  the bells of St. John;
He's chock full of holes,
  peal the bells of All Souls;
Must go to the forge, say
  the bells of St. George;
But what's to be done,
  once more peals St. John;
Bang'd if I know, tolls
  the big bell of Bow.*

Finally, at the suggestion of George Airy, the Astronomer Royal, the decision was made that the bell was not so damaged that it could not be used, since the crack only went partway through the sound bow. To prevent it from spreading further, the bell was first rotated one-eighth of the way around so that the crack was at the point of least stress when the bell was struck. When metal reverberates after being struck, it oscillates in waves, with low, or nodal, points occurring in eight places around the bell, alternating with eight points of greatest oscillation. By rotating the bell one-eighth around, the crack was placed at one of these nodal points of low oscillation.

Second, a lighter hammer was used, something many had been pressing for all along. A strong floor was also built under the bell in case it actually broke, so that it would not damage the clock mechanisms below.

"WESTMINSTER **QUARTERS**"

One of the best known and best loved qualities of Big Ben is the music played by the quarter bells. Known now as the "Westminster Quarters," the music was originally created for Great St. Mary's Church, the university church of Cambridge, in the late 1700s and is based on a passage from Handel's *Messiah*. The figure below shows the musical phrases associated with each quarter bell.

As can be seen, in ringing the last quarter, the note B is played at the end of the third measure and again at the beginning of the fourth. Since the bell cannot be played that fast in succession, the fourth quarter bell has two hammers to play the notes.

After it was chosen to be the music for the tower, the "Westminster Quarters" became so popular that it is now one of the most frequently used chimes in the world. On a YouTube video put out by Parliament in 2015 called "The Chimes of Big Ben," a lovely rendition of the "Westminster Quarters" is played followed by the deep sound of Big Ben calling out the hours. The video is particularly vivid because the camera is placed inside the bell tower, so the viewer has a close-up view of these magnificent bells as they are ringing.

One of the beautiful clock faces on the Elizabeth Tower. Each face is twenty-two feet in diameter and is made up of 312 pieces of opal glass fitted together like a stained-glass window.

Finally, a small hole that had been dug out of the bell to gauge the depth of the crack was left to help prevent further expansion of the crack. With all this decided, the bell resumed ringing, and, although the sound was a bit "off," it became a familiar sound to the English people. Most people are not even aware the bell has a crack.

One of the most beloved qualities of the tower is the beauty of the four-sided clock. Each clock face is twenty-two-and-a-half feet in diameter and fits into a square, ornately decorated, gold-and-black frame. The minute hand is fourteen feet long, the hour hand nine feet long, and the Roman numerals each two feet high. Each clock face is made up of 312 pieces of opal glass fitted together like a stained-glass window. A couple of the pieces of glass in each face can be removed so workers can go outside to perform maintenance on the clock. The clocks are particularly beautiful when lit up at night.

> **One of the most beloved qualities of the tower is the beauty of the four-sided clock. Each clock face is twenty-two and a half feet in diameter and fits into a square, ornately decorated, gold-and-black frame.**

Big Ben achieved its role as the nation's bell many years after it was first rung as the hour bell of Parliament. This role developed during wartime, in World War I, but particularly in World War II.

During World War I, the lights in the clock tower were extinguished and the bells silenced so that the Houses of Parliament would avoid detection by zeppelins, the large German airship bombers that flew low over the city. This silence came to an end at eleven o'clock in the morning on November 11, 1918, when the bells rang out to celebrate the Armistice that ended the war. Today, the Sunday closest to November 11 is observed in England as Remembrance Day. Every year at eleven a.m. on that day, the bells ring in honor of all those lost in war.

During World War II, the lights were again extinguished in the tower as part of the overall blackout of London, but the bells were still rung because bombers now flew so high that the sound of the bells was no longer a threat. By this time, the sound of Big Ben had become an internationally known sound on British radio. All through the siege of Europe and the bombing of Britain, Big Ben continued to ring, a symbol of wartime resistance and survival for many people, not just in Britain and Europe, but around the world. Even on the night of May 11, 1941, when bombs destroyed parts of the Parliament buildings and smashed the glass in the south clock face in the tower, the bells rang. When all the bells in the city rang out in 1945 to celebrate the end of the war, it was a momentous occasion.

The clock tower and Big Ben have played many roles in popular culture. Big Ben was rung as part of the opening and closing ceremonies of the 2012 Olympics in London, and is always rung on New Year's Eve—the quarter chimes ringing out the old year and Big Ben ringing in the new. The tower and the bells feature in many advertisements, in musical compositions, and in the visual arts. They have also played a role in a number of movies, one

of the most dramatic being the 1978 movie *The Thirty-Nine Steps*, where a bomb is placed in the clock room timed to go off when the minute hand reaches 11:45. In order to prevent this, the hero climbs out on the clock face and hangs on the minute hand just as it approaches 11:45, stopping the clock until the bomb is dismantled. This scene was filmed on location outside on the actual clock face.

Big Ben has also played a role in ceremonies of state. It tolled for the funeral of King Edward VII in 1910, George V in 1936, and George VI in 1952. When Winston Churchill died in 1965, rather than tolling the bell, the bell was silenced from 9:45 in the morning, when the funeral started, until midnight. It was also silenced for the funeral of Margaret Thatcher. In 2012, the clock tower was formally named the Elizabeth Tower in honor of Queen Elizabeth II on the occasion of her Diamond Jubilee.

There are a few bells in the world that attain iconic stature because of their size, their sound, or their role in history. The Tsar Kolodol in Russia, the Yongle bell in China, and the Chion-in bell in Japan are a few of these bells. Big Ben is another. Not the largest bell in the world nor the most melodic, yet Big Ben has become the iconic symbol of London, as well as an international symbol of courage and resilience in the face of danger, a role that still inspires people throughout the world.

PART IV

THE BELLS OF EU AND RUS

ROPE
SIA

The famous bell tower at Bruges in Belgium is home to many memorable carillon concerts. This is where Nannie and her friends would listen to the carillon concerts as they sat at tables around the market square.

THE "SINGING TOWERS"

Around 1500, something unusual happened in a small region along the North Sea. In the cities of the Low Countries, bells in church and city towers were transformed into musical instruments. And thus the carillon was born.

—LUC ROMBOUTS, *SINGING BRONZE: A HISTORY OF CARILLON MUSIC*

Carillons are the largest musical instruments in the world, requiring their own towers to house them. They are also some of the world's most fascinating instruments, often having more than sixty bells played by a single musician from a central console. The music flows out from the tower over long distances and can be anything from Mozart to show tunes.

Groups of bells that are sounded harmoniously are called chimes. A carillon is a specific kind of chime, one that has at least twenty-three bells arranged in chromatic order, meaning that it includes both the white and black notes of the piano. The bells are hung in a large metal frame at the top of a bell tower that has open windows or sides so the music can flow out into the air. In a carillon, the bells are hung fixed in place or "dead," and the clapper is pulled against the inside of the bell to make it ring. Attached to each clapper is a wire that goes down to a playing console in a room below the bells.

The playing console is set up much like a piano keyboard, but the keys are long, rounded, wooden batons or levers that the carillonneur plays with the outer sides of his loosely held fists. When a baton is pushed down, it pulls the

A typical carillon keyboard has rounded levers for the small and medium bells and foot levers for the large bells. Using both hands and feet, a talented player can create a wide range of beautiful music, from show tunes to Bach.

clapper wire so that the clapper strikes the inside of the bell. While the keyboard is used to sound the medium and smaller bells, there is a row of elongated foot pedals to ring the larger bells, similar to the pedals on a pipe organ. Today, carillons usually have four or five octaves of bells, although some have more.

Carillons originated in Europe, and most of their history and development took place there, particularly in the Netherlands and Belgium. However, my own experience with carillons has been in the United States, mainly with the Bok Tower carillon in Florida, one of the world's most unusual carillons and the one I researched and visited. While there, I was able to meet with Geert D'hollander, the resident carillonneur and one of the world's finest players and composers. Although the Bok carillon is in America, it is part of a tradition that is deeply rooted in Europe.

Carillons evolved from the development of mechanical clocks. Before the invention of the mechanical clock, time was measured either with water clocks, which were not reliable, or by following the natural progress of the sun through the day. In the late thirteenth century, a mechanical clock was developed in Europe that used the controlled power of gravity to give a more uniform unit of time.

In the fifteenth and sixteenth centuries, one of the greatest reasons for such clocks was to inform people of the time in the growing industrial towns and cities where the work day was beginning to be regulated. Most of these towns and cities already had tall, often elegant, municipal or church bell towers whose bells were rung for civic and religious occasions. If the new clocks were installed in these towers, their bells could also be used to sound the time.

Initially, a tower watchman would strike the bell, giving the number of hours. Then, mechanical robots called jacquemarts or clock-jacks were used that were able to move and strike the hour. Many of the clock-jacks became famous and are still in use today, such as the one on the clock tower in St. Mark's Square in Venice. Eventually, the clock mechanism was attached directly to a hammer mounted on the outside of the bell that could be lifted by the clock mechanism and then released so it would strike the bell.

A problem arose at this point in that the bell would often have started striking before people were aware of it, so they lost count of the number of hours. To alert people that the clock was about to strike, a warning bell was sounded, which became known as the fore-stroke. The forestroke was then expanded to two bells, a higher pitched bell sounding first followed by a bell pitched one third lower, giving the now familiar chime of ding-dong or ting-tang, also found in cuckoo clocks.

Originally, only the number of the hours was sounded on the bell, but, eventually, smaller bells were used to signal the half hour and then the quarter hours, the largest bell still being reserved for striking the hours. As more and more bells were added to the forestroke

and as more parts of the hour were rung, what had started as a series of signals turned into a new kind of music.

This music evolved in two directions. First, as more bells were used in chiming the clock, the wheels controlling the bells were brought together in a drum, which rotated mechanically to ring them. There were holes in the drum where pins were put to control which bell would ring when, thus providing the desired melody, similar to a music box or player piano. Drums were then developed with removable

The St. Mark's bell tower in Venice where mechanical robots called clock-jacks still ring the bell.

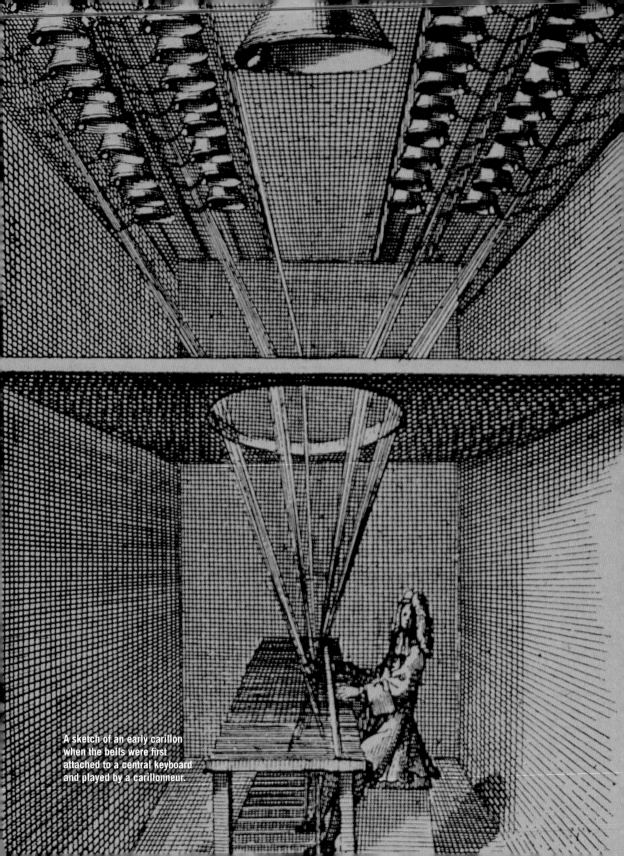

A sketch of an early carillon when the bells were first attached to a central keyboard and played by a carillonneur.

pins so that different melodies could be programmed on a single drum. Eventually, these mechanical drums were used to ring elaborate melodies on a large number of bells no longer attached to clocks.

The true carillon, however, developed in a

major trading centers in the late Middle Ages and were flourishing with the development of industrialization. This was also the golden age in the art of Rembrandt, Rubens, and Vermeer.

Part of the culture in the Low Countries was a strong sense of municipal pride, and the

---

The true carillon, however, developed in a different way. Rather than attaching the bells to a revolving drum, they were attached to keyboards played by musicians, who became the first carillonneurs. The advantage of this is that a person playing on a keyboard can elicit a wide range of sounds, introducing skill and imagination. . . .

---

different way. Rather than attaching the bells to a revolving drum, they were attached to keyboards played by musicians, who became the first carillonneurs. The advantage of this is that a person playing on a keyboard can elicit a wide range of sounds, introducing skill and imagination into the playing of the music, while a mechanical drum can only produce a constant set of sounds. The flexibility of this artistry became a defining characteristic of carillon music.

By the end of the sixteenth century, the mechanisms of the carillon were in place. While the mechanical clock was adopted throughout Europe and in other countries, the carillon developed mainly in the Low Countries, which then included the Netherlands, Belgium, and parts of northern France. The important cities of this region—Bruges, Ghent, Antwerp, and Amsterdam—had become

major cities competed for prestige and economic and artistic preeminence. Creating beautiful, tall towers, like the bell tower at Bruges, Belgium, was part of that competition, as was vying for the largest and best carillons to place in those towers. By this time, there were a number of founders in the Low Countries creating carillon bells. However, a major problem remained, which was that the bells were not well tuned and often sounded discordant. The knowledge of how to successfully tune a bell had not yet been discovered in the West.

In the seventeenth century, three uniquely talented men emerged who changed the history of the carillon and of bell founding. The first was Jacob van Eyck, the town carillon player of Utrecht who, although blind, had an uncanny sense of hearing. Where before bells had been analyzed and tuned as a whole, van

The famous St. Rumbold's Tower in Mechelen, Belgium, which became the home for the revolutionary carillon playing of Jef Denyn in the late 1880s.

Eyck started to analyze the partial notes of the bell and argued that it was these partials that had to be tuned. He identified the five main partials we now accept as key to tuning: the fundamental, the octave below the fundamental, the third, the fifth, and the octave above the fundamental. He also argued that, for bells, the correct third to be tuned was the minor third, not the major third, as was traditional in tuning other instruments. The minor third is what gives bells their often plaintive sound.

To try out his theories, van Eyck needed bell founders to work with, and two bell founders appeared, the Hemony brothers, who would become some of the most famous bell founders in history. François Hemony and Pieter Hemony were born in France and learned bell founding there. After spending time in Germany, they settled in the city of Zutphen in the Netherlands, where the city ordered a carillon from them for its Wine House. When the city also hired van Eyck to act as a consultant for the project, these three talented men came together, sharing their knowledge to develop a new way of tuning bells.

The Hemonys accepted van Eyck's belief in the need to tune the five main partials of a bell, rather than trying to tune the bell as a whole. To do this, they cast their bells with extra thickness, which became known as the tuning reserve, and then put each bell upside down on a lathe that was rotated by five or six men. As the bell rotated, the founders cut away metal on the inside of the bell at the places van Eyck identified as containing the key partial notes, stopping at the moment when that partial came into tune. The Hemonys cast metal bars to act as tuning references; van Eyck only needed his own acute hearing. When completed in 1646, the new carillon so far surpassed anything known before that a new standard was established for well-tuned bells.

In 1657, François Hemony accepted an offer from the city of Amsterdam to move there and set up a foundry. Seven years later, his brother joined him. In Amsterdam, they continued to cast well-tuned carillons for many of the cities of the Netherlands and Belgium. In their lifetimes, the two brothers cast fifty-one carillons, many of which still exist today, a rich legacy of this turning point in the history of Western bells.

When the Hemony brothers died, they took most of their specialized knowledge of bell tuning with them, leading to a decline in the quality of new bells and, in turn, a decline in the quality of carillon music. Combined with several wars, when many bells were confiscated for their metal, and social and economic changes, carillons lost favor in the eighteenth and nineteenth centuries. But, at the end of the nineteenth century, a carillon renaissance began due to the skill of a single carillon player.

Jef Denyn was born in the town of Mechelen in Belgium in 1862. His father, Adolf, was the official carillonneur for the town, playing the carillon in the famous St. Rumbold's Tower. Over time, the father lost his sight and sent his son into the tower to play. Jef had a knack for mechanical things and wanted to study engineering, but the family prevailed, and, in 1887, he was appointed the Mechelen town carillonneur at the age of twenty-five.

As Denyn began to play more regularly, exhibiting a remarkable musical gift, he became increasingly unhappy with the carillon mechanism—the keyboard and the wire arrangement that attached the keys to the clappers of the bells. The wires were often loose, which made controlling the clappers difficult. With his mechanical mind, he started improving the mechanism, first at St. Rumbold's and then at other carillons in Belgium and the Netherlands, which gave the player

greater control over his bells.

With better control, Denyn developed exciting new ways of playing the carillon. In particular, he became a virtuoso in playing tremolos, the quick repetition of notes that create the illusion of a sustained note. One of the limitations of playing bells is that the player has no control over the sound of a bell after it is struck. The strike note sounds sharply and quickly and is followed by a muted decay of aftersounds. With tighter control over the bells, a carillonneur could play more rapidly, so the sounds could meld together into a controlled musical effect, greatly adding to the range of sounds available to the player. Denyn was particularly effective when he combined the tolling melody of a tune on the bass bells with a tremolo played on the small, high-toned bells.

As Denyn employed these new techniques on the improved carillon, his playing began to be noticed. At the request of one of the town aldermen, he started giving Monday evening concerts at St. Rumbold's in the warm months. The first concert took place in August 1892, transforming the role of the carillon from an accompaniment to market and municipal activities to a concert instrument.

The response to the concerts was slow at first, but gradually, they became better known. In 1906, members of the Language and Literary Conference came to Mechelen to hear Denyn play, and they were so impressed that they wrote articles about it and advertised the concerts all over Europe. Eventually, as many as 30,000 people were attending the concerts, many brought in on special trains from Brussels and Antwerp just for the occasion.

For all Denyn's accomplishments, however, the fundamental problem of playing on poorly tuned bells remained. People were so used to the sounds of the bells that they accepted them, but just as Denyn was starting to achieve his fame, an Englishman rediscovered the knowledge of tuning bells lost after the deaths of the Hemony brothers.

The English cleric Canon Arthur B. Simpson was a lover of bells and became increasingly incensed at the poor quality of English bells, as well as those imported from the Low Countries. After studying the acoustics of bells, he discovered, as van Eyck had so many years earlier, that it was the five main partials that had to be tuned, not the bell as a whole. He appealed to founders to try his method, but only one founder responded, John Taylor of Loughborough. Together, they started producing bells, the first well-tuned, modern carillon being cast by Taylor in 1904. Eventually, other founders followed their lead and began producing well-tuned bells, first in England and later in the Netherlands and Belgium. With Denyn's musical genius bringing the art of carillon music to a new

AN EVENING AT **MECHELEN**

Jef Denyn Concert | August 18, 1913

In these northern countries the day is long even in late August, and it was still twilight. Against the southern sky, framed in by two dark trees in the foreground, rose the broad, rugged tower of St. Rumbold's. High up, near the top of the tower, from a narrow opening shone out a faint, dull light.

After the bell ceased striking (eight o'clock), and the vibration of its deep and solemn tone had died away, there was silence. So long a silence it seemed, so absolute, that we wondered if it ever was to be broken. Then pianissimo, from the highest, lightest bells, as if not to startle us, and from far, far above the tower, it seemed—indeed as if very gently shaken from the sky itself—came trills and runs that were angelic! Rapidly they grew in volume and majesty as they descended the scale until the entire heaven seemed full of music. Seated in the garden we watched the little light in the tower, where we knew the unseen carillonneur sat at his clavier and drew the music from his keys, and yet as we watched and listened, we somehow felt that the music came from somewhere far beyond the tower, far higher than that dim light, and was produced by superhuman hands. Sometimes in winter after icicles have formed, there comes a thaw, and one by one they tinkle down gently and timidly at first; then bolder in a mass they come till, like an avalanche, they crash down with a mighty roar. All of this the music suggested. It was low, it was loud; it was from one bell, it was from chords of many bells; it was majestic, it was simple. And every note seemed to fall from above, from such heights that the whole land heard its beauty.

William Gorham Rice
Carillons of Belgium and Holland

high and with well-tuned bells now available, carillons once again became the "singing towers" of Europe.

The year 1922 was singular in the history of the carillon. A great gathering took place in Mechelen, where Jef Denyn celebrated his

---

Today, there are more than 600 carillons in the world. Found in twenty-nine countries, there are noted carillons in Japan, South Korea, New Zealand, Germany, and South Africa.

---

thirty-fifth anniversary as carillonneur, the first carillon congress took place, and, most important, the first carillon school was established, the Mechelen Carillon School (later renamed the Royal Carillon School "Jef Denyn") headed by Denyn. These three events were celebrated with lavish concerts in St. Rumbold's Tower.

One of the speakers at this gathering was William Gorham Rice, an American who often visited the Netherlands and was fascinated by carillons and their music. After researching carillons and speaking to people associated with them, he started publishing books and articles about carillons and giving talks on them around the United States. Over time, he developed a wide readership and, through his passionate advocacy, he introduced the carillon to America.

In the same year as the Mechelen gathering, the first two carillons were installed in America, a Taylor's carillon at the Church of Our Lady of Good Voyage in Gloucester, Massachusetts, and a Gillett & Johnston carillon at the Metropolitan Church in Toronto. Both had twenty-three bells. Other carillons followed, and, by 1939 and the beginning of World War II, sixty carillons had been installed in the United States and Canada, mostly in churches, but also at schools and universities, in parks, and in municipal buildings.

After World War II, a new growth in carillons took place in Europe. During the war, there was massive destruction of bells when they were melted down for armaments or destroyed by bombs. These bells needed to be replaced, and most of the new bells were produced by two Dutch founders, Petit & Fritsen and Royal Eijsbouts, who were now using the Simpson system of tuning and producing well-tuned bells. In the Netherlands, fifty new carillons were created between 1946 and 1960; in Belgium, twenty new carillons were added. Once more, carillons flourished in their traditional home.

North America also entered a new era of carillon growth after World War II when a number of major carillons were installed at such places as the University of Kansas and the Washington National Cathedral. By then, the Guild of Carillonneurs of North America had been established, which became influential through its conferences, competitions, journal, and its publication of carillon music. Many of the new carillonneurs attracted to the American carillons were gifted composers and

The Bok Tower carillon in Lake Wales, Florida. Patterned after St. Rumbold's Tower but with Florida colors and materials, it is the center of a lovely garden refuge where concerts are played each day. A number of noted carillonneurs have played here over the years.

An early Taylor carillon, Bok Tower is the centerpiece of a lovely, fifty-acre nature refuge that was created in central Florida by Edward Bok, a Dutchman who came to the United States as a child and made his fortune in publishing.

contributed to a rich body of American carillon music that continues to grow as part of what has become a distinctive North American carillon movement.

Today, there are more than 600 carillons in the world. Found in twenty-nine countries, there are noted carillons in Japan, South Korea, New Zealand, Germany, and South Africa. But almost 70 percent of today's carillons are still found in the three carillon countries of the Netherlands, Belgium, and the United States.

One of the finest—and most unusual—of these carillons is the Bok Tower in Lake Wales, Florida. An early Taylor carillon, Bok Tower is the centerpiece of a lovely, fifty-acre nature refuge that was created in central Florida by Edward Bok, a Dutchman who came to the United States as a child and made his fortune in publishing. He had a winter home in the Lake Wales region and envisioned turning the barren Florida land into a sanctuary for plants and birds, and for people who could come

there to find peace in a crowded world. Bok hired Frederick Law Olmsted Jr., one of the most noted landscape architects of his day, to fill the area with rich gardens of native plants and quiet walkways. Remembering the carillons of his youth, Bok decided to build a carillon as the center of his garden refuge, modeled after the famous St. Rumbold's Tower in Belgium.

In 1926, Bok contracted with Taylor to cast the bells. Two years later, they were shipped from Liverpool to Jacksonville, Florida, where they were sent by railroad and truck to the tower site. A large hole had been left in the side of the tower while it was being constructed, and the bells were lifted through this opening into the top of the tower. Bok hired Anton Brees, a noted Belgian player, to be the first resident carillonneur, and the tower, bells, and gardens were officially dedicated on February 1, 1929, by Calvin Coolidge, the president of the United States.

The Bok carillon has sixty bells; the largest, the bourdon, weighs more than 22,000 pounds, while the smallest weighs twelve pounds. Together, the bells weigh almost sixty-two tons. They are hung in rows in a rectangular structure housed at the top of the tower, the largest bells on the bottom and the smallest on top. Surrounding the carillon are large, vertical windows thirty-five feet high and ten feet wide that are covered by wire netting to keep birds from flying into the room.

When I visited Lake Wales in February 2016, I was pleased to meet with Geert D'hollander, the Bok Tower carillonneur. He had studied and taught at the Mechelen carillon school and also played at St. Rumbold's in the place that Jef Denyn played his famous concerts and where there are still Hemony bells in use. Belgian, he came from his post as city carillonneur of Antwerp in 2012 to become only the fourth carillonneur in the almost ninety-year history of the tower. Four days a week, from Thursday to Sunday, he plays concerts at one o'clock and three o'clock in the afternoon, as well as on holidays and special occasions. The tower is more than 200 feet high, so the music can be heard from a great distance, but visitors can also have an intimate view of him playing on a video screen that is set up near the base of the tower. As an internationally known player and composer, his music makes the tower sing with beautiful

The quality of carillon music depends on the instrument, the music being played, and the skill of the player. Watching Geert D'hollander play on the video outside the tower, I could see the skill he brought to the instrument.

renditions of classical and popular music.

On the day I visited, we met at the base of the tower early in the morning. After exchanging greetings, he took me on a tour of the tower. First, we took an old Otis elevator to the sixth floor, which is his office, a warm room with a piano, desk, and sitting area where he works and teaches. Since this was as far as the elevator went, we climbed the narrow spiral staircase to the seventh floor, which houses the carillon keyboard where he plays, although there is also a practice keyboard on a lower floor where he can experiment and compose music.

We next went up more steps to the top floor, the bell chamber. As we stepped out into the chamber, I was startled by the three largest bells hanging just over my head. They were grand, beautiful bells. When I turned around, I saw two photographs framed on the wall; one of Jef Denyn sitting at a carillon console and one of Denyn with the two other men who evaluated the Bok bells at Taylor's before they were shipped to Florida. A distinctive man— short with bushy white hair—he seemed right at home in the Bok Tower.

The quality of carillon music depends on the instrument, the music being played, and the skill of the player. Watching Geert D'hollander play on the video outside the tower, I could see the skill he brought to the instrument. When playing military or heavy music, which is often played on holidays, he strikes the batons firmly with the outside of his fists. But when playing other music, he often uses an open hand, as well as a fist, which gives him the flexibility to sound more notes at a time with greater sensitivity, adding more color

to a piece. Usually, the color is added on the higher bells, while the middle bells carry the melody, and the large, bass bells add the beat and undertone, but this is not always the case. In his playing, Geert creates a wide range of sounds on all the bells, from trills to rolls to somber bass beats. His hands seem to float over the keys, rising and falling with enormous grace. It is inspired, virtuosic playing.

When I talked with him, he emphasized how important it was to understand your instrument and its location. Each of the 600 carillons in the world is different and has to be played differently. The weight of the bells, their height off the ground, how well they are tuned, and their own individual resonances must all be taken into consideration. Geert has played many carillons around the world and said there is a great variation in how well they can be played. It also makes a difference where they are located. He said that in a city like Antwerp, he plays energetically to match the pace of city life, but in Lake Wales he plays quietly to match the peace of the garden. City music would sound harsh in the country, while country music would be bland in the city. This is also true in composing carillon music; it must fit both the instrument and the setting. Geert's graceful playing can be seen and heard on the Bok website at www.boktowergardens.org.

As I was getting ready to leave, I was again reminded of how generous bell people are in sharing their knowledge and their love of bells. As I turned to go, Geert said he would play something for me, and, as I walked away from the tower, the lovely strains of "Danny Boy" floated out over the gardens.

The bell cemetery in Hamburg, Germany, where bells were sent after being confiscated during World War II. The bells were melted down and their metal used for armaments.

THE BELLS OF WAR AND PEACE

Ring out the thousand wars of old,
Ring in the thousand years of peace.

—ALFRED, LORD TENNYSON

As I was researching the stories for this book, I was repeatedly surprised when I read about bells being melted down for armaments in wartime, only to be recast as bells in peacetime. I didn't remember hearing about this in American history, although, when I looked into it, I found many examples from the Revolutionary and Civil Wars. But the experiences of other countries have been so devastating that the story of bells seems incomplete without the story of the role they have played in war. It also seems incomplete without acknowledging the role they have played in commemorating and celebrating peace.

WAR

A tragic affinity has always existed between bells and war. Most bells are made of bronze, an alloy that is roughly 80 percent copper and 20 percent tin, both metals that are used extensively in armaments. There is a long history of countries at war melting down bells and using the metal to make cannons, ammunition, airplane parts, and other weapons of war. Sometimes, these bells had even been cast from armaments used in earlier wars, an eerie recycling of a scarce and expensive resource.

Some of the most dramatic destructions of bells took place during World War II, when Germany removed more than 150,000 church bells from its own churches and the churches in the countries it occupied. We know a great deal about this confiscation because, in 1945, Percival Price, the American carillonneur and bell historian, was commissioned to study church bells lost during the war. His report, *Campanology: 1945–1947*, revealed the story of what happened to these bells.

Germany did not have extensive natural resources of copper and tin and was dependent on imports for these metals. As the buildup of the Nazi war effort proceeded in the late 1930s, imports were not adequate. In March 1940, the government ordered that all decommissioned bells and all bell metal in foundries be made available for military reserves. At the same time, an inventory and classification of church bells was ordered, with the bells classified into four categories of value, starting with recently cast bells and working up to the most important historical bells, particularly bells from the Middle Ages and the three historical carillons of Berlin, Potsdam, and Darmstadt.

The least valuable and most numerous bells, category A bells, were to be taken down and sent to smelting refineries for processing. Although there were a number of these refineries, the most important ones were in Hamburg, which is where most of the bells confiscated in the war were sent. Category B and C bells were to be taken down and held in warehouses until they were needed, while the most precious category D bells were to be left in their towers. In addition, each parish church was allowed to keep one bell, the one they deemed most valuable.

The first category A bells arrived in Hamburg in December 1941, where they were broken down, melted, and separated into their component parts. By the end of the war, approximately 90,000 category A bells had been melted down, along with about 10,000 other German bells. In all, German bells provided almost 300,000 metric tons of copper and 14,000 metric tons of tin to the war effort. More than 80 percent of German bells were destroyed this way.

As Germany advanced into other European countries, they began requisitioning the bells of those countries. First were Poland and Czechoslovakia, where requisitions were heavy. Before the war, Poland had about 33,000 bells; 22,500 were confiscated and 20,800 were destroyed, 63 percent of the prewar total. Czechoslovakia had 15,000 bells before the war; 12,000 were confiscated and 11,400 destroyed, 76 percent of the prewar total.

The next countries to lose their bells were the Netherlands and Belgium. Each country had about 9,000 bells before the war, and each had about half confiscated and destroyed, 4,660 in the Netherlands and 4,220 in Belgium. In both countries, a four-fold classification system was set up, similar to the one being used in Germany. In the Netherlands, the government had already carried out an inventory of the country's bells in case it needed the metal itself. In doing so, it had marked the most historic and important bells with an "M" for "Monument." The "M" bells, plus additional important bells, were protected as category D bells, including many important carillons. The Dutch government also undertook a study of the bells to be confiscated, which delayed their being shipped to Hamburg and aided in identifying some of them after the war.

In Belgium, there was more flexibility in how the bells were confiscated. All carillons were exempt as long as they were regularly played, as were bells cast before 1450. The rest of the bells were put in a historical classification system: category A bells were those cast after 1850; category B bells between 1790 and 1850; category C bells between 1700 and 1790; and category D bells before 1700. Category A, B, and C bells were taken down and shipped to Germany. Belgian authorities were also able to delay some of these shipments while gathering information on the bells.

France fared better than the other European countries because the leaders of the collaborationist Vichy government made an agreement with the Nazis to provide metal statues instead of bells, thus preserving many of their bells.

Italy, however, fared poorly. Before the war, Mussolini had made an agreement with the Vatican that half of the weight of Italy's bells could be "mobilized" for the war effort. By the end of the war, 42 percent of Italy's bells had been confiscated and destroyed.

The requisition and destruction of bells in the occupied territories did not take place without resistance. Particularly in the Netherlands and Belgium, historically famous bell ringing countries, religious authorities protested that destroying the bells was against the Geneva Convention and a moral crime. This caused only a slight modification of the German program.

More successful were the efforts to hide or bury bells before they could be taken. Belgian railway workers often pushed confiscated bells off the trains headed for Germany. Other bells

Germany did not have extensive natural resources of copper and tin and was dependent on imports for these metals. As the buildup of the Nazi war effort proceeded in the late 1930s, imports were not adequate. In March 1940, the government ordered that all decommissioned bells and all bell metal in foundries be made available for military reserves.

were put on barges and sunk. In northern France, the town of Sedan saved its bells by having some local citizens pose as German soldiers who came in a truck and "confiscated" the bells and buried them for safekeeping.

Also, since carillons were exempt in Belgium, people took valuable swinging bells and attached them to carillons to disguise them. In the Belgian town of Ath, St. Julian's Tower had once had a carillon, but it was destroyed by fire in 1815. The townspeople assembled swinging bells from other churches into a mock carillon in the tower and played a recording of carillon music regularly to show that their "carillon" was being played, thus saving these bells.

Of course, confiscation wasn't the only threat to bells during World War II. Many other bells were lost during the war from bombing and fire. After the war, Price estimated that an additional 5 percent of the bells in Germany, 2 percent in Belgium, 10 percent in the Nether-lands, and 10 percent in Italy were destroyed. Unfortunately, many of the bells still hanging in these countries were their finest bells, those that had been exempt from confiscation. All three of the most important carillons in Germany that had been put in the protected D category were destroyed by Allied bombing. Several famous Hemony carillons were destroyed in the Netherlands and Belgium, and Rouen Cathedral in France lost its bells.

When the war was over and Germany was divided into zones under the jurisdiction of the Allies, Hamburg fell under British jurisdiction. At the time, it was estimated that 14,000 bells were still in the refineries and yards in Ham-burg, most of them category B and C bells.

The return of these bells to their original homes took a number of years, complicated by arguments about whether German bells should be used as reparations to the Allies for the damage inflicted on them and, in the case of the Eastern European countries like Poland, the realities of the emerging Cold War.

Eventually, the arguments for reparations were rejected, and the bells were returned, first the bells of the countries that had been occupied and then the German bells. The scrap metal found in the Hamburg refineries was also sent proportionally to the various countries with the understanding that it could only be used to make new bells. Since the postwar demand for bells to replace those lost was so high and metal still scarce, this provided a beginning for the process of rebuilding the lost bell heritage of Europe.

World War II is a well-documented case of the relationship between bells and war. Most other wars have similar stories where not only Christian bells but Buddhist, Taoist, Confu-cian, and civic bells have been sacrificed for war purposes.

PEACE

The bells of war have always been bells of sorrow. The bells of peace are first bells of remembrance and then bells of hope.

At the end of a war, countries need physical restoration, but they also need emotional restoration as people begin to mourn their dead. As a tribute to the dead, war memorials have been built in many places, and bells have often been chosen for such memorials, their deep tones acting as a solemn expression of such sorrow.

The Bell for the Fallen at Rovereto, Italy, was cast in 1924 as a bell of remembrance. It is rung every evening to remember soldiers killed in war.

One impressive example of such a bell memorial is the Bell of the Fallen in Rovereto, Italy. This large bell was cast in 1924 with bronze from the guns of all the nations that had engaged in World War I. Baptized Maria Dolens (the grieving Virgin Mary), the bell is rung every evening in remembrance of Italian soldiers killed in war and also in remembrance of all soldiers killed in war. Engraved on the bell are the constellations that appeared in the sky at dawn on the day World War I began and the constellations that appeared at sunset on the day the war ended.

A particularly poignant example of a bell memorial is the memorial in Khatyn, Belarus, a tiny village that originally had twenty-six houses. On March 22, 1943, German occupying forces surrounded the village to exact revenge for a German officer killed by partisans. The townspeople were rounded up and locked in a barn that was then set on fire. Some of the people were able to break down the door but, as they ran out, they were gunned down. The rest died in the fire. In all, 149 people were killed, including 75 children. All the other buildings in the town were burned.

Khatyn was one of many hundreds of Belarusian villages destroyed during World War II. In the 1960s, it was chosen as the site for a war memorial commemorating the more than two million people who died in Belarus during the war. One part of this memorial is a set of chimneys constructed on the sites where each of the twenty-six burned houses stood. The chimneys are reminders of the original brick chimneys, all that was left in the village after it was burned. Each chimney has a plaque remembering the family that lived in that house, and at the top of each chimney is a bell. These twenty-six bells are rung regularly and have become the voice of the memorial.

Although so many of the battles of World War I and World War II were fought on European soil, a large number of the soldiers who fought there came from countries outside Europe, particularly the United States, Canada, and Australia. At the end of the wars, each of these countries created its own memorials to mourn their dead.

One of the loveliest memorials is the Peace Tower at the Houses of Parliament in Ottawa, Canada, which has a fifty-three-bell carillon from the English firm of Gillette & Johnston. Dedicated on July 1, 1927, the Peace Tower commemorates the Canadians who lost their lives in World War I. The inaugural concert was attended by the Prince of Wales and was broadcast during the first coast-to-coast live radio broadcast in Canada. At the concert, the Canadian prime minister declared the carillon to be the "the Voice of the Nation."

Another powerful memorial is the University of Sydney War Memorial Carillon, which was dedicated on Anzac Day, April 25, 1928.

> **One part of this memorial is a set of chimneys constructed on the sites where each of the twenty-six burned houses stood. The chimneys are reminders of the original brick chimneys, all that was left in the village after it was burned.**

One of the chimneys symbolizing the homes destroyed in the small town of Khatyn in Belarus during World War II. The bells on the top of the chimneys are rung in remembrance of those lost and have become the voice of the Khatyn memorial.

The Peace Tower at the Canadian Houses of Parliament in Ottawa has a fifty-three-bell carillon that commemorates Canadian lives lost in World War I.

Anzac Day is Australia's most patriotic holiday, commemorating the first major military campaign conducted by Australian and New Zealand forces at the battle of Gallipoli in World War I. Housed in the university's historic clock tower, the carillon has fifty-four bells that ring in remembrance of the members of the university who died in World War I. On a plaque listing those to be honored is inscribed the following, with the names listed below.

These also be held in grateful memory
And shall be sung forever by the bells

In addition to the desire to memorialize the dead, after a war there is often a deep recoiling from the horrors of war and a desire to move past these horrors toward a more hopeful world of peace. This feeling has inspired the creation of many bell memorials dedicated to the ideal of peace. Rather than being in just one country, however, many of these peace memorials are located in many countries, reflecting the desire for a more universal vision of peace. Not surprisingly, the largest of these efforts, the World Peace Bells, was instigated by Japan, which suffered the atomic bomb attacks on Hiroshima and Nagasaki at the end of World War II.

After the war, Chiyoji Nakagawa, a business-man and mayor of the Japanese city of Uwajima, came to believe in the need for a world peace movement. He proposed that ringing a temple bell could be a tangible symbol of such a

THE **NATIONAL CARILLON**

A war memorial was also planned for Washington, D.C. after the end of World War I. Designed to be a national carillon, it was to be placed in a 300-foot tower on the National Mall near the White House and would hold fifty-four bells, one for each of the forty-eight states and six territories. Included in the bell metal would be bronze from German cannons, while the tower was to have stones incorporated in it from Reims, Verdun, Leuven, and other European cities destroyed in the war. Sadly, this carillon was never built.

movement, an audible prayer for peace. In 1950, he had his first peace bell cast for the Taihei Temple in Uwajima, which would replace a temple bell seized by the military during the war. The bell, called the Bell of Banzai for Absolute Peace, had coins from twenty-six countries included in its metal. It became the prototype for the World Peace Bells that followed.

After attending a meeting of the United Nations as an observer in 1951, Chiyoji Nakagawa created a plan to have the Japanese people present a similar bell to the United Nations as a symbol of peace. Coins gathered from sixty nations were incorporated in the bell. Called the Japanese Peace Bell, the bell was shipped to New York and dedicated on

The Japanese Peace Bell housed in a lovely replica of a Shinto shrine at the United Nations headquarters in New York. It is one of many similar peace bells installed in countries around the world.

The peace bell at Cowra, Australia, is an example of the world peace bells. The bells are designed alike but housed in different structures native to each country.

June 8, 1954, in the West Court Garden of the UN headquarters.

Housed in a lovely replica of a Shinto shrine, the bell is just over three feet tall, two feet in diameter at the rim, and weighs about 250 pounds. Inscribed on one side of the bell are Japanese characters that say "Long live absolute world peace." The bell is rung twice a year. On September 21, the International Day for Peace, it is rung by the UN secretary-general to pray for world peace and to open the UN General Assembly. It is also rung on the vernal equinox, which is the first day of spring and the celebration of Earth Day.

In 1982, the World Peace Bell Association was founded in Tokyo to carry on Chiyoji Nakagawa's work. Supported by the ambassadors of more than 120 countries, the association pledged to further the goals of world peace by casting and installing duplicate UN peace bells in countries around the world.

The first two bells were installed in Japan in 1988. In 1989, bells were installed in Turkey, Germany, and Poland. In the 1990s, bells were placed in Mexico, Australia, Mongolia, the Philippines, Austria, Canada, Brazil, Argentina, and Ecuador. Since 2000, bells have been placed in the United States, Spain, Uzbekistan, New Zealand, and Argentina. Although the

structures housing the bells differ from country to country, reflecting the culture of each country, the bells are all the same and look like the one in Cowra, Australia.

A different series of peace bells has been created by the World Choir Games, an international competition of choirs modeled on the Olympics that meets every two years in different cities around the globe. Each meeting has a peace bell designed and cast for it that is rung in the opening and closing ceremonies to call all nations to sing and celebrate together in peace. The organization believes that bringing people together to sing also brings their cultures together in better understanding.

The 2016 games were held in Sochi, Russia, and were attended by more than 20,000 people from more than seventy countries. The lovely bell created for these games is shown on page 174. Previous games had been held in Austria, South Korea, Germany, China, the United States, and Latvia. In contrast to the

The lovely Sochi Peace Bell was designed for the World Choir Games when they were held in Sochi, Russia, in 2016. The World Choir Games aim to promote peace and understanding among nations.

World Peace Bells, the bell for each of the choir games is unique, ranging from the Sochi Russian bell to Chinese temple bells to traditional American bells, reflecting the culture of the host city.

Finally, another moving series of peace bells is the Dharma Peace Bells that the Light of Buddhadharma Foundation International has been placing at key sites in the life of the Buddha. Founded in 2002 in the United States, the mission of the foundation is to support and strengthen these historical sites through physical restoration, pilgrimages and teaching projects, chanting ceremonies, peace walks, and the donation of the dharma bells. The bells have been placed at the site of the birth of the Buddha, the place he is believed to have received enlightenment, many of his places of pilgrimage, and the site of Nalanda University, the great monastic Buddhist university. The hope is these dharma bells will bring with them the power of the message of peace that the Buddha brought to the world. The photo on the next page shows the stately bell placed at Sarnath, where the Buddha gave his first teaching of the Dharma.

These are just a few of the peace bells that can be found around the world. Each of them echoes the desire of people to break out of the cycle of war and peace that has characterized human history, as well as the history of bells.

The peace bell at Sarnath is one of the Dharma Peace Bells that the Light of Buddhadharma Foundation International places at important places in the life of the Buddha. Sarnath is where the Buddha gave his first teaching of the Dharma.

The Tsar Kolokol, the largest bell in the world, was cast in Moscow in 1735. The bell cracked after casting during a fire at the Kremlin. One hundred years later, it was raised from its casting pit and placed on a platform in the Kremlin with its cracked piece leaning against the platform. The bell was never rung.

RINGING THE ZVON:

THE BELLS
OF RUSSIA

The sound of Russian bells is utterly mystical, filled with multiple layers of meaning and significance, powerful in its effects on the human soul.

—HIERODEACON ROMAN

One of the first bells I encountered in my study of bells was the Tsar Kolokol, by far the largest bell in the world. Standing just over nineteen feet tall, the bell is sixty feet in circumference around its rim, has a diameter of nineteen feet, and weighs more than 430,000 pounds. The bell was cast in Moscow in 1735, but cracked after casting. Today, the bell sits at the base of the Ivan Velikij Bell Tower in the Kremlin with its large cracked piece leaning next to it, a vivid symbol of Russia's long history as a bell-ringing nation.

The Tsar Kolokol (kolokol is the Russian word for bell) is one of the many monumental bells that were cast in Russia in the seventeenth and eighteenth centuries, the peak of Russian bell founding. Besides their enormous size, one of the unique qualities of these bells is that they developed in lineages or dynasties.

The Tsar Kolokol was the fourth and final bell in the most famous of these lineages. The first was the Godunov Bell commissioned by Emperor Boris Godunov and cast in 1599 by Andrej Chokhov, the most famous founder of the day. At more than 78,000 pounds, it was the biggest bell ever cast in Russia at that time. The bell was hung in a wooden tower in the Kremlin and rung for important state and religious occasions. Two ropes were attached to its heavy clapper, one extending out to each side, and it took twelve men on each rope to swing the clapper back and forth.

After the Godunov Bell was destroyed in a fire in the Kremlin in the mid-1600s, Tsar Aleksei Mikhailovich ordered the pieces of the bell to be recast as part of a much larger bell. The new bell, which became known as the First Aleksei Mikhailovich Bell, was cast in 1654 by a pair of father and son founders named Danilov and weighed almost 290,000 pounds, the clapper alone weighing 9,000 pounds. When rung, its deep boom could be heard for more than four miles from the center of Moscow. However, efforts to ring the bell even more loudly caused the bell to crack within a year.

After the bell cracked, the tsar immediately commissioned a new, young founder named Grigor'ev to recast the bell. Grigor'ev had an enormous pit dug in the Kremlin for the casting, with five brick furnaces around it for melting the metal. The mold was constructed and placed in the pit, and, after being melted in the furnaces, the metal was poured into the cast, where it cooled for three days before the cast was removed and the bell cleaned and polished. The bell was raised with an elaborate system of ropes and pulleys into its wooden tower. Known as the Second Aleksei Mikhailovich Bell of 1655, the new bell weighed at least 360,000 pounds and took 100 men to ring with four ropes. When rung, the sound was described as a small earthquake, breaking glasses and dishes in homes throughout Moscow. Later hung in a masonry structure, the bell was destroyed in another Kremlin fire in 1701. For over thirty years, the pieces of the bell remained in a heap on the ground where they fell.

The last bell in the lineage was the Tsar Kolokol, cast in 1735, shortly after Anna Ivanovna became empress of Russia. The empress ordered a new, even larger, bell that would include the remains of the 1655 bell and commissioned Ivan Motorin, then the most admired founder in Moscow, to cast it. Motorin started by making a 400-pound model of the bell, and then had the casting pit dug thirty-three feet deep and thirty-three feet in diameter near the Ivan Velikij, or Ivan the Great, Bell Tower in the Kremlin. The bottom of the pit was strengthened by an iron grating laid over oak timbers dug into the earth, while the walls of the pit were lined with bricks and horizontal timbers held in place by iron beams. The furnaces were constructed around the pit, and artisans were brought in to design the elaborate ornamentation that would be carved into the bell mold, including a full-length portrait of the empress.

Finally, in November of 1734, the metal was loaded into the furnaces, prayers were said in the Kremlin's Uspensky Cathedral, and the furnaces were fired. All went well until the hearthstone under two of the furnaces malfunctioned, allowing hot metal to seep out. Motorin stopped the process, but then decided to go ahead with just the two remaining furnaces. After finding additional sources of metal, including 600 old bells that were melted and reused, he tried again. But when the furnaces were started, a third one failed, and Motorin had to abandon the effort. About three months later, he died without completing

The Tsar Kolokol at the Kremlin.

his great work, and his son Mikhail took over. One year later, Mikhail successfully cast the new bell.

Now the challenge was to raise this huge bell. The plan was to build a belfry right over the casting pit, so the bell could be raised vertically without having to be moved to a different location. But before plans were approved for the raising of the bell, another fire took its toll on the Tsar Kolokol dynasty. On May 29, 1739, the Feast of the Holy Trinity, fire again raged through the Kremlin. A wooden shed that had been constructed over the casting pit to aid the casting process caught fire, tumbling burning logs down onto the bell. Firefighters, with the best of intentions, poured

cold water into the pit to put out the fire. Because the bell metal had become so hot, the shock of the cold water caused a seven-foot-tall piece of the bell to break off from the sound bow. This silenced the great bell, which remained in its deep pit for the next 100 years. Although never rung, the pitch of the bell was later estimated to be two octaves below middle C, with the hum tone an octave lower, near the lower end of human hearing.

There were many proposals to raise, restore, or recast the bell, but none of them were accepted until the reign of Nicholas I, when a proposal was approved to raise the bell and move it to a platform where it would rest permanently. A large hoisting derrick was built over the bell pit, and, on July 23, 1836, the bell was successfully raised. The bell was rolled on logs up a gentle slope to the granite pedestal that had been built for it, and the hoist was used to lower it in place. The large broken piece was placed on the ground, leaning against the pedestal. A few years later, the bell

which was the one true religion he should adopt for his own pagan kingdom. The envoys journeyed to Bulgaria to study Islam, Khazar to study Judaism, Germany to study Roman Catholic Christianity, and Constantinople to study Eastern Orthodox Christianity. When they returned, they overwhelmingly reported

---

The large broken piece was placed on the ground, leaning against the pedestal. A few years later, the bell was consecrated as a chapel and its inside used as a place of worship, the equivalent of a two–story church.

---

was consecrated as a chapel and its inside used as a place of worship, the equivalent of a two-story church. No longer a place of worship today, the Tsar Kolokol stands as a monumental sculpture of Russian technological achievement.

Although these monumental bells are a unique part of the history of Russian bells, they are only a few of the thousands of bells that rang out for centuries from churches and monasteries throughout the country. All of these bells were an inherent part of Eastern Orthodox Christianity, the religion that permeated Russian life from the tenth century until the Russian Revolution in the early twentieth century. The story of Russian Orthodox Christianity is also the story of her bells.

The story began in 987 when Prince Vladimir, then ruler of "Kiev and all Rus," sent envoys out to study the major religions of the neighboring countries in order to decide

that the Eastern Orthodox Christianity of Constantinople was the most beautiful and compelling of all religions. After attending a festival service in the great Hagia Sophia, they said, "We knew not whether we were in heaven or on earth. For on earth there is no such splendor or such beauty, and we are at a loss to describe it." After being baptized, Vladimir destroyed his pagan idols, built churches in their place, and converted his kingdom to Orthodox Christianity.

This was a profound decision for the cultural and spiritual development of Russia and for the development of Russian bells. Seated between East and West—and influenced by both over its history—Russia's conversion to Orthodox Christianity placed it within the great Byzantine Empire that was the center of Christianity for much of its first millennium. Although born of a common heritage, Christianity developed into two branches early

FLOGGING **THE BELL**

Some bells had surprising fates in Russia. In the sixteenth century, the bell in the cathedral in the town of Uglich, northwest of Moscow, was rung to gather townspeople together in protest of the suspected murder of a child by agents of the Tsar. When the authorities tried to quell the rebellion and stop the bell from ringing, the bell ringer locked himself in the belfry and refused to stop. Eventually the rebellion was put down, but, in retaliation, many of the citizens were executed, put in prison, or exiled to Western Siberia. The bell was treated as being as guilty as the people. It was taken down from the tower, flogged 120 times, had its clapper removed, and then exiled to Siberia with the people.

on, one in the Greek-speaking East and one in the Latin-speaking West. By the time Emperor Constantine converted to Christianity in 306 and moved the seat of government from Rome to Constantinople, the western parts of the empire were already starting to decline. Although Rome always remained the "first among equals" of the jurisdictional centers of Christianity, invasions by Germanic tribes and repeated sacking of the city led to the breakup of the Western territories. As the Christian West slowly entered the Dark Ages, the Christian East— led by the great cities of Alexandria, Antioch, Jerusalem, and Constantinople—flourished.

When Russia became part of the Byzantine Empire in the late tenth century, the two branches of Christianity had already become two distinct churches—the Eastern or Greek Orthodox Church and the Roman Catholic Church—which were increasingly divided by irresolvable differences in theology and practice. In 1054, less than a century after Russia's conversion, the two churches formally separated in what became known as the Great Schism. It was the Greek or Eastern Orthodox Church, with its 600 years of splendid art, architecture, and spirituality, that Russia inherited.

Of all the differences that divided the two churches—the date of Easter, the wording of the creeds, whether the pope or the scriptures were the ultimate authority—the most important difference for Russian bells was the mystical quality of the Orthodox service as expressed so vividly by Vladimir's envoys when they said they could not describe its heavenly splendor and beauty. While the Western Church developed within an environment of rational thought and rich language, the Orthodox Church believed that faith could reach a reality beyond reason and that language itself was too narrow to express that reality. In the Orthodox Church, the celebration of the divine mystery of Christianity was something to be directly experienced and adored, a communion with the Living God that engaged all the senses—sight, sound, taste, smell, and touch—in a total aesthetic and spiritual experience.

The visual expression of this experience was icons, the ethereal images of the Christian pantheon painted on wood that are so identified

(LEFT): A Russian icon, one of the visual expressions of the divine mystery of Russian Orthodox Christianity that personify sacred personages, such as Christ, the Virgin Mary, and the Apostles. (ABOVE): Although Russian Orthodox bells look like Western bells, many of their most important features are more like the bells of the East.

with Byzantine and Russian art. Images of Christ, the Virgin Mary, the Apostles, saints, martyrs, and episodes and symbols of Christian history were all portrayed in rich colors of gold, red, greens, and blues. Icons were not realistic paintings; they were spiritual paintings that captured the essence of a holy person and invited believers to a living communion with that person. Such devotional icons were universal parts of worship; they filled church walls, were carried in processions, and were placed in homes and other places of daily life. They were visual gospels that personified beauty and veneration.

The aural counterpart of icons in the Orthodox service was bells. Bells were the voice of God, as icons were the spiritual presence. Hung in low towers next to Orthodox churches, they were played in intricate patterns called zvon. Most of the Orthodox

service was chanted; only the sermon was spoken, so the service itself was intensely musical, greatly enhanced by the bell music that enveloped it.

Although Orthodox bells were visually similar to Western bells, with rounded shoulders and flared waists, many of their important features were more like the bells of the East. Like Eastern bells, they were hung "dead," meaning they were fixed in place and did not swing. To ring the bell, a rope was attached to the clapper and pulled against the inside of the bell by the ringer. Usually, the ringer held the clapper near the lip of the bell with the rope taut so he just had to press the rope or flick it to make the bell ring. By directly controlling the clapper this way, the ringer had a great deal of flexibility; he could play loud or soft, fast or slow, and with many variations in rhythm. This gave him more control than

At the Danilov Monastery in Moscow, the bell ringer must ring many bells at once during the service.

with swinging bells, whose regular rhythm and beat were hard to change.

When there was more than one bell, ringing became complex. For two bells that were not too heavy, one ringer could ring one bell with each hand. To accommodate three bells, the ropes of two bells could be attached to each end of a wooden grip. The bell ringer would twist his wrist back and forth, sounding each bell in turn, called "milking the cow." Additional bells might be attached to the ringer's elbow or arm. For larger, heavier bells, the clapper ropes were attached to a foot pedal, often with the help of pulleys. Often, one ringer could ring up to six or seven bells.

With many bells, there was more than one ringer, each in charge of several bells, and the ringers had to watch carefully so as not to interfere with one another's ropes. For a very heavy bell, there were two ringers for the bell, one standing on each side, who would push the clapper back and forth in a steady beat.

Percival Price, in his monumental work *Bells and Man*, reports that, when Russians first saw the swinging bells of Western churches in early silent films, they laughed. They couldn't understand why you would move a heavy bell to hit a light clapper, rather than move a light clapper to hit a heavy bell.

Like Eastern bells, Orthodox bells were also untuned. Where European bells were tuned to a particular note and could be played harmoniously with other tuned bells, Orthodox bells were chosen for the richness and complexity of their individual sound. It was the character of the bell that mattered—whether it was sonorous with rich tones and overtones—rather than its ability to create harmony. The richer the sound of the bell, the more it became the voice of God played out in sound and space. Bells, as aural or singing icons, had a spiritual place in the Orthodox sacrament not experienced in the West.

Although hung in towers like Western bells,

The richer the sound of the bell, the more it became the voice of God played out in sound and space. Bells, as aural or singing icons, had a spiritual place in the Orthodox sacrament not experienced in the West.

signaling the time for services. Eventually, a much larger semantron was developed that could be hung in a central place where all could hear it. By the eighth century, semantra, both large and small, were in common use in Orthodox monasteries and, increasingly, in Orthodox churches.

A skilled player could play a wide variety of sounds on the semantron, creating different patterns and rhythms depending on the size, shape, and thickness of the semantron and the kind of mallet used to strike it. For example, using a two-headed or double mallet could add pace and complexity to the sound. Used for centuries in the Orthodox Church, even after bells started to be imported from Europe, the semantron can still be found in remote monasteries today. The pulsing, rhythmic sound of the semantron became the basis for Russian bell ringing, which over time evolved from a signal to the complex and rich art called zvon.

Zvon is built on the interaction of three different sizes of bells played in intricate and varying patterns: large bass bells, middle-sized alto and tenor bells, and small soprano bells. The large bells provide the pulse, the metronome for the music. The middle bells provide the rhythm, the pattern for the music, while the small bells provide the trill, the adornment that runs through the ringing.

An example of how these bells can be played is found in a short article "Ring Like the Masters of Old!" published by Blagovest Bells on their website www.russianbells.com. You start with an even, slow pulsing of the bass bells, then add the intermediate rhythm of the alto and tenor bells, and finally the trill of the

Orthodox bells were also played differently. Since the distinguishing quality of each bell was its unique sound, the relationship of bells to one another was whether they had higher or lower pitches, not whether they were in harmony. Arranging the bells this way reflected the most distinctive characteristic of Russian bell music, which was that it was based on rhythm, not melody; it was the music of the drum, not the piano, and had its origins in the use of the semantron as a signaling device in the early years of the Orthodox Church.

In the monasteries of Egypt and Palestine, it was the tradition to call monks to services by knocking on their individual cell doors with a wooden hammer or mallet. This changed with the development of the semantron. A semantron is a long, narrow, wooden board struck with a mallet by one of the monks as he walked around the monastery, its sound soprano bells. With five bells, number 5 being the largest, this would sound like:

---

*Start with a large bell pulsing 5 . . . 5 . . . 5 . . . sounding **bong, bong, bong**.*
Add two medium bells striking 3-4-3, 3-4-3 in the intervals between the large pulses sounding ding-dong-ding . . . ding-dong-ding.
*Combining these bells would sound **bong**-ding-dong-ding-**bong**-ding-dong-ding-**bong** . . .*
Then on top of this add the trill of the soprano bells sounding ching-a-ling, ching-a-ling, ching-a-ling.
End by ringing all the bells together.

This example can be expanded in many ways, such as changing the tempo of the bass bells, adding a more complex pattern for the alto and tenor bells, or changing the trill surrounding the peal, with all maintaining the pulse or rhythm of the whole. It can also be changed by adding more bells, increasing the density of the music. Taken together, the sounds of the bells are like a chorus, with bass, alto, tenor, and soprano bells singing together in a polyphonic rhythm.

Just as a painter creates a landscape, Russian bell ringers use these building blocks to create a soundscape, a complex musical score that expresses the liturgy of the service or the nature of a special occasion, such as Easter or a funeral. The music of the soundscape usually has several movements like a symphony, each movement containing a series of repetitive, rhythmic phrases. The movements are the structure of the zvon, while the phrases are the expressive art created by the ringers. Like change ringing, zvon is an intricate and complex art. Zvon players, however, can improvise within the fixed larger structure of their music, while change ringers are constrained by the preordained sequences of their music. This demanding and complex bell music permeates the Orthodox service and is a rich part of what has been called Russia's "conversation with God." Wonderful examples of zvon can be heard on the website www.russianbells.com.

In addition to its rich texture and complex composition, another important dimension of Russian bell ringing is how the ringing itself is elevated to a spiritual experience. The role of the bell ringer is not only to give a fine musical performance; his deeper challenge is to create an "inspired" peal that embodies the theological meaning of the service, a sound image that reaches people's hearts and souls. He must become one with his music. On Easter, he becomes jubilant; for a funeral, he becomes sorrowful; for a procession, he gives a measured beat. A moving description of this higher calling was given by Hierodeacon Roman, the head bell ringer of the Danilov Monastery of Moscow, at a talk at Harvard University in 2008 on the occasion of the monastery bells being returned after being held in safety at Harvard during Soviet rule. He said:

The church bell is a symbol with many meanings ... But more than anything else the bell sound is tied together with the voice of God. The voice of God summons the people, the voice of God is the voice of our conscience; it is a call to kindness in our hearts, changing our lives for the better.

The challenge of the bell ringer is to create music that expresses both the voice of God and the powerful effect that voice can have on the human soul.

He starts by creating a bond between himself and his bells, gaining a sense of the skill of the craftsman who originally cast each bell, maybe many centuries ago. He then reminds himself of the particular quality of each bell and how it is best combined with the other bells. Next is his contemplation of the nature of the service or occasion at hand. What is the religious and emotional nature of the occasion? How does he feel about it? How do his bells fit in with the other elements of the service—the architecture of the building, the music of the chanting and the hymns, the icons? How can he create a soundscape that expresses all this? Slowly, he comes to a point of quiet contemplation and inner peace. Again, from Hierodeacon Roman:

SAVING **THE DANILOV BELLS**

The seven-hundred-year-old Danilov Monastery is one of the most important monasteries in Russia; it is the seat of the Patriarch and the home of some of Russia's most famous bells. During the Soviet era, like other Russian bells, the Danilov bells were slated for destruction and the monastery turned over for secular use. Thomas Wittemore, an American Byzantium specialist, heard about the bells and urged a friend of his, Charles R. Crane, a noted philanthropist, to try to save them. Crane agreed to purchase the bells from the Soviet state and transport them to Harvard University for safe keeping. At the time, a clock tower was under construction at Lowell House, one of the Harvard residential houses. The clock tower was redesigned as a bell tower, and the bells were shipped there in 1930. It was a magnificent peal of eighteen bells, ranging in size from twenty-two pounds to thirteen tons, cast between 1682 and 1907, and noted for the beauty of its ringing.

At the end of the Soviet era, the Danilov Monastery was returned to the Russian Orthodox Church. The buildings were restored and some substitute bells were put in the bell tower. Soon suggestions were made that perhaps Harvard would repatriate the bells. The conversation went on for twenty-five years before an agreement was reached where Harvard would return the Danilov bells. In the summer of 2008, the Danilov bells came home seventy-eight years after they had been given refuge at Lowell House.

In these elaborately decorated Orthodox bells, each clapper is attached to a rope that is pulled by the ringer to sound the bell.

He then expands this profound inner world, this internal sense of peace, to the wider world, shares it with others, and through the pealing of the bells creates an aural-spatial icon of the mass. This icon, this image, includes the austere poetry of Byzantine hymns, the warmth of the morning sun during the Liturgy, the golden glitter and ancient patterns of the vestments seen through the smoke of the censer, the scent of incense, the words of the priest, the sense of freshness and profound spiritual peace, contentment, flashes of exultation.

Bells, as aural or singing icons, are transformational and have a spiritual place in the Orthodox sacrament not experienced in the West.

For more than 900 years, Eastern Orthodox Christianity permeated the culture of Russia. For much of that time, Russia was a major leader of the church. Russia also had one of the finest histories of bell founding and created one of the richest traditions of bell ringing and bell music. But all this came to an abrupt end in 1917 with the Russian Revolution and the winning supremacy of Soviet communism.

Soviet communism was militantly atheist, and gradually, most of the churches and monasteries of Russia were closed. It is estimated that, by 1941, 98 percent of the churches and monasteries in the country had stopped functioning and their bells silenced, which included at least 1,000 monasteries and 60,000 churches. A large number of the bells were melted down and transformed into armaments and agricultural implements as part of Russia's plans for military and economic development. Behind the destruction of the bells was the repression of the religious practices of Orthodox Christianity. Bell founding came to an end, and, over the seventy-four years of Soviet rule, much of the knowledge of traditional bell founding and bell ringing was lost.

Since the breakup of the Soviet Union in 1991, the deep roots of Orthodox Christianity in Russia have begun to grow again, carrying with them a renewal of bell founding and bell ringing. In 1992, permission was given to once again ring the bells in the Moscow Kremlin on Easter morning. Since then, thousands of churches and monasteries have reopened in Russia, and thousands of others are being rebuilt. Foundries have come to life, and the art of making bells is recovering. Russia is once again becoming a major center for bells in the world.

The art of bell ringing and the actual bell music have been more difficult to recover. Few pre-Soviet ringers were still alive, and little of the music was ever written down. Some of the music has been recovered from Russian Orthodox churches founded abroad by Russians who emigrated during the Soviet era, and other music has been recovered from monastery records and folk memories. In 2002, when the Patriarchate of Moscow issued the preliminary "Typikon of the Russian Orthodox Church," the official manual for Orthodox bell ringing, it brought together all the information that had been gathered by that time, a major step forward in reclaiming the art and practice of Russian bell ringing.

Reindeer are indigenous to the cold, Arctic climate, migrating from inland pastures in the winter to warmer pastures on the coast for the summer, stopping in the spring for the calving season and in the fall for the mating season.

ARCTIC NORWAY

He also introduced me to that for which there are no words—that special note which is the sound of the harmony which has existed for thousands of years between people and Nature in Sami country.

—THE PAINTER JOHN SAVIO IN THE SAMI PLAY *GESAT* BY NILS GAUP AND KNUT WALLE

In the spring of 2001, I was reading a book called *We Die Alone* by David Howarth about the harrowing experience of a World War II Norwegian resistance fighter who escaped a Nazi raid by retreating into the snow-clad mountains of northern Norway. He survived for some time with the help of partisans from the coastal towns who brought him supplies when they could. But he was slowly dying from frostbite and malnutrition, and his only hope was that the Sami reindeer herders who migrated over these lands would find him and take him over the border to Sweden and safety. But they were late that year, and didn't come and didn't come. Finally, as he was near death, he heard a loud snuffling and jangling of bells over his head. Looking up, he saw a bunch of reindeer gathered around with their heads poking down toward him. The herders had come just in time. They loaded him on a sled and took him over the border to safety, where he not only survived but recovered enough to rejoin the resistance movement later in the war.

I always intended to write a story about animal bells, and, after reading the book, I decided to write about reindeer bells. As I started to do my research, however, I found a deeper and more compelling story than I anticipated. More than other animal bells, reindeer bells have been deeply woven into the fabric of reindeer herding and Sami life. The reindeer have provided almost all the material necessities of life, such as food and clothing, and also created the structure and contours of daily life as the Sami people followed the reindeer through their annual migration. I also found that reindeer bells have been used in more subtle and sophisticated ways than other animal bells, not just as warning devices but to most of the world knows them. But it is a foreign and imposed name; the people always knew themselves as Sami, and today their identity is increasingly recognized by the outside world.

Reindeer are indigenous to this cold, Nordic area with almost half of their migratory lands

---

I also found that reindeer bells have been used in more subtle and sophisticated ways than other animal bells, not just as warning devices but to help organize the internal structure and behavior of the herd. Reindeer herding is an art, and the bells are an important part of that art.

---

help organize the internal structure and behavior of the herd. Reindeer herding is an art, and the bells are an important part of that art. As I became fascinated with these bells, I made contact with people in northern Norway and arranged to go there to meet some of the Sami reindeer herders.

For thousands of years the Sami people followed the reindeer across the top of Scandinavia and the Kola Peninsula of Russia. Long before the modern borders of Norway, Sweden, Finland, and Russia were carved on the land, the Sami had developed a life rich in history, culture, and song. It was a life of economic self-sufficiency centered on the family and in deep harmony with nature. At some point, this ancient race of people was given the name Laplanders or Lapps by visiting Europeans, and it is by this name that

within the Arctic Circle. Originally the reindeer were wild, and the Sami people were hunters who moved with the deer as they migrated. They followed the deer inland to the tundra in the winter, where the deer could dig down in the snow and subsist on lichen, and then outward to the coast in the summer, where they thrived on tender new grasses. In the fall, the migration was interrupted for the mating season and, in the spring, for the calving season. Each year, the deer would follow the same paths, stopping in the same places at about the same time. The Sami only followed them; the deer determined the pace and movement, the rhythm of life in accord with the seasons. Deer were killed as needed, and all the animal was used—the meat for food, the hide for clothing and tents, the sinew for thread, and the antlers for domestic and decorative items.

About 400 years ago, a change took place in the relationship between the Sami and the reindeer, when the Sami moved from being hunters to being pastoralists. Separating the wild deer into family herds, the Sami took ownership of these herds, the deer now becoming the property of the herders and the herders taking direct responsibility for their own herd. Domesticating the reindeer did not substantially change the pattern of Sami life: the families still followed the reindeer in migration over the same land, the reindeer providing the direct sustenance of food and clothing for their lives. What did change was the relationship of the herder to the herd. Rather than depending on nature and chance for the family's well-being, the herder could now exercise some degree of control over the deer. The herder could not change the migratory pattern, attuned as it was to the seasons, the food supply, and the reproductive cycle of the deer, but could work to manage the size and safety of the herd. The herd was the family's wealth; the bigger and healthier the herd, the better off the family would be.

With the shift to pastoralism, the natural dangers that always threaten deer in the wild, particularly predators and bad weather, become direct threats to the herder and his family. In the summer, when the new calves are young and vulnerable, eagles often swoop down, capturing the calves and carrying them away. Other times, ground animals, such as wolves and lynx, stalk the young deer. In the winter, bad weather becomes a danger if ice makes it difficult for the deer to reach their fragile supply of lichen buried under the snow.

A gray-and-yellow ground cover like moss, lichen is rich in the carbohydrates reindeer need to endure in the cold, often subzero climate. If the lichen is covered with ice, the female deer cannot get enough food, so, when spring comes, these weakened mothers give birth to frail calves, many of whom die or become easy prey to other animals. In a good year, a herder expects to lose about 20 percent of the herd's calves to natural death and predators. In an exceptionally bad year, up to 80 percent may be lost, a devastating loss to any herd.

Although they can do little about predators and bad weather except to exercise vigilance, there are things herders can do about another threat to their herds, the deer's constant proclivity to stray, which makes herding an endless process of finding and rounding up stray deer. To control the herd, a herder needs a deep and intimate knowledge of his deer, the kind of knowledge that only comes from years of experience. Good herders know each of their deer by sight, even in a herd of 500 or more. It is fairly easy to identify whether a deer is male or female and how old it is by its antlers. But the herder also knows each individual deer by its shape, walk, and behavior. He knows the lineage of each deer, its temperament, how it acts in the herd, what its history of fertility is if it is a female, and how it performs in the mating season if it is a male. And herders know how to "read" the moods and movements of the herd. The Sami language has more than 500 words relating to reindeer, a codification of this precise and technical knowledge.

An old, handmade reindeer bell worn down to a soft patina.

Another way a good herder can control the herd, however, is with the artful use of bells. Reindeer tend to form groups within a herd, clustering around deer that are calm and act as leaders. This natural, internal dynamic gives the herd a cohesiveness it otherwise would not have. Using their intimate knowledge of the herd, herders can enhance this natural process by putting bells on some of these select deer, amplifying their effect on the rest of the herd. The challenge is to place the right bells on the right deer in the right places within the herd.

A good herder watches the deer for three or four years before deciding if a particular deer should have a bell, watching how the deer acts within the herd and how the herd responds. If he has a calming effect on the other deer and they group around him, he is a good choice. But the herder must also choose the right bell. Each bell has a different tone, and the deer respond differently to different bells. Usually, a herder wants a bell with a low, melodic tone that carries a far distance; shrill and high tones are irritating, rather than calming. The herder tries a bell on the deer to see how it works. If the other deer respond to it, the bell stays on that deer; if not, another bell is tried. Just as herders know each of their deer, they also know the sound of each bell. In the dark or in bad weather, a good herder knows by listening to "which bells are missing" and therefore to which deer are missing: the belled deer and probably some or all of the deer that follow that particular bell.

Besides carefully choosing the deer and the bells, the herder also has to decide how many bells to have in the herd and where they are to be placed—in the front of the herd, the middle, the back, or the sides. Because only a few deer in the herd have bells, where they are

Reindeer linger near the ocean, where the winds keep summer insects away and they find the protein-rich grasses they love to eat.

placed forms the internal structure of the herd, each bell becoming a magnet for part of the herd. The herder is building that structure when choosing how many bells to have and where to place them. Since each herder tends to have an opinion about this, placement is unique to each herd. It is the combination of the right deer, the right bells, and the right placement that enhances the cohesiveness of the herd, so the bells become a special means of communication among the deer and between the herder and the deer.

When the deer are at pasture spread out over the tundra or hillside, the sound of their bells is quite fragmented—a clang here and there as the deer reach down for food or move from place to place. But when the herd is on the move for migration, at roundup, or going from one pasture to another, the melody and rhythm of the bells becomes clear. In addition to the bells placed within the herd, there is a special reindeer—the bell reindeer—that is chosen to lead the herd. The bell reindeer must have the same calmness as other belled deer, but he also must be comfortable with people, which many reindeer, still wild animals, are not. The bell reindeer is trained to be led by a rope in front of the herd, so when the bell reindeer moves forward, the rest of the herd follows, the sound of his bell creating the cadence for the herd. The steady ringing of his bell, along with the rhythmic ringing of the other bells within the herd, become the song of the reindeer as they move across the land.

When the herd is on the move, so are the Sami people. As the day lengthens after the long, dark night of winter, the deer grow restless and are ready to move. The families pack their winter homes, load the sleds, and start off. Led by the bell reindeer, the herd starts toward the coast, mostly traveling at night when a firm crust forms on the snow, making travel by sleigh easier. When they reach their traditional calving grounds, they stop while the new calves are born and gain strength. Then they go on to the summer pasture, usually by the ocean where the winds keep summer insects away and where they find the protein-rich new grasses that are such an important part of their diet. Here they grow and gain weight and, after molting, begin to develop new coats. Some of the herds even swim to one of the many islands off the coast for their summer pasture, the herder leading them from a boat. Holding the rope of the bell reindeer, the herder takes its bell, holds it out of the water, and rings it in a steady cadence. The deer enter the water and, submerged to their necks, swim across the divide, following the bell reindeer. The whole herd becomes a maze of antlers crossing the water.

During the long days of summer while the deer are at pasture, the Sami people have time to fish in the rivers, hunt for wild game, carve and sew bone and deerskin artifacts, and enjoy the light and warmth of the long days. As fall approaches, the deer again become restless. Mushrooms appear, the deer's favorite food, which make them fat and sleek. They are now reaching the peak of their annual growth and strength.

With fall, the days get darker, and there is often rain and fog. This is roundup season, when the deer are separated after mingling

Reindeer swimming to an island for their summer pasture.

during the summer, when many families work together. Wooden corrals are placed strategically just over the top of a hill where the deer cannot see them, and the deer are led over the hill by the bell reindeer into the outstretched arms of the corral fence and into the corral. Most corrals are constructed as a series of circles, the first being quite large and the last rather small. As the deer enter the largest circle, the herders start the process of culling them with the skillful use of lassos. The new calves have the family mark cut into their ears, and those designated for slaughter are shunted off to a separate corral. Some of the deer are driven into the next smaller circle, where the process continues. Finally, they are driven into the last corral, which is shaped like a daisy, with a central circle surrounded by petal-like smaller circles. Here the herders lasso their own family deer and pull them into one of the side corrals. Roundup is the most frenetic time of the year, the air resounding with the noise

of shouting men, snorting deer, and the constant jangling of bells.

When the deer are marked and separated, the Sami again pack up and follow the deer to their traditional mating grounds. The birch trees that fill the landscape are turning a rich gold, and frost is in the air. The mating process takes a few weeks, the males losing their antlers at this time. Finally, the herd heads farther inland toward their winter pasture.

The winter months are cold and dark. The sun is below the horizon from late November until late January. But the moonlight shines off the snow, giving some light, and there is the magical presence of the Northern Lights, whose many shimmering colors grace the sky. Page 200 shows the northern lights shining over one of the lavvus, or Sami tents. The winter is a time of rest for the herders and their families.

As the Sami people move with their deer on migration, they carry their culture with them,

For the Sami, it is not only the gods who have such powers but nature itself, for the natural world—the sun, moon, stars, mountains, and rivers—is animated by such supernatural forces.

A Sami lavvu or tent reflected in the shimmering Northern Lights.

particularly their religion. Like most religions, the Sami religion is based on a belief in supernatural forces that affect people's lives and destinies. For the Sami, it is not only the gods who have such powers but nature itself, for the natural world—the sun, moon, stars, mountains, and rivers—is animated by such supernatural forces. As a person travels through life, he or she is surrounded by this living world of spirits. There is much a person can do to appeal to these spirits, particularly being careful to give respect to the natural world, never taking more than is needed, and renewing rather than depleting its resources. There are also special places, often mountains or rock formations, that are sacred places where people can offer sacrifices and ask the spirits to look favorably on them, blessing their herd and the health and prosperity of their families.

Much has changed since the days when the Sami traveled freely across the land, following the reindeer and their own way of life. These changes came in two waves; the first took over a century, the second just a few decades. Sami life started to change when the Norwegian people began moving farther and farther north, settling in Sami lands. First came the Lutheran missionaries with their strict sect of Christianity that was so dramatically at odds with the Sami religion. Then came settlers, whose language and culture also were deeply at odds with Sami life. As their numbers grew, the settlers began asserting cultural and religious superiority over the Sami people, attempting to subsume them into Norwegian culture. The Sami were portrayed as an inferior and ignorant people in need of transformation, and their ways of life denigrated. As they gained control of the area, the Norwegians began suppressing vital parts of Sami life. The Sami's shamanistic religion was forbidden, and most of the sacred drums were destroyed. Also, the Sami were no longer allowed to use their own language, Norwegian names replacing both family and place names. The loss of their names was particularly devastating to the Sami because their names identified their kinship relations, their place in their larger families. Just as the Sami language has a specialized vocabulary for reindeer, it also has a special vocabulary for kinship relations. By losing this, they lost the history of their identity.

Although this long process of "Norwegianization" loosened the ties of the Sami to their culture, it never succeeded in destroying these ties. Underneath the veneer of acculturation, many of the ancient Sami ways survived. But in the 1960s and 1970s, a second and much more rapid wave of change began with the introduction of the snowmobile. Within a few decades, this "tin-plated reindeer" became a staple of reindeer herding, changing both the economics of herding and the relationship of the herder to the deer. With snowmobiles, people could move rapidly, no longer needing to stay close to the herd; people could come out with supplies or to check the herd and go back to more permanent homes. As a result, the herders no longer followed the herd; they drove the herd ahead of them with the new machines, eventually even using helicopters for herding and transportation. The roar of the

THE **NOAIDI'S DRUM**

In the Sami religion, the most important intermediary between the people and the spiritual world is the Sami religious leader, the noaidi or shaman, who uses his sacred drum to reach and interpret the spiritual world. The drum is a beautiful, oval-shaped drum covered with the figures that symbolize the Sami journey through life—the light-filled symbols of the gods, sun, and moon, the everyday symbols of animals, boats, and lavvus, and the darker symbols of evil and death. Colored with the juice of the bark of the alder tree, these symbols are drawn in the same shapes and forms as the ancient rock paintings found in the area. They are also drawn in a special design that links the symbols together in dynamic ways. By "listening" to the drum, the noaidi can trace patterns through these symbols that help reveal the past and foresee the future. With the help of the drum, the noaidi can enter a trance and be transported to the spiritual world to find help and healing for the people. The sacred drum is the Sami's portable altar and a symbol of their deep spirituality.

machines and the smell of the exhaust replaced the peace of the tundra and the rhythmic melody of the bells. Bells were still used, but they became less important. Herding became a business, as much as a way of life, and reindeer bells were one input to that business, rather than a special link between the herder and herd. Also, instead of the hand-forged bells always used by herders in the past, rather cheap-looking, mass-produced bells came on the market.

As the snowmobile was technologically transforming reindeer herding, Sami lands were becoming increasingly attractive as places for mining, hydroelectric plants, and recreation as the economic growth of the country spilled north. Due to new government policies that not only regulated reindeer herding but dictated when and where the Sami could fish in the rivers or use the land, discontent grew among the Sami people. All this discontent came to a head in the late 1970s when the Norwegian Parliament proposed damming the Alta River, a main river in the area, for a hydroelectric plant, a project that would flood some Sami towns and reindeer migratory routes. This threat galvanized the Sami people. Joined by Sami from Finland, Sweden, and Russia, by environmentalists from around the world, and by other indigenous people such as the Inuit, the Sami people engaged in a massive civil protest. After a long siege, the government removed the protesters by force and went ahead with the dam, although on a smaller scale than originally planned. This event became the catalyst for a political and cultural renaissance for the Sami people.

The heart of this renaissance was the Norwegian government's eventual acceptance that the Sami were historically and culturally a separate people. Gradually ending much of the practice of "Norwegianization," this opened up the space and energy for a reclamation of Sami heritage. During the next twenty years, the Sami language was restored to

world through active participation in the World Council of Indigenous People. After so many years, the Sami were regaining their cultural heritage.

In the summer of 2001, I visited the northernmost area of Norway where the largest number of Sami people live, and where, with the help of Terje Tretnes, my Sami guide

In the summer of 2001, I visited the northernmost area of Norway where the largest number of Sami people live, and where, with the help of Terje Tretnes, my Sami guide and interpreter, I was able to talk with a number of reindeer herders, particularly older herders who remembered life before the snowmobile.

the schools, Sami family and place names re-emerged, Sami political organizations were founded, the Sami flag was reclaimed, and a Sami Parliament was established that, although only advisory, grew in status and influence. A Sami theater was created, Sami cultural and art museums were established, and Sami literature began to flourish. Sami achievements were also increasingly recognized by the outside world. The exquisite Sami movie *The Pathfinder* by Nils Gaup received an Oscar nomination in 1990 for best foreign film; an increasing amount of Sami poetry and fiction was translated into other languages; and Sami silver and carved bone work became recognized for its beauty and artistry. The Sami also joined the international cultural and political efforts of other native people around the

and interpreter, I was able to talk with a number of reindeer herders, particularly older herders who remembered life before the snowmobile. As a way of introducing me to Sami life, Terje first took me inland to the towns of Karasjok and Kautokeino in the winter grazing lands, the centers of Sami population and culture. Here we saw the Sami Parliament—a beautiful building of glass, wood, and stone filled with light and art—the Sami museums and cultural centers, the Sami theater, and the Sami flag in its bright blue, red, green, and gold colors.

We then visited with a number of the older herders. As Terje brought me as his guest to each home, I was continually struck by the embracing warmth of the Sami families, their informality, humor, and gentle harmony. One

Herder Mahtis Mahttisen Somby.

conversation I vividly remember was with Aslak A A Mienna and his wife, Lilly. Aslak fondly recalled how he had spent much of his youth traveling with the herd and how, in the dark of winter, it was the sound of the bells that kept the family company and told them where the deer were. He also talked about how he had been forced to go to boarding school for four months a year when he was seven; how only Norwegian was spoken at the school, so he had no idea what was going on; and how scared and lost he felt until his last year when a Sami maintenance worker at the school took an interest in him and taught him to ski. He talked about games they used to play as children, lining up antlers on the ground and trying to lasso them, or playing make-believe where one person played a herder, another a deer, another a wolf, and so on. It was partly

through these games that children learned about the deer and herding. And he told the story of how, when it was very cold in the winter, the children would throw cups of hot water into the air that would instantly freeze and come down as snow.

Another visit I fondly recall was with Mikkel M Eira, whose wife, Marit, was a noted singer. Mikkel spoke of the freedom he knew in his younger days as a herder; despite the cold, the snow, and the hardships, he was free to follow the deer over the land, managing his herd with his own experience and knowledge. Then, he was subject only to nature, not to other people; now he is subject to the cash economy and outside culture that has penetrated Sami life. He missed the old ways deeply, and, although he knew his children liked the advantages of the new life, he mourned what had been lost.

After leaving the inland towns, we traveled to the coast to the island of Magerøya, where Terje's own family herds were for the summer. Here we visited with two of his uncles who spend their summer months in the small fishing village of Skarsvåg. We were now 250 miles above the Arctic Circle, but the weather was surprisingly mild because the Gulf Stream protects much of this coast. As we drove over the island, I could see the deer spread across the rolling gray-and-green hills, their mottled summer coats blending with the landscape. When we stopped, I could hear the music of their bells drifting on the wind. At one point I was taken by a lovely picture of a mother and calf standing in silhouette against the hills, the calf standing in front, a miniature version of its mother. With their long, straight backs, small heads, and thin legs, they looked like the line drawings on the shaman's drum.

We visited a long time with Mahtis Mahttisen Somby, one of Terje's uncles, who showed me a wonderful reindeer bell that had been made by a Sami man over fifty years ago. The bell was like a piece of ancient wood, smoothed down by time to a gleaming patina. Shaped in the traditional flat, rectangular form, the bell had been hand-forged from a sheet of metal that had been cut out, bent and riveted at the

sides, and then coated with brass to prevent it from rusting.

We also visited with Johan Kemi, Terje's other uncle. Both men recalled their earlier life traveling with the herd, living in lavvus, following reindeer time, and feeling great pride in themselves, their work, and their herds. They talked about their intimate knowledge of the deer and how they chose and placed the bells in the herd. And they described with amusement how a bell reindeer could walk so gracefully that its bell would not sound, deliberately confusing both the herder and the other deer.

We then headed back to Karasjok to complete my visit. In Karasjok, we made one

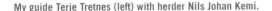

My guide Terje Tretnes (left) with herder Nils Johan Kemi.

last stop, this time to visit Nils Johan Kemi, the son of one of the uncles we had met on the island. Nils represented the new generation of herders. One of the fascinating things about modern Sami society is that there are multiple generations living together who have different experiences and views of Sami life. The oldest generation, now dwindling, remembers the age-old Sami ways, but also lived under the repressive policies of Norwegianization. The middle generation came of age at the time of the Alta protests, many becoming political activists determined to throw off repression and advocate and practice traditional Sami life. Now there are new generations who want to do it their own way, neither accepting outside interference nor being restricted to Sami customs. Having grown up with the snowmobiles, herding regulations, and increasing economic and social opportunities, these all seem normal to them. They do not miss the intimate contact with the deer because they never knew it, having spent their childhoods in school, rather than with the herd. Sami culture is deeply important, but not sacred to them. They are looking for a middle road, one that is their own. Understanding that they have to know the Norwegian language and culture in order to successfully navigate modern life, they still rely on the strength and pride of their Sami heritage and take nourishment from their close family ties and deep bonds with nature. The snowmobiles, cell phones, and Nike sneakers are all there, but, underneath, the noaidi's drum, the song of the bell reindeer, and the eternal lure of the land still live.

In the beginning was the White Reindeer. The whole world was created from him. His veins became the rivers and the lakes. His fur became the woods and the fields. His eyes became the stars in the heavens. And his heart was buried deep in the earth where it grew invisible strings to all living things. These are the invisible bonds that tie us one to the other and to all of nature. As long as the heart is beating, the earth is alive. So, if you ever feel lost in your life, lean down and listen to the heartbeat. It will help you find your way.

SAMI LEGEND

A reindeer in the morning sun.

PART V

AME

THE BELLS OF

RICA

The Liberty Bell with its famous crack held in its strong wooden yoke.

THE LIBERTY BELL

Proclaim Liberty Throughout the Land unto all the Inhabitants Therein

—LEVITICUS 25:10

I mages of the Liberty Bell have become so ubiquitous in American culture that it is easy to forget the real bell behind the images. When I went to Philadelphia to see the bell, I was surprised at how powerful it is. Framed by its heavy wooden yoke, the bell is large and shines in the light. The bottom edge of the bell is uneven where people have chipped off souvenirs over the years, but the inscriptions are easily read: the quote from Leviticus cited above and the identity of the bell and its founder. The famous crack is quite startling, rising at an angle almost two-thirds up the side of the bell, not a hairline crack but a wide crack with file marks along its edges where efforts were made in the past to fix it. The two-dimensional representations of the bell on everything from T-shirts to stamps have indeed flattened and diminished the image of the bell. Seeing it in its three-dimensional reality reveals its rugged and engaging personality.

The Liberty Bell is a colonial bell that was forged a quarter of a century before the United States became an independent nation. It has always been in Philadelphia, the city founded by William Penn in 1682. Nestled between the Delaware and Schuylkill Rivers,

acquired in the nineteenth century. Last was its role as a contemporary symbol of civil rights, of liberty achieved—and not achieved—in the twentieth and twenty-first centuries. Each of these stages symbolizes a different understanding of what liberty meant for the country.

For many years in early Philadelphia, a small bell that hung from a tree behind the State House was used to call people to meetings of

To commemorate the anniversary of the Charter, the new bell would be inscribed with the quote, "Proclaim Liberty Throughout the Land unto all the Inhabitants Therein." The quote was taken from the book of Leviticus in the Bible, in which God speaks to Moses on Mount Sinai, proclaiming the laws the people should follow.

just inland from the Atlantic coast, Philadelphia became the political center for the American colonies, the place where the Declaration of Independence and the Constitution were written and the first capital of the new nation. Its State House was considered the finest building of its time, and the Liberty Bell resided there for more than 200 years, until it was moved to a nearby pavilion.

The history of the Liberty Bell is complex, evolving in four distinct phases. First was its role commemorating the fiftieth anniversary of the colony's first constitution, the reason the bell was commissioned and the least known role of the bell. Next was its role as a witness to the American Revolutionary War and the events leading up to it. Third was its role as an icon of liberty and patriotism, a role it only

the assembly, to ring in the New Year, and to announce important events. By the late 1750s, however, Philadelphia had become a center of commerce with over 14,000 people, and it was felt that a more resonant and dignified bell was needed. At the same time, the colony was approaching the fiftieth anniversary of the Charter of Privileges that William Penn had established as the colony's constitution. A new bell would be a celebratory way to mark that anniversary.

The land that became Pennsylvania was granted to William Penn by King Charles II in 1681 in payment of a debt owed to Penn's father. A Quaker, Penn wanted his colony to personify the Quaker value of religious freedom and to have some degree of popular sovereignty. After a number of earlier attempts to institute these values, Penn proposed his Charter of Privileges, sometimes called the "Charter of Freedoms," which was adopted in 1701. This new constitution guaranteed religious freedom, strengthened the separation of the church and state, supported a popularly elected assembly, and created a better balance between the governor, legislature, and judiciary. It became a model for other states and, eventually, for the U.S. Constitution.

To commemorate the anniversary of the Charter, the new bell would be inscribed with the quote, "Proclaim Liberty Throughout the Land unto all the Inhabitants Therein." The quote was taken from the book of Leviticus in the Bible, in which God speaks to Moses on Mount Sinai, proclaiming the laws the people should follow. Among them was that, every fifty years, the people should celebrate the exodus of the Israelites from slavery in Egypt. The freedom of the Israelites would be a metaphor for the freedom granted the colonists. This is the first understanding of the meaning of the bell.

In November of 1751, Isaac Norris, the speaker of the assembly, wrote to the colony's agent in London to get a 2,000-pound bell. At this time, there were a few small bell foundries in the New England colonies but none near

The Philadelphia State House, considered the finest building of its time in the American colonies, was the original home of the Liberty Bell.

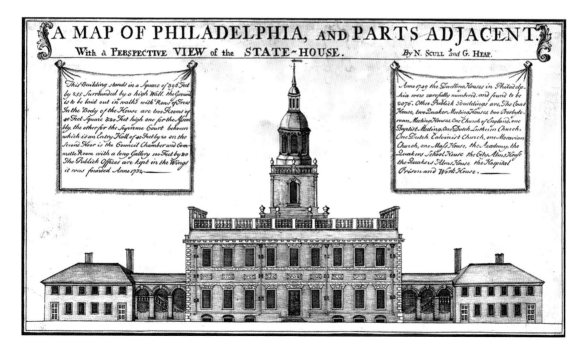

Philadelphia and none that had ever cast a bell of this size, so it made sense to send back to England for the bell.

The London agent contacted Thomas Lester, the master founder at Whitechapel Bell Foundry, and commissioned the bell. Near the end of August in 1752, the bell arrived on the ship *Hibernia* after a rough, eleven-week crossing. After being brought ashore and taken to the State House, the bell was mounted on a temporary stand to test its sound. On the first stroke, the bell cracked at the brim. Isaac Norris wrote back to England that he was mortified by this failure.

Many theories have been suggested as to why the bell cracked—faulty packing on the ship, the rough sea voyage, a too-brittle mix of metal, or faults in the founding, although Whitechapel has always denied the last two. Whatever the reason, the cracked bell was now useless. While debating whether a ship could be found to send the bell back to England, two local metalworkers, John Pass and John Stow, came forward and asked to recast the bell. Although they were inexperienced at casting anything of this size, they were given the commission. After carting the bell to their small foundry, they made a new mold for it and then smashed the bell into pieces small enough to fit in their furnace. The metal was melted and poured into the new mold, and, on March 10, 1753, the mold was opened, revealing a lovely bell. But when the new bell was hung to test it, its sound was a terrible thud, rather than a melodious ring. Pass and Stow immediately set about recasting the bell, and three months later, in June, 1753, they succeeded. This third

version of the bell was hoisted into the bell tower that had been built on the south side of the State House and was first rung to convene the assembly on August 27, 1753. The bell was five feet, three inches tall and weighed 2,080 pounds, the largest bell ever cast in the colonies.

These were turbulent times for the American colonies, and the Pass-Stow bell, now known as the State House Bell, became a witness to these times, tolling out the major milestones on the journey to independence. The background to the eventual split between England and the colonies was the effort by Britain to raise revenue to refill its coffers after recent wars and to help pay for the cost of its colonies. To raise these funds, Britain began imposing direct taxes on a wide range of goods, starting with the Sugar Act of 1764 and followed by the Stamp Act, the Townshend Act, and a number of similar acts during the 1760s and 1770s.

The colonists resisted what they saw as unfair taxation, mildly at first but with increasing vigor as British policies became more burdensome and belligerent, affecting many basic goods, such as tea. Skirmishes started breaking out between colonial militia and English troops. Boston was the center of much of this resistance and was the site of the famous Boston Tea Party, when the colonists dumped English tea into the harbor. In retaliation, Britain closed the Boston harbor and took over its government. Finally, in 1775, a major confrontation took place when British troops from Boston marched to Lexington and Concord outside the city to take over munition stores there. By now, militia troops had grown, and they fought off the British, successfully pushing

PAUL REVERE AMERICAN BELL FOUNDER

Most people have heard the story of Paul Revere and how he rode to warn the colonial militia in Lexington and Concord that the British were coming at the beginning of the Revolutionary War. What is not as well known is that Paul Revere was one of the country's first important bell founders.

Revere was a noted silversmith before the Revolutionary War and also worked in copper and other metals. After the war, he established a small metal foundry, but it wasn't until he joined up with Colonel Aaron Hobart, already a bell founder, that he turned his art to bell making. After learning from Hobart, Revere cast his first bell in 1792. This and his other early bells were not considered successes, having harsh and weak tones. But he learned as he went along, and his greatest achievement came in 1817 when he cast a wonderful bell for the famous King's Chapel in Boston, where it still rings today. Of the hundreds of bells recorded in Revere's stock book between 1792 and 1817, over half have been located in recent times. Many of these bells have colorful histories of service on ships, churches, and civic towers, mostly in New England, but as far away as Singapore, where Revere's daughter lived. His business was eventually carried on by his sons and grandsons and is an important chapter in the history of American bell founding.

them back to Boston. What had been rebellion now turned into war.

The separate and diverse colonies had attempted to unite in their resistance to what they increasingly saw as British tyranny. In September 1774, they convened the First Continental Congress in Philadelphia to issue strong protests of British policy, but took no direct action. In May 1775, however, less than a month after the battles of Lexington and Concord, a Second Continental Congress was convened, which went on to pass the Declaration of Independence, the official declaration of war. In just ten years, what had begun as a minor economic protest had unexpectedly escalated into a major political confrontation that would split the colonies off from Britain into an independent nation, an outcome neither side could have imagined a few years earlier.

The State House Bell rang for almost all of these occasions, gathering the people of the city to hear the news. Nearly 8,000 people gathered the day the bell rang to proclaim the news of the battles of Lexington and Concord. The bell also rang when Benjamin Franklin was sent to London to protest how the colonies were being treated and when George Washington was appointed to head a new Continental Army. But its most famous ringing was when the Declaration of Independence was first publicly read on July 8, 1776.

The Declaration had been signed on July 4, but, since it had to be printed and distributed, it was not publicly read until the eighth. According to contemporary accounts, all the bells in the city rang between eleven a.m. and noon on that day to summon the people to the

On arriving in Allentown, the bell was hidden under the floorboards of the Zion Reformed Church, where it remained for almost a year before it was safe to bring it home to the State House.

State House. At noon, Colonel John Nixon mounted the platform and read the Declaration. When he finished, all the bells rang again. War had been declared, and the bell had now taken on new meaning as a symbol of political protest.

Just over a year after this great celebration, the British captured Philadelphia. After the Continental Army lost the Battle of Brandywine, it became clear that the city was in danger. As part of the evacuation of supplies and men from the city, the State House Bell and ten other bells were removed, not just for patriotic reasons, but because if left behind, the British could use the metal to make ammunition.

Loaded on the wagon of John Jacob Mickley, the State House Bell became part of a train of wagons that left Philadelphia for refuge in Allentown, about fifty miles away. At one point during the trip, Mickley's wagon broke down, probably due to the heavy weight of the bell, and the bell was transferred to another wagon. On arriving in Allentown, the bell was hidden under the floorboards of the Zion Reformed Church, where it remained for almost a year before it was safe to bring it home to the State House.

After the war and the establishment of Philadelphia as the new nation's capital, the State House Bell continued to ring to announce or commemorate important occasions. It rang when the Peace Treaty was signed in 1783, when the Constitution was adopted in 1787, when new states entered the Union, when new presidents were inaugurated, and on every Fourth of July. It mourned the death of George Washington in 1799 with a muffled peal, as it did the deaths of all the signers of the Declaration of Independence. In 1800, the national capital was moved to Washington, DC, and the State House Bell no longer played the role of the nation's bell. However, it continued to ring in Philadelphia for important national and local occasions.

While tolling the death of John Marshall, the chief justice of the Supreme Court, in July 1835, the bell developed a hairline crack. Although rarely rung after that, it could still produce a tone. Eleven years later, in February 1846, the decision was made to take a chance and ring the bell to celebrate the anniversary of Washington's birthday. During the ringing that day, the crack widened so much that the bell

The State House bell, later known as the Liberty Bell, was rung to celebrate the occasion of the signing of the Declaration of Independence in Philadelphia in 1776.

became mute. As reported in the Philadelphia newspaper the *Public Ledger* on February 23:

The Old Independence Bell rang its last clear note on Monday last in honor of the birthday of Washington and now hangs in the great city steeple irreparably cracked and dumb. It had been cracked before but was set in order for that day by having the edges of the fractures filed so as not to vibrate against each other, as there was a prospect that the church bells would not chime upon that occasion. It gave out clear notes and loud, and appeared to be in excellent condition until noon, when it received a sort of compound fracture in a zig-zag direction through one of its sides which put it completely out of tune and left it a mere wreck of what it was.

It is not surprising that the original crack was made much worse by the heavy tolling that day, but what caused the crack in the first place?

Like the earlier Whitechapel bell, there are many theories as to why the original crack appeared. Perhaps the metal was fatigued after being cast three times. Perhaps there was a minuscule imperfection in the final Pass-Stow recasting that slowly spread over the seventy years the bell was rung before the hairline crack appeared. Perhaps the fall while being removed from Philadelphia during the war caused a problem. Although metallurgists have made tests on the bell in recent years, we probably will never know why it cracked. But the ringing for Washington's birthday was the end of its life as a ringing bell.

However, it was during this same period, when it seemed the bell's life was at its end, that it began to acquire its next identity. In the 1830s and 1840s, as the nation began to split over issues of slavery and states' rights, abolitionist groups started using images of the bell and its inscription on their publications, calling it the Liberty Bell. The image and name appealed to people's imaginations, and the bell began to enter the public mind as a potent symbol of freedom. A process of metamorphosis began that changed the bell from being an important, but not widely known, participant in history to a widely recognized symbol of that history. Writers started telling often fanciful stories about the bell in popular magazines and books. Songs and poems were written about it, and, in 1848, the now mute bell was taken down from the tower in the State House—by then known as Independence Hall—and placed in a prominent position where people could see and touch it.

The popularization of the bell came to a peak at the Centennial Exposition held in Philadelphia in 1876 to celebrate the country's hundredth birthday. Such expositions were becoming a popular way of celebrating history, while showing off a city or country's industrial, technological, and cultural progress. They were giant promotional fairs. More than ten million people came to the Philadelphia Exposition, including representatives from fifty countries who displayed their own accomplishments in individual pavilions. A huge replica of the Liberty Bell was created and placed in a prominent place. Included in the bell was the metal from four cannons: one British and one American cannon from the Battle of Saratoga in the Revolutionary War and one Confederate and one Union cannon from the Battle of Gettysburg in the Civil War. Thousands of people also came to Independence Hall to see the real bell, while entrepreneurs marketed images of the bell on every conceivable object from toys to buttons. At the Philadelphia Exposition, the Liberty Bell came into its own as a cultural icon of freedom, patriotism, and American values.

The exposition was also the beginning of an unusual chapter in the bell's life. Other cities having expositions or other celebrations wanted people in their cities to see the bell, and requests started coming to Philadelphia to have the bell travel. After considerable discussion of whether the now fragile bell should be moved, the decision was made to send it to the New Orleans World Industrial and Cotton Exposition in 1885. This was the first of seven trips the bell made across the country over the next three decades: to Chicago (1893), Atlanta (1895), Charleston (1902), Boston (1903), St. Louis (1903), and San Francisco (1915). Each of these trips was accompanied by bands, processions, speeches, bunting, and flowers. Even at the smallest stops, people turned out in large numbers to celebrate the bell, while others saw it from the side of the train tracks as it passed through the countryside. It was a thirty-year, countrywide parade for the Liberty Bell.

After the San Francisco trip, the bell was considered too fragile to travel, even though a metal brace had been installed inside the bell. However, the bell continued to play a national role. For special occasions, it was tapped gently with a rubber hammer in place of being rung. In 1915, it was tapped when the first transcontinental telephone call was made, connecting Philadelphia with San Francisco. It was tapped for Franklin Delano Roosevelt's fireside chats, at the time of the Normandy landing, and in celebration of the end of World War II.

The bell also became the face of Liberty Bond drives to finance World Wars I and II. In 1918, 25,000 soldiers stood together to fashion a "Human Liberty Bell" at Fort Dix, New Jersey, to promote the cause. At one point, fifty-five full-sized replicas of the bell were cast, one for each of the states and territories and one for the District of Columbia. Ford Motor Company provided red, white, and blue trucks to carry the bells to the state capitals, where many are prominently displayed today.

As the country entered the middle years of the twentieth century, however, a fourth, more complex, identity for the Liberty Bell emerged. The turmoil of the Vietnam War, the battles for civil rights, and the counterculture rebellion of many young people punctured the aura of patriotism that lingered over the country after World War II. The bell, with its inscription to proclaim liberty to "all the people," became a symbol of the liberties not yet achieved by a large number of the American people.

The roots for this emerging identity had been planted 100 years earlier when the abolitionists chose the bell as their symbol for ending slavery. In the late 1800s and into the early 1900s, the women's suffrage movement also took the bell as its symbol for the right of women to vote. Suffragists had a large replica of the bell cast that they took around the country as part of their campaign. But the identification of the Liberty Bell with these earlier protest movements was overwhelmed during these years by its role as a symbol of the political freedoms achieved in the Revolutionary War.

With the changes in the culture in the 1960s and 1970s, the balance shifted from celebrating these earlier achievements to the incomplete agenda of freedom and justice still facing the country. In this period, the bell became an important symbol of the civil rights movement. In 1959, Dr. Martin Luther King Jr. laid a wreath at the bell in observance of Freedom Day, the anniversary of Abraham Lincoln's signing of the declaration that led to the passage of the Thirteenth Amendment. In 1963, the Philadelphia chapter of the Congress of Racial Equality (CORE) staged a sit-in there to protest the lack of federal support for voting rights in the South. Many demonstrations for and against the Vietnam War were staged there, and it was the place chosen by Ralph Nader to celebrate the first Earth Day.

When the national bicentennial celebration was being planned for 1976, leaders in Philadelphia were concerned that the crowds would be too big to allow enough people to see the bell in the narrow confines of Independence Hall, so they moved the bell to its own nearby pavilion. Although this solved the problem of access to the bell, it also subtly changed the identity of the bell by separating it from the historic context of Independence Hall. Going forward, Independence Hall remained a major historical site, while the bell continued to take an active role in the ongoing battle for freedom and justice.

Since the terrorist attacks on the country in 2001, American political attitudes have become even more complex, with a resurgence of patriotism being thinly layered over the ongoing divisions in the country. More recently, political and racial conflicts have deepened the divides. Although there are now some security restrictions on the space around the bell's pavilion, marches and sit-ins continue, particularly on the Fourth of July. In 2020, there were Fourth of July marches for the Black Lives Matter movement and for transgender rights. The Liberty Bell started as a commemorative symbol, became a symbol of protest, then an icon of achievement, and now is a vivid part of the struggle to find new understandings of what liberty means for the American people.

Suffragists took a replica of the Liberty Bell around the country to advocate for the right of women to vote.

Classic railroad bell

TRAINS, CABLE CARS, AND CIRCUS WAGONS

Come all you rounders if you want to hear
The story of a brave engineer;
Casey Jones was the hogger's name,
On a big eight-wheeler, boys, he won his fame.
Caller called Casey at half-past four,
He kissed his wife at the station door,
Mounted to the cabin with orders in his hand,
And took his farewell trip to the promised land.

—"CASEY JONES," AN OLD RAILROAD SONG

The second half of the nineteenth century and the first half of the twentieth century were exciting times in American history. During these years, the country went from being an agrarian society to an industrial one; from a parochial nation to an international power; from horses and buggies to automobiles and trains; and from home entertainment to the mass entertainment of radio and television. Many wonderful bells were part of these changes, but three particularly intrigued me because of the history they carried with them: bells on trains, on cable cars, and on circus wagons. Because the country is blessed with a rich network of small museums, the history of these bells is well chronicled in the B & O (Baltimore & Ohio) Railroad Museum in Baltimore; the Cable Car Museum in San Francisco; and the Circus World Museum in Baraboo, Wisconsin.

TRAINS

It was an extraordinary accomplishment when the locomotives of the Central Pacific Railroad and the Union Pacific Railroad moved forward the last foot on May 10, 1869, to complete the transcontinental railroad at Promontory Point, Utah. The Central Pacific Railroad had laid 690 miles of track east from Sacramento, California, while the Union Pacific had laid 1,087 miles of track west from Omaha, Nebraska. The locomotive of the Central Pacific was the Jupiter, while the Union Pacific engine was the #119, both famous engines of the era. Gleaming on top of each locomotive was a classic railroad bell.

The completion of the transcontinental railroad transformed the future of the United States. At that time, there were few pioneer settlements between the Missouri River and California. Settlers had been traveling west to find new homes, but the numbers were small. The biggest expansion had come from speculators following the discovery of gold in California and silver in the Nevada Territories. At that time, it took four to five difficult months to cross the continent by wagon train and six months to reach California by ship traveling around the tip of South America.

The transcontinental railroad cut the time to reach the West Coast to a few weeks, radically changing the settlement of the West. New settlers founded towns along the railway lines, and goods were now quickly transported across the country. Also, a telegraph line had been installed along

Jupiter, the Central Pacific locomotive, which had come east from Sacramento, California, and Engine #119, the Union Pacific locomotive, which had come west from Omaha, Nebraska, met at Promontory Point.

The "Best Friend of Charleston," an early vertical train engine with no cab.

the tracks as the railroad was being built, which provided instant communication. When the last spike was driven in to complete the railroad, the telegraph line was attached to it so that a signal could be sent to cities and towns all across the country announcing the event.

Bells had been used on trains since their earliest days in the 1830s and 1840s. Small bells and crotals had always been used on horse-drawn vehicles, such as sleighs, carriages, and streetcars, to warn people of their presence. However, horse teams could be stopped fairly quickly to avoid collisions. Heavy metal engines took a long time to stop before automated brakes were developed. And trains moved much faster than horse-drawn vehicles, many reaching fifty to sixty miles per hour, even in the early days, making them a menace to people and animals. Much louder and more sustained warning devices were needed. Bells were one of these warning devices.

Usually made of bronze, railroad bells were classically shaped and quite large and heavy, most weighing over 100 pounds. The bells

were held in a yoke, which was connected to a stand on top of the engine. Fixed to the yoke was a handle or crank with a rope running back into the engine cab. When the engineer wanted to sound the bell, he pulled the rope to set the bell swinging. Usually, the bell was rung when the train was entering or leaving a station and when it was approaching crossroads in the country.

The other warning signal used on trains was the steam whistle, which created the long and often plaintive sound people associate with trains. Steam engines, first developed in England and then in the United States, work by converting water into steam, which becomes the energy that pushes pistons back and forth in cylinders attached to the train wheels, creating the forward and backward motion of the train. The same steam was used to sound a whistle. Like the bell, the whistle was used to warn people that the train was entering or leaving a station or approaching a crossing. Often crew members developed distinctive patterns of sound with their bells and whistles that were recognized as a train pulled into a station. There was even a poem written in 1893 by L. R. Andrews called "The Clang of the Bell," in which each stanza described the sound of a different train bell.

The earliest engines were actually vertical, rather than horizontal, and had no cab or attachments. They only had the engine and a following car or tender that held the water and fuel. By mid-century, the more familiar horizontal shape had developed, which had a cab to protect the crew from the weather. Transcontinental Engine #119 is a good example of the new trains and also a good example of how bells were placed on these trains.

Train #119 had both a steam dome and a

Engine #119, one of the two engines that met at Promontory Point in Utah to complete the transcontinental railroad in 1869, has a gleaming bronze bell mounted on top.

A BELL **FOR ADANO**

The change to diesel engines surprisingly led to a new chapter in the life of many railroad bells. In the late 1940s, a Pulitzer Prize–winning book by John Hersey called *A Bell for Adano* became a best seller. The book tells the story of an American soldier who found a bell for the small Italian town of Adano to replace the town bell that had been melted down to make bullets in World War II. The Southern Railroad used the popularity of this story to advertise that it was donating one of its old railroad bells to a church in North Carolina to replace a bell destroyed by fire. The unexpected result of this public relations effort was that railroads starting receiving hundreds of letters asking for the used bells that were being scrapped as diesel engines came into use. The Southern, along with many other railroads, started sending these bells to mission churches, schools, and charitable institutions all over the world, where many of them still ring today.

running in front of the engine was a pilot or cowcatcher, which had been developed to keep animals that were struck by the train from going under the engine and derailing it. It was the two cowcatchers that touched when the engines met at Promontory Point.

Engine #119 was part of the heyday of steam engines in the mid-to-late nineteenth century when bright colors, elaborate mountings, and shining bronze were used to showcase train engines. Train crews took pride in their engines and polished and painted them regularly. When a train was getting ready to leave a station, people could see steam clouds swirling around the wheels and hear the blasts of the steam whistle, the ringing of the bell, and the familiar *chug, chug, chug* of the train as it accelerated out of the station.

In the later years of the nineteenth century, the look of the engines started to change as practical concerns began to overrule aesthetic concerns and most engines were painted black. Although this removed most of the colorful look of the engines, it actually made the polished bronze bells stand out more sharply.

More drastic changes took place in the 1930s and 1940s when trains became stream-lined to make them more wind resistant and modern in appearance, and all the distinctive features of the earlier engines disappeared. After World War II, most trains changed over to the more powerful and economical diesel engines, and warning signals were automated. Today, when most passenger trains pull into a station, an automated horn is sounded, a far cry from the bells and whistles of its colorful ancestors.

sand dome. The steam dome, just in front of the cab, collected the steam to drive the engine. The steam whistle was on the top of the steam dome. In front of that was the sand dome, painted red on #119, where sand was fed down onto the track to give traction when the rails were wet or slippery. The bronze bell was mounted between the sand dome and the smokestack. Mounted in front of the smokestack was an elaborate lantern, and

A cable car bell in the Cable Car Museum in San Francisco.

CABLE CARS

Another historic type of bell can be found on cable cars. Quite different from the classically shaped train bells, cable car bells are shaped like a shallow cup and, rather than having a clapper, they are struck by a hammer that hits the inside of the bell when pulled by a rope. The bell is mounted on the top of the cable car, and the rope is threaded down into the car, where it is pulled by the driver. Rung when the cable car stops and starts at each location on its route, as well as a warning when crossing busy intersections, the sound of the bell is sharp and clear and usually rung in a double ring of *clang-clang*.

Cable cars are most associated with the city of San Francisco, where they were first put into service in 1873, just four years after the completion of the transcontinental railroad. The genius of the cable car was that it had no power of its own; it gripped onto a cable that ran in a channel embedded in the street between its wheels. Just over an inch in diameter, the cable moved at a constant nine-and-a-half miles per hour. At the end of each line was a power house that had huge wheels powered by steam engines. The cables were wound around the wheels, and, as they rotated, the cables were fed in and out of the building. The grip itself was a heavy pincer, which was attached under the car and controlled by a long lever inside the car. When the grip operator moved the lever, the pincer clamped onto the cable, and the car was pulled along with it. To stop the car, the cable was released and additional brakes applied.

Cable cars were one of the first alternatives to horse-drawn streetcars for transportation in urban areas. After their success in San Francisco, they were adopted in Chicago, New York, Kansas City, Denver, and many other cities, although their service was short-lived in most places. In 1888, the electric streetcar was developed, which was cheaper to install and run and eventually began to replace cable cars. However, some cities still retained their cable cars, particularly if, like San Francisco, they had steep hills that electric streetcars could not climb or if people did not like the appearance of the overhead wires that powered the streetcars.

San Francisco probably would have resisted

A cable car coming up a steep hill in San Francisco.

POWELL AND MARKET

HYDE AND BEACH FISHERMANS WHARF

16

Rainforest Cafe

Cable cars are most associated with the city of San Francisco, where they were first put into service in 1873, just four years after the completion of the transcontinental railroad.

the changeover to electricity, but much of the choice was taken out of its hands. The massive earthquake and fire of 1906 destroyed large areas of the city and much of the cable car system. As the city rebuilt, it replaced the system with electric streetcars, except where steep hills still required the cable cars.

In the 1920s and 1930s, internally powered buses started to come into service, which eventually replaced both cables and electric lines and were capable of going up the steep San Francisco hills. In the late 1940s, the mayor of San Francisco proposed shutting down the remaining parts of the cable car system, but this caused such a public outcry that a referendum was passed requiring the city to keep its remaining lines in service. The cable cars had become part of the city's culture, as well as a growing tourist attraction.

Today, there are three cable car lines still in operation. The Powell-Mason and Powell-Hyde lines run roughly north and south over the city, while the California Street line runs east and west. Together they run forty cable cars, each with either one or two bells, so the *clang-clang* of the bells is still regularly heard in the city.

In addition to the daily ringing of the cable car bells, there is one other time you can hear the bells ring in San Francisco. Each July, a cable car bell-ringing contest takes place in Union Square among the different cable car crews. After preliminary trials a few weeks earlier, seven finalists are chosen for a ring-off, where contestants are judged on the style, originality, and skill of their ringing.

Standing inside the cable car, each ringer has two minutes to showcase his or her talent. To get the most versatility out of the bell, the ringer holds the bell rope so that the hammer is close to the inside lip of the bell, which allows small flicks of the rope to sound the bell. The ringer then creates a pattern of rings— long, short, fast, slow, loud, soft—that produces a rhythm unique to that player. Each ringer also has a personal style; one flicking the rope back and forth between the hands, another using just the wrists, and another using the whole body to move back and forth around the car and even leaning back over the seats with feet off the ground. Given the simplicity of the bell, the ringers created a surprisingly rich range of sounds. In 2016, Cassandra Griffin became the first woman to participate in the contest. When asked about her technique, she said, "I just work my wrists. It's like dancing from the wrists."

CIRCUS WAGONS

Bells of a different kind are found on the Ringling Brothers Bell Wagon. Not used for signaling or as a warning device, these bells were part of the music and spectacle of the American circus.

One of the most colorful expressions of American culture is the circus. In its heyday in the late 1800s, there were more than thirty circuses traveling the country. In that era, particularly if you lived in a small town, circus day was one of the most important days of the year. This was before radio, television, or other forms of entertainment were readily available and before there was much widespread knowledge of distant countries and cultures.

The Ringling Brothers Bell Wagon, one of the most unusual and popular wagons that took part in the elaborate circus parades that circus companies put on to advertise their shows.

The circus brought acts from China, Japan, and Africa and featured elephants, camels, and tigers, as well as daredevil acrobats and beautiful women. It was exotic, dangerous, and wonderful fun. On the day the circus came to town, everyone turned out to see the show.

First came the circus parade. Before there were extensive railroads, circuses traveled by wagon, and, early on, performers found that people were so eager for their arrival that it made sense for them to stop outside of town, put on their costumes, and turn their entrance into town into a show. This became the circus's main form of advertising, for, if excited by the free parade, people would buy tickets for the performances later in the day. Always ready to cash in on a new idea, circus owners started decorating their wagons in more and more elaborate ways and adding music and other forms of entertainment to the parade. At its height, the circus parade was often miles long, with marching bands, beautifully costumed

performers, richly carved wagons pulled by teams of up to forty horses, and lions and tigers in gilded cages. It became a grand pageant, an event in itself, as well as a wonderful enticement to see the show.

Many famous circus wagons were part of these parades, but one of the most famous was the Ringling Brothers Bell Wagon. The Ringling Brothers followed P. T. Barnum as the most successful circus owners of their era, dominating the field during its Golden Age from about 1880 to 1920.

The Ringling parades were filled with different kinds of music. There were brass bands playing on top of the wagons and air and steam calliopes. Calliopes are instruments with a series of upright brass pipes of different sizes—like organ pipes—that emit strong, whistling music when air or steam is forced through them. This whistling music became one of the distinguishing features of circus parades. Another parade instrument was the

The bell player's seat.

una-fon, a series of flat pieces of metal of differing tones that played tunes as they were struck with small clappers like a chime. Carried in circus wagons, they added another sound to the parade music.

The bell wagon added a new kind of music to the parade. Constructed on an open framework, there were nine large bells of graduated sizes: three on each side, one in the front, one in the back, and one on top in the center. The wagon was red with rich gold carvings—winged and helmeted maidens at each corner and a fierce mask with carved garlands coming out of its mouth in the center on each side. Encasing the bell player's seat at the rear of the wagon were two large winged beasts sitting back on their haunches. The wheels of the wagon were intricately painted, white with gold-and-black streaks that created a dizzying pinwheel of color as the wheels turned.

Attached to the clapper of each bell was a thick wire running under the wagon and connected to one of the nine white, spring-primed levers standing a foot tall at the player's seat at the back of the wagon. Sitting in the seat, the musician pulled the levers so that the clappers struck against the insides of the bells. The player had to move quickly, crossing his hands over and under to reach each lever in time to keep the rhythm flowing. Since there were only nine bells, the range of notes was limited, but more than adequate to play the hymns and songs popular at the time. Some of the favorites were "My Old Kentucky Home," "Yankee Doodle Dandy," "Nearer, My God, to Thee," and "Rock of Ages." There had been a few bell wagons before the Ringling's, but nothing so grand. Usually drawn by six large Percheron horses, it was a striking feature of the Ringling parade.

The Ringling brothers grew up in Baraboo, Wisconsin, a lovely, small town on the banks of the Baraboo River, where they started their circus and created their bell wagon. They were still a young circus at the time and wanted a unique wagon for their parade. In 1892, they commissioned the Moeller Bros. Wagon Works in Baraboo to build this special wagon. The Moellers, skilled artisans and first cousins of the Ringlings, supplied most of the Ringling wagons. The bells were cast by the Centennial Bell Foundry in Milwaukee and were big, ranging from fifteen to twenty-eight inches in height and weighing a total of 4,300 pounds. The bell foundry mounted the new bells on the large oak frame and shipped it to the Moellers, who fitted it onto the undercarriage they had built for it.

The wagon then had to be "flashed up," or decorated, by adding the wooden carvings that gave circus wagons their rich appearance. The carvings for the bell wagon came from the Milwaukee Ornamental Carving Company, also a frequent supplier for the Ringlings. The carvings they made for the new wagon were lovely and had a great sense of movement and animation, as did most of the circus wagon carvings of that period; today, these carvings are considered important pieces of American folk art. After being paraded through the streets of Baraboo in the spring of 1893, the bell wagon began a long career as a favorite Ringling wagon.

Many of these circus wagons can be seen today at the Circus World Museum in Baraboo. In the early 1900s, the Ringling brothers moved their headquarters to Connecticut, and many of the lovely buildings in Wisconsin fell into disuse or were converted to other purposes. The founding of the Circus World Museum in Baraboo in 1959 allowed the buildings that were left to be reclaimed. These wonderful old buildings, painted in their original colors of red and green, are now National Historic Landmarks.

The center of the Circus World Museum, however, is its famous collection of circus wagons that were gathered up over the years from the fields and barns where they had been abandoned. The museum has more than 200 of these restored wagons. In the summer, some of these wagons can also be seen when the museum puts its circus wagons on a train to Milwaukee, where it mounts a full circus parade, recreating much of the thrill and spectacle of the American circus.

Train, cable car, and circus wagon bells are just a small part of the legacy of this era of expansion in American history, but each highlight one part of the culture of that era; the romance of the railroad, the urban allure of the cable car, and the pure excitement and fun of the American circus.

The restored *Fitzgerald* bell at the Great Lakes Shipwreck Museum at Whitefish Point, Michigan.

THE
FITZGERALD
AND THE
EREBUS

S hip bells have a long and colorful history. They have been the music that marked the rhythm of the day, the alarm sounded in times of danger, and the dirge tolled for the dead. Originally, bells were the clocks of a ship. Without actual clocks, there had to be a way to tell time in order to assist navigation and regulate the crew's day. Since ships at sea needed to be manned at all times, the day was divided into six four-hour watches, each watch being further divided into eight half-hour segments. Originally, these half-hour segments were measured by sandglasses. At the end of each half hour, when the sand ran out, a sailor turned the glass and rang the bell to announce the time. The first half hour was one bell, the second two bells, and so on up to eight bells, which was the signal to change the watch.

The ringing of the bell was a familiar part of a sailor's life.

Bells were also rung to gather the crew to meals, for meetings, for prayer, and to signal when visitors came on board. And they were often rung to ward off evil spirits because, like early Christian bells, ship bells were thought to have mystical powers. Because the sea held so many unknowns, sailors felt beset by supernatural forces and believed ringing the bell would ward off these forces. And all sailors knew stories of hearing the bell of a drowned ship ringing beneath the sea, an eerie reminder of the lingering tragedy of a lost ship. Sometimes this ringing could be explained by currents from storms pushing the clapper against the sides of the bell; sometimes there was no logical explanation.

With clocks, electronic navigation equipment, modern communication equipment, and the decline of many superstitions, bells no longer serve many of the functions they once did. But

When the *Edmund Fitzgerald* entered service on the Great Lakes in 1958, she was the largest ship ever to sail there and she became the largest ship ever lost there.

one of the most fascinating things about ship bells is that they were always more than their functional role; they were a physical emblem that embodied the personality and identity of a ship. The sound of the ringing of the ship's bell, with its tones and after-tones, became the "voice" of the ship, carrying with it an ongoing sense of life. Even after a ship was gone, the memory of the ship and her crew often lived on in her bell.

Two bells that have lived on after their ships were lost are the bell of the *Edmund Fitzgerald*, a huge freighter that went down in the Great Lakes in 1975, and the bell of the *Erebus*, one of the ships of the famed Franklin Expedition, which went down in the Arctic in 1845.

THE *EDMUND FITZGERALD*

Does anyone know where the love of God goes
when the waves turn the minutes to hours?
The searchers all say they'd have made
    Whitefish Bay
if they'd put 15 more miles behind'er.
They might have split up or they might
    have capsized,
they may have broke deep and took water;
and all that remains is the faces and the names
of the wives and the sons and the daughters.

—Gordon Lightfoot
"The Wreck of the Edmund Fitzgerald"

Carved into the land by glaciers 10,000 years ago, Lake Superior is the largest body of fresh water in the world and one of the coldest and deepest. It is the most western of the five Great Lakes that anchor the center of the North American continent, and its long shoreline borders the states of Michigan, Wisconsin, and Minnesota, and the Canadian province of Ontario. Superior is 350 miles long, more like an inland sea than a lake; if lined up along the eastern coast of the United States, it would reach from Boston to Philadelphia.

On a lovely summer day, Lake Superior can be blue and inviting, but, when the early winter storms come, it can be cold and threatening, a forbidding prelude to the snow and ice of the long winter months. During such a storm on November 10, 1975, the giant iron ore carrier the *Edmund Fitzgerald* went down just seventeen miles from the sanctuary of Whitefish Bay at the eastern end of the lake. She went down so fast that no distress message was sent; without witnesses or survivors, we still do not know what happened to this massive 729-foot freighter. The twenty-nine men aboard were lost and still rest with the ship 535 feet beneath the sea.

Twenty years after the *Fitzgerald* went down, the ship's stately bell was retrieved by a diver and brought up to serve as a memorial for the ship and her crew. At the same time, a new bell engraved with the names of the men was taken down and put back on the ship, which is now a gravesite. Each year on November 10, the *Fitzgerald*'s bell is rung at a commemorative ceremony at Whitefish Point.

The *Edmund Fitzgerald* was named after the president of the company that owned her, a common practice for lake freighters, but she was affectionately called "*Big Fitz*" or "*Fitz.*" When she was launched in 1958, she was the largest ship ever to enter fresh water. She was the first of the 730s, a new class of freighters that would dominate lake shipping for many years. At that time, the size of lake freighters was dictated by the size of the locks connecting Lake Superior with the other Great Lakes, for the *Fitz* and ships like her were the transportation system for carrying the iron ore of the Mesabi Range at the western end of Lake Superior to the steel mills of Cleveland, Gary, and Detroit.

Shipping developed on the Great Lakes as trade grew; canoes were replaced by sailing schooners and lake steamers that were, in turn, replaced by freighters. Lake freighters evolved as a pragmatic way to increase the amount of cargo that could be carried on a ship. Much of the space on steamers was taken up with steering and power equipment, so the amount of cargo they could carry was limited. As bulky timber, copper, and iron ore became the main freight, greater cargo capacity was needed. The solution was to separate the steering from the power equipment, pushing the steering equipment forward to the bow and the power equipment back to the stern, leaving space for large cargo holds in between. This created the silhouette we know today: a tall forward superstructure followed by a long, low deck and then a tall aft superstructure. The *Fitz*'s superstructures were painted a gleaming white in contrast to the deep red of the hull, and each had the name of the ship spelled out in bold, black letters.

Map of Lake Superior

AND THE ROUTE OF THE *FITZ*

Thunder Bay

Canada
United States

The *Fitz* route

Michipicoten Island

Caribou Island

Minnesota

Lake Superior

Two Harbors

Whitefish Point

Duluth

Whitefish Bay

Superior

Michigan

Wisconsin

CANADA

Lake Superior · Ontario · Quebec

Wisconsin · Lake Michigan · Lake Huron · Lake Ontario · New York

Michigan · Lake Erie

Illinois · Indiana · Ohio · Pennsylvania

UNITED STATES

The pilot house was the command center of the ship. On the *Fitz*, the pilot house was at the top of the forward superstructure, a spacious area with thirty-one large windows that curved gracefully around three sides, giving a panoramic view of the water and sky. On top of the pilot house was a twelve-foot radar scanner mounted on a tall platform, as well as other electronic and navigational equipment. Directly in front of the radar scanner was the ship's bell, which was anchored by three stanchions, one thick stanchion shaped like a question mark that curved around the back of the bell and two thinner ones near the front that completed the tripod that held the bell in place. Made of brass, the bell was twenty-one inches in diameter across the lip and weighed 200 pounds. Like most ship bells, the *Fitz*'s bell was stationary, rung by pulling a rope attached to the clapper against the inside of the bell. Also, like most ship bells, it was not finely tuned; it had a sharp clanging sound that echoed across the water. Many lake dwellers remember the clanging of the freighter bells passing back and forth across the lake as part of their childhood.

Although we do not know what happened in those few minutes in the early evening of November 10 when the *Fitz* foundered, we do know about the storm she was in and about the communications she had with other ships before she fell silent. The *Fitz* left the docks in Superior, Wisconsin, at the western end of Lake Superior just after two o'clock on a lovely Sunday afternoon, an unseasonably warm and sunny day for November. She had just loaded 26,116 tons of taconite into her three holds, taconite being the small pellets of concentrated iron ore that were her usual cargo. She was headed for the Great Lakes Steel Company complex near Detroit, a trip of about five days across Lake Superior, through the Soo Locks into Lake Huron, and then down Lake Huron to Lake Erie. It was a typical run, one she did over and over during the shipping season.

However, November is a time when violent storms often hit the Great Lakes. If cold Arctic air from Canada collides with the lingering warm air of autumn farther south, spiraling winds can develop that reach hurricane force. The most treacherous time of year on the lakes, it was always a risk for owners to send their ships for one last run before the close of the season. Of the more than 6,000 ships on the bottom of the Great Lakes, two-thirds went down between September and December.

One of these storms, considered by many to be the worst in thirty years, overtook the *Fitzgerald*. On Saturday, the day before the *Fitz* sailed, the storm began to develop in the Oklahoma Panhandle over a thousand miles away. By Sunday, the storm had gained strength and moved northeast over Kansas and Iowa, heading directly for Wisconsin and Lake Superior. Although the weather was fine when the *Fitz* sailed Sunday afternoon, the storm caught up with her in the early hours of Monday morning, causing massive waves and heavy rain. Given the deteriorating forecast, the *Fitz* decided to team up with the *Arthur M. Anderson*, another freighter traveling nearby, and take the northern route across the lake, which would give them some shelter from the winds. As shown on the map, they then angled down between Michipicoten and Caribou

Islands and on toward the shelter of Whitefish Point at the eastern end of the lake. By now, the winds were gusting to almost 100 miles an hour.

Around three-thirty that Monday afternoon, as the ships came out from between the islands, Captain Ernest McSorley of the *Fitzgerald* radioed the *Anderson* that she had topside damage and was listing. A little later he reported that the ship had lost her radar scanner and was sailing blind, asking the *Anderson* to be her eyes as they kept heading toward Whitefish Point. In the early evening, at 7:10, the first mate of the *Anderson* radioed the *Fitz* to tell her that there was a ship headed out of Whitefish Bay on her heading, but that she would clear it with no trouble. Almost as an afterthought, the mate asked the *Fitz* how she was making out. Captain McSorley replied, "We are holding our own." At that point, the ships entered a snow squall, and the *Fitz* disappeared into what the *Anderson*'s captain later described as a white blob at the center of the *Anderson* radar screen. Fifteen minutes later, the snow suddenly cleared, and visibility became quite good. But when the officers of the *Anderson* looked at the radar, they could not see the *Fitz*. Scanning the horizon for her visually, the only ships they could see were three ships farther away coming out of Whitefish Bay. Although they could not believe it, the unimaginable had happened: the massive, technologically sophisticated *Fitzgerald* was gone. And she was gone so fast that there had been no radio message, no SOS, or call for help. Just seventeen miles from the sanctuary of Whitefish Bay, she had lost her battle with the storm.

Over the next few days, search efforts were made, but little debris was found. A U.S. Navy aircraft picked up evidence of two large objects on the lake bottom, but it wasn't until the next spring that an unmanned Navy underwater vehicle called CURV-III was sent down to photograph the wreck. The photos showed the ghostly presence of the ship lying broken in two pieces on the bottom of the lake, the bow sitting upright covered in mud, with her pilot house windows twisted and broken, and the stern resting upside down at almost a right angle to the bow and 170 feet away. It was utterly still now around the ship. Her colors were leached away in the dark water, and everything was shades of misty gray. No bodies were seen, and, in the very cold temperatures of the lake, bodies do not decompose, so they would not be expected to rise.

At first the loss seemed unbelievable to the families of the crew. As the reality sank in, the tragedy became all the deeper because there could be no funerals, no way to grieve, for the ship would always be the gravesite for these men who could never be brought home. Over time, there were more excursions to the site of

Painting of the *Edmund Fitzgerald* broken in two pieces on the seabed.

The *Fitzgerald* bell was brought up on July 4, 1995 to serve as a memorial for the men who died when the ship went down. A new bell with the names of the lost crew was taken down and placed on the wrecked ship as a tribute to the men from their families.

the wreck, but none of the expeditions were able to solve the mystery of the *Fitzgerald*.

In 1995, a different mission to the *Fitzgerald* took place in which the families' desire for a more tangible memorial for the men came together with new technology and the leadership of the Great Lakes Shipwreck Museum at Whitefish Point. Thomas Farnquist, the head of the Great Lakes Shipwreck Historical Society and the Shipwreck Museum, had been involved in two of the earlier expeditions as well as the original search for the *Fitz*. In the fall of 1994, he was asked to meet with some of the families at the Mariners' Church in Detroit to talk about the growing number of dives to the wreck, which was upsetting family members. The outcome of that conversation was that the families asked that something be brought back from the ship to act as a memorial and that the ship be declared a gravesite that could no longer be visited. The families wanted the bell that was known to be intact on the roof of the pilot house. If brought back, the long-silenced bell could become a living memorial for the ship. With the help of the Canadian Navy ship HHCS *Cormorant* and her two submersibles, special photographic equipment from the Sony Corporation, and the participation of Emory Kristof, a noted underwater photographer from *National Geographic*, the mission took place on July 4, 1995, and the bell was successfully raised.

Like the day the *Fitz* sailed out of the harbor

of Superior, Wisconsin, twenty years earlier, this July 4 was sunny and warm. The families gathered on ships out on Lake Superior at the site of the wreck. The two submersibles from the *Cormorant* positioned themselves underwater at right angles to the bell on the pilot house roof, triangulating their powerful lights with the light on the "Newtsuit" worn by Bruce Fuoco, the thirty-seven-year-old diver. Using an underwater torch, Fuoco cut through the bottoms of the thin front stanchions holding the bell and most of the way through the heavy back stanchion. He had already placed thick canvas straps around the tops of the stanchions and attached them to a lift line. When everything was ready, he cut through the rest of the back stanchion, and the bell separated from the ship and was lifted to the surface, where it broke free into the sunlight. The families and crews of the ships cheered as the bell appeared, still perfectly intact, although now a deep red, almost mahogany, color from its twenty years under water. The new bell that had been engraved with the names and ranks of all the lost crew members was taken down to replace the original bell on the pilot house roof as a tribute to the men from their families.

The historical society sent the bell to Michigan State University, where experts carefully removed the rust and restored it to its original condition. On November 10, 1995, a dedication ceremony was held at the Shipwreck Museum at Whitefish Point where the "Call to the Last Watch" was performed. The restored bell was tolled once in memory of each man lost on the *Fitz* by a member of that man's family and then one more time in honor of all the mariners lost on the Great Lakes. This memorial ceremony for the *Edmund Fitzgerald* and her crew is now held at Whitefish Point every November 10.

The *Edmund Fitzgerald* was a memorable ship. She was one of the best-known ships on the Great Lakes and the largest ship ever lost there. And the mystery surrounding her loss has never been solved. For these reasons alone, the *Fitzgerald* would live on in Great Lakes' history. But the story of the *Fitzgerald* has grown into a legend, due, in large part, to the haunting ballad "The Wreck of the *Edmund Fitzgerald*" by Canadian songwriter Gordon Lightfoot. Capturing the mystery and tragedy of the *Fitzgerald*, the ballad went to the top of the music charts, bringing the story to a wider audience and making it part of popular culture.

THE *EREBUS*

Another mysterious ship lost at sea was the *Erebus*, which disappeared in the Arctic in 1845. Like the *Fitz*, the *Erebus* was overcome by the powers of nature, and, also like the *Fitz*, her bell was later brought up as a symbol of the ship.

The islands of the Arctic archipelago stretching across the top of Canada are remote and forbidding, dark many months of the year and constantly subject to fierce gales and subfreezing temperatures. In the nineteenth century, the great dream was to find a passage through these islands that would link the Atlantic and Pacific oceans, the fabled Northwest Passage that would open up a new trade route to the East. But Arctic summers are short. In good years, there are six to ten weeks from July to September when the ice breaks up enough for ships to travel into the islands. In bad years, much of the ice never breaks up, and, if caught, ships can be frozen in the ice for years and often crushed by its pressure. At that time, only parts of the Arctic had been charted; it was one of the last frontiers.

On May 19, 1845, an expedition to find the Northwest Passage set out from England led by Sir John Franklin. The expedition had two ships, the *Erebus* and the *Terror*, which were the most technically sophisticated and well provisioned ships that had ever attempted the Arctic passage. Although tiny and frail compared to the *Fitzgerald*—they were three-masted wooden sailing ships, each just over 100 feet long—the *Erebus* and the *Terror* had originally been built as warships and were heavily timbered to withstand the shock of cannon fire. For the Arctic trip, the hulls of

A sketch of the *Erebus* and the *Terror*, the two ships lost from the Franklin Expedition to the Arctic in 1845.

the two ships were further reinforced with heavy timber and the bows covered in iron plates. Both ships had seen service in Antarctica and had experience in polar climates.

The Franklin ships were also the best provisioned ships ever to attempt the Arctic. They carried the newly invented "canned" food that was supposed to provide "fresh" food that could help prevent scurvy, as well as tons of coal, salted meat and fish, pickled vegetables, dried fruit, lemon juice, chocolate, tea, and rum. They had extra sails and machine parts, more than 2,000 books, and a hand organ. Assisting Franklin were James Fitzjames, captain of the *Erebus*, and Francis

Crozier, captain of the *Terror*, both experienced explorers. In addition to these leaders, there were 21 officers and 105 crew, for a total of 129 men.

After crossing the Atlantic, the ships reached Greenland, where they took on additional supplies. On July 12, they left Greenland to cross Baffin Bay and were seen two weeks later by whaling ships just as they reached Lancaster Sound, their entrance to the Arctic islands. The *Erebus* and the *Terror* were not seen again until they were found more than a century and a half later. The largest and best equipped expedition that England had ever sent to the Arctic just disappeared, with the greatest loss of life in the history of polar exploration.

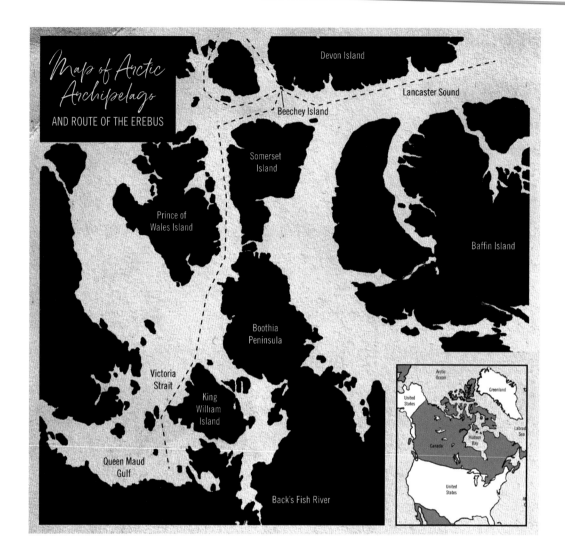

Map of Arctic Archipelagos

AND ROUTE OF THE EREBUS

Devon Island

Lancaster Sound

Beechey Island

Somerset Island

Prince of Wales Island

Baffin Island

Boothia Peninsula

Victoria Strait

King William Island

Queen Maud Gulf

Back's Fish River

Arctic Ocean

Greenland

United States

Labrador Sea

Hudson Bay

Canada

United States

Unraveling this mystery became a long process of trying to fill in the map of where the ships journeyed and what happened to the men. The map above traces the route of the ships as it was eventually reconstructed, starting with the final sighting of the ships by the whalers at the entrance to Lancaster Sound. In 1848, when the ships had not been heard from in over three years, the British Admiralty sent out a relief expedition, and, by 1850, eleven British and American ships were

searching. One of them found the remains of a camp, some artifacts, and three graves on Beechey Island, where it turned out the ships spent their first winter in 1845–46. But the most important find came in 1859, when an expedition sent by Lady Jane Franklin, Sir John Franklin's wife, found a cairn on the northwest coast of King William Island that contained a letter, the only written document ever found from the ships. The letter had been written at two different times. The body of the letter was written in May 1847 and reported that the two ships had wintered the previous year at Beechey Island and had then been beset in the ice off the coast of King William Island, where they wintered in 1846–47, but all was well. However, around the margins of the letter was

nia, frostbite, starvation, and perhaps lead poisoning and botulism from badly sealed cans of food. Later search parties found artifacts and bones all along the coast of King William's Island and on the northern shores of the Adelaide Peninsula on the mainland. The last

---

Obviously, things had gone terribly wrong. The deaths of twenty-four men, including Franklin, was highly unusual compared to other ships that had been forced to winter in the ice. The decision to abandon the ships was also unusual, probably reflecting despair after two years of being frozen in the ice with dwindling supplies.

---

a second letter written almost a year later saying that, on April 25, 1848, the crew had deserted the ships. Sir John Franklin was dead, as were eight other officers and fifteen men, and the remaining crew planned to try to reach Back's Fish River on the mainland.

Obviously, things had gone terribly wrong. The deaths of twenty-four men, including Franklin, was highly unusual compared to other ships that had been forced to winter in the ice. The decision to abandon the ships was also unusual, probably reflecting despair after two years of being frozen in the ice with dwindling supplies. Whatever the reasons, the men left the ships and started south, heading toward the Back's Fish River on the mainland, which could lead them to a Hudson Bay Company outpost, the closest possible source of relief. But the men slowly died from a lethal combination of scurvy, tuberculosis, pneumo-

remains found were still far north of Back's Fish River and any hope of survival.

Some of the search parties also gathered testimony from local Inuit tribes who had seen the two ships and the survivors. They described starving men, a large group of them on King William Island and a smaller group on the mainland. They also insisted that one of the ships had been seen much farther south than where it had been frozen in the ice, suggesting that it had drifted with the ice pack. At first discounted, this proved to be correct when a Canadian search team finally found the *Erebus* south of King William Island in Queen Maud Gulf in 2014, more than 150 years later.

Like the group that brought up the *Fitz*'s bell, the 2014 Canadian search party was a consortium of public and private groups led by Parks Canada. Including four ships and the most advanced technology for underwater

The first view of the *Erebus* when she was discovered in Queen Maud Gulf in 2014, more than 150 years after she went missing.

The first indication that the search this year might be different was the discovery of a relic on a small island in the eastern part of Queen Maud Gulf. Identified as part of a davit used to raise and lower small boats, the relic had the broad arrow mark that identified it as belonging to the British Royal Navy. Since this was the first artifact found in modern times that could be linked to the lost ships, the group moved their search closer to the island.

The search was conducted by a towfish, a side-scan sonar that was pulled behind one of the ships where it could detect objects for almost 250 feet on either side. The towfish was pulled back and forth over the search area, rather like mowing a lawn, as one crew member commented. On September 7, as members of the team were watching the sonar screen, the ghostly presence of a ship slowly scrolled into view. Unbelievably, they had found the *Erebus*, still intact on the ocean floor after all these years.

Because the ship was discovered so late in the season, only a few dives could be made on it before the weather closed in. On the first dive, one of the divers saw the ship's bell lying on its side among the marine life on the upper deck and called up, "I found the bell, I found the bell." The group decided to remove this one artifact from the ship because of its emblematic value, being the "ceremonial

exploration, this was by far the largest and best equipped attempt to find the lost ships.

Two search areas had been identified for the trip: the primary one was at the site where the ships had been locked in the ice in Victoria Strait, and the second farther south in Queen Maud Gulf, the area noted by Inuit observers. But the weather was bad, and ice blocked Victoria Strait, just as it had in the Franklin years. This pushed the group to focus its main attention on the southern site.

heart and soul" of the ship, as one of the members of the group put it.

On the last dive, the bell was brought up. Clearly seen on it was both the broad arrow mark of the Royal Navy and the year 1845, the year the ship left Britain. The bell itself was covered in a green patina acquired during all those years underwater. The photo on the next page shows members of the Parks Canada team examining the bell after it was brought up. It was then taken to Ottawa to be restored, while a remarkable 3D replica of it was created to be the centerpiece of an exhibition about the discovery of the ship for Canadian museums and educational programs. The Parks Canada video "Ship's Bell from HMS

The *Erebus* bell discovered by divers on the deck of the ship was brought up as a symbol of the lost ship.

Parks Canada's Ryan Harris, Jonathan Moore, and Dr. Douglas Stenton (left to right) examining the bell after it was recovered.

Erebus" (November 10, 2014) brings together fascinating footage of exploring the bell while it was still on the *Erebus* deck and the later efforts to restore it.

After the success of the expedition, expectations were high for finding the *Terror*. However, it wasn't until two years later, in the fall of 2016, that the *Terror* was found, also in Queen Maud Gulf. In 2017, the *Terror*'s bell was found, and, in 2019, divers were able to film the insides of both ships. Led jointly by the Inuit and Parks Canada, a multi-year program is now underway to research,

document, and preserve these historic ships.

The *Fitzgerald* gained renown from the ceremonies surrounding its bell and from Gordon Lightfoot's song "The Wreck of the *Edmund Fitzgerald*." The *Erebus* and the *Terror* were renowned because of the great mystery surrounding their loss and the adventure of their discovery. They also had a popular ballad written about them by the Canadian singer and writer Stan Rogers called "The Northwest Passage." Its refrain has the same haunting quality as Lightfoot's song, the haunting quality that surrounds all ships lost at sea.

Ah, for just one time I would take the Northwest Passage
To find the hand of Franklin reaching for the Beaufort Sea.
Tracing one warm line through a land so wild and savage
And make a Northwest Passage to the sea.

—Stan Rogers, "The Northwest Passage"

The International Space Station travels 17,600 miles per hour at 230 miles above the Earth and circles the Earth every ninety minutes, going through sixteen sunrises and sunsets each day.

THE INTERNATIONAL SPACE STATION

All this world is heavy with the promise of greater things and a day will come, one day in the unending succession of days, when beings who are not latent in our thoughts and hidden in our loins shall stand upon this earth as one stands upon a footstool and shall laugh and reach out their hands amidst the stars.

—H. G. WELLS

H G. Wells spoke these famous words in a speech he gave in 1902, expressing his dream of the endless potential of humanity to enter the world of space. Today, his dream has become reality. Humans have walked on the moon, built a space station for research and human habitation 230 miles above the Earth, put telescopes into space beyond the Earth's atmosphere that can look back in time to the earliest days of the universe, landed robotic vehicles on Mars, and sent robotic probes to explore Jupiter, Saturn, Uranus, Neptune, and Pluto. Two of these probes have now entered interstellar space.

The story of space exploration has been a story of remarkable technology and human courage. New worlds of knowledge have opened for us, as we explored the outer planets and been overwhelmed by the stunning photos sent back from deep space. There have been tragedies, such as the losses of the *Challenger* and *Columbia* space shuttles, and political setbacks, as we learned how difficult it is to sustain public support for space programs over multiple generations. But, despite the obstacles,

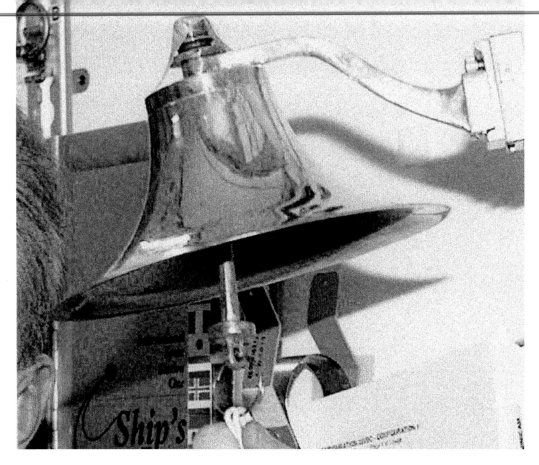

A small brass bell attached to the side of the Space Station that is used to mark ceremonial events.

our scientific imagination and human thirst for knowledge continue to push us forward. Today, we are poised on a new era of space exploration, including plans to live and work on the moon in preparation for human exploration of Mars. There is still much to dream about.

Within the grand story of space, however, there is another story, the story of a simple bell that is attached to the side of one of the modules of the International Space Station. Made of gleaming brass, the bell is quite small, about six inches high and eight inches across the bottom, and has a flaring lip. Its clapper is attached to a small, white rope that is pulled back and forth to ring the bell. In the micro-

gravity of space, this clapper "floats" inside the bell, drifting to one side or the other as it is affected by air currents in the space station. To ring the bell, an astronaut has to hold on to the side of the station so as not to float away, and then pull the rope sharply. It takes practice to get a crisp, clear note. Traveling 17,600 miles per hour, this simple bell circles the Earth every ninety minutes, going through sixteen sunrises and sunsets each day.

The International Space Station (ISS) is one of the most challenging engineering projects undertaken in the history of humanity—the construction of a complex the size of a football field made up of more than 100 parts brought up in pieces from Earth and assembled in the emptiness of space. Working together, sixteen nations—the United States, Russia, Canada, Japan, Brazil, and the eleven nations of the European Space Agency—have built this scientific laboratory that now orbits the Earth, staffed by rotating international crews.

After years of planning, in November 1998, the first module, *Zarya* (sunrise), was launched into space from Russia. A few weeks later, the American space shuttle *Endeavour* was launched carrying the second module, *Unity*, in its cargo bay. When *Endeavour* came close to *Zarya*, Mission Specialist Nancy Currie used the shuttle's robotic arm to capture *Zarya* and mate it to the *Unity* module. After two spacewalks to complete the attachments, the *Endeavour* crew entered the new station, completing the first step of constructing the ISS. Over the next two years, astronauts using the American shuttles and the Russian Soyuz vehicles brought up supplies, such as clothing, exercise equipment, spare parts, and medical equipment; they attached foot restraints, bags of tools, and other equipment to the outside of the station; and they delivered and installed connecting trusses for the station.

Finally, in November 2000, the first permanent crew consisting of Commander William M. Shepherd, Pilot Yuri P. Gidzenko, and Flight Engineer Sergei K. Krikalev arrived on board. Next to come were blue-and-gold solar panels and the main research module *Destiny* from the United States. Italy supplied *Leonardo*, the first of three Italian modules used as moving vans to bring up experiment racks and supplies and take back completed experiments

OUR EYES **IN SPACE**

On December 25, 2021, the James Webb Space Telescope was launched from French Guiana, and, after traveling almost a million miles, reached its planned orbit on January 24, 2022. At launch, the telescope was a tightly compressed bundle of advanced science, what one astronomer likened to a chrysalis, that would start to unfold as it journeyed into space; first antennas would come out to enable communications, then a giant sunscreen would unfold, and, finally, when the Webb reached orbit, the twenty-one-foot segmented mirror, the heart of the telescope, would snap into place. With the Webb, scientists can look back in time and space to the earliest moments of the creation of the universe, much further back that they could with the earlier Hubble Telescope. This greatly enhanced vision will allow them to see the first stars and galaxies being formed, greatly expanding our knowledge of the origins of the universe. The Webb is another giant leap forward into the vast unknown realms of space.

and trash. Canada supplied the fifty-five-foot robotic arm used for moving equipment around outside the station and for lifting equipment in and out of the cargo bays of the shuttles. By the time it was completed, the station included additional scientific and storage modules, a bigger and more

The union of the Russian module *Zayra* and the American module *Unity* began the construction of the International Space Station.

sophisticated habitation module, and a large number of human and scientific experiments.

The construction of the space station was an amazing feat. One imagines a world of giants building with Tinker Toys out in the vastness of space, creating this architecture of the future. But what is also amazing is the incredible beauty surrounding the astronauts as they built and now work on the station. When they look up, everything around and above them is the black void of space, punctuated in the distance by the millions of stars and galaxies of the universe. Below them, the Earth is a vibrant globe showing deep blue oceans, swaths of green forests, and swirling white clouds. It is an extraordinary setting for a bell.

Putting a bell on the space station was the idea of astronaut Jeff Ashby. A highly decorated Navy captain, he served as a pilot for numerous combat missions and as a test pilot for many of the most advanced aircraft. Raised in the Rocky Mountains of Colorado, he became an astronaut in 1995. He flew his first space mission as pilot of the shuttle *Columbia* in 1999 when the Chandra X-Ray Observatory was deployed in orbit. He then flew two missions to the space station, one as pilot of the shuttle *Endeavour* in 2001 and one as commander of the shuttle *Atlantis* in 2002.

When Ashby first became involved in the space program, he began thinking about how traditions developed in the Navy for life at sea

Astronaut Jeff Ashby conceived of the idea of having a bell on the space station and arranged to have it taken up just before the first crew arrived.

might be relevant to life in space. Spaceships have many similarities to ships at sea, and much seagoing terminology has been adopted on spacecraft; for example, the different levels of a spacecraft are called decks, the command center is the bridge, and a ship's log is kept. But the similarity that fascinated him the most was that both enclose a small group of people in a contained space for long periods of time away from home. In the Navy, a number of traditions exist that help establish an environment of good order on ships. When out at sea, particularly under the stress of danger, such traditions help maintain an environment of discipline and respect. As astronauts travel farther from Earth for longer periods of time, life on board will have similar needs for discipline and respect. So Ashby's question was how some of the benefits of naval traditions could be introduced into life in space.

Since many of these naval traditions center on the use of a ship's bell, Ashby initiated the idea of putting a ship's bell on the International Space Station. In a phone interview I had with him after he returned from his first flight to the space station, he described the story of how this particular bell was chosen and taken to the station. First, he went to the Naval Aviation Museum in Pensacola, Florida, and enlisted the support of the curator, Buddy Macon. Rather than using a historic naval bell, they decided it should be a new bell that would represent the people of all the countries, not just be associated with the United States. The bell would stand as a symbol for the international status, continuity, and accomplishments of the space station.

After the Naval Aviation Museum supplied a bell, a plaque was attached across its outer lip that had miniature replicas of the flags of all sixteen countries on it, the same logo of flags that is on the ship's log. Then a tiny hole was drilled in the bell and three symbolic flecks of metal were soldered into it—a fleck of gold from Alan Shepard's Annapolis ring representing the pioneer astronauts, a fleck of metal from *Mir*, the early Russian space station, and a fleck of metal from the bell on the USS *Enterprise*, a historic naval ship, also the name of the famous spaceship on *Star Trek*. The bell was taken up to the station on the first shuttle trip.

A problem arose, however, when the bell was rung on the station. The addition of the plaque and the tiny metal fragments had dulled the tone of the bell on Earth, but, in the microgravity of space, the tone changed further, becoming quite flat. The astronauts decided to take the bell back down and replace it with one that had a better tone. Jeff got the second bell at a marine store in the Houston area and, in a friend's garage, fashioned an attachment to it that could slide into the camera mounts on the station. The new bell was taken up in September 2000 by shuttle pilot Scott Altman, just before Commander Shepherd and the first permanent crew arrived.

A few weeks after the permanent crew settled in, they received their first visitors, the crew of the shuttle *Endeavour*, who were bringing up solar panels. Before entering the station, shuttle Commander Brent W. Jett requested, "Permission to come aboard," and station commander Bill Shepherd replied, "Permission granted." The bell was rung as

Commanders Brent Jett (left) and Bill Shepherd (right) float on either side of the bell for its first ceremonial ringing.

the official welcome. A smiling picture of Brent Jett and Bill Shepherd floating on either side of the bell captures this first ceremonial moment.

Jeff Ashby first saw the bell in place in April 2001 when he served as pilot for the shuttle *Endeavour* that brought the Canadian robotic arm and *Raffaillo*, one of the Italian cargo vans, to the station. In recognition of his role in introducing the bell to the ISS, the station crew asked Ashby to ring the bell to welcome his own crew on board. In describing this visit, Ashby's enthusiasm for his work and love for

the story of the bell was evident. He said he hoped the bell would become part of the history of the space station and all it accomplished.

In the years since Bill Shepherd welcomed the first visitors to the space station, the use of the bell has evolved in many of the ways Ashby envisioned. No longer representing just naval traditions, the bell has acquired the larger meaning of symbolizing the continuity and international status of the ISS.

For example, when a new crew arrives on the station, the bell is now rung for the "change of command" ceremony to signal the smooth transition of authority. When the Expedition Five crew replaced the Expedition Four crew on the station in 2002, outgoing flight engineer Dan Bursch said:

Welcome everyone to International Space Station Alpha for the change of command. The change of command ceremony is a time-honored tradition that formally restates the continuity of the authority of command to the assembled ISS crew members. The change of command of the ISS shall be an instantaneous transfer of total authority, responsibility and accountability from one individual to another.

He then reported on the state of the station and wished the new crew well. The bell was rung for this ceremony.

The bell is also rung to welcome other visitors on board, particularly the crews of the vehicles who bring supplies and experiments to the station. For instance, when the shuttle *Endeavour* flew to the station in June 2011, ISS flight engineer Ron Garen rang the bell and said, "*Endeavour* arriving. Welcome to the International Space Station." When the shuttle left the station to go back to Earth, the bell was rung and Garen said, "*Endeavour* departing," and then he wished the departing crew "Fair winds and following seas," a lovely seafaring

phrase for a safe journey often used now in this parting ceremony.

There was also an unusual time when the bell was rung to greet visitors. In June 2005, astronaut John Phillips testified by video before the U.S. House Subcommittee on Space and Aeronautics from the space station. The station crew rang the bell to welcome the House representatives to the station for the video testimony.

After July 2011, the United States stopped sending space shuttles to the station and instead relied on the Soviet Soyuz vehicles to bring astronauts and supplies back and forth from Earth. However, in May 2020, a public–private partnership between NASA and SpaceX launched a new kind of capsule called Crew Dragon to the station carrying two NASA astronauts, Doug Hurley and Bob Behnken. As the astronauts came through the connecting tunnel into the station, station commander Chris Cassidy said, "Bob and Doug, we're glad to have you as part of the crew," and then rang what the news media called the "traditional" ship's bell, a tribute to how much the bell has become part of the life of the station.

In October 2021, Blue Origin, another private space company, sent a small group of passengers on a short trip to space. Included among the passengers was William Shatner, the then ninety-year-old actor who played Captain Kirk on *Star Trek*. As the passengers stepped onto the ramp leading into the space capsule, they each rang a lovely silver bell hanging there. A spokesperson for Blue Origin said the company wanted to introduce their passengers to this tradition of welcome long found on the

The launch of a shuttle from Cape Canaveral in Florida showing the massive clouds and exhaust as the solid rocket boosters were ignited for lift-off.

International Station and in the Navy.

Since I could not see the bell in person, I decided the closest I could come was to attend the launch of a space shuttle. After applying for admission, I attended the launch of space shuttle *Discovery* at Cape Canaveral in Florida

back up, the solid rocket boosters were ignited for lift-off, and immense clouds of white exhaust engulfed the launchpad. With great majesty, the shuttle lifted above the billowing clouds and, after a few seconds, started to arc to the east over the Atlantic Ocean, its plumes

It is hard to describe being at a shuttle launch, for it has little in common with watching a launch on television. I was overwhelmed by the danger, the power, and the beauty of it. When the voice of Mission Control approached T-minus 1 second, it felt as though my heart was stopping, and I couldn't breathe. Then, as the shuttle lifted off so gracefully, rising higher and higher in the dawn light, my whole body seemed to lift with it.

in March of 2001. We gathered at the Space Center at four in the morning on Thursday, March 8, and were bused to the launch pad at about five a.m. It was cold—about forty-five degrees—and dark. As we lined up along a small river across from the launchpad, it was very quiet, except for the cries of birds circling overhead.

Discovery lifted off from Cape Canaveral right at dawn. It was a beautiful launch. The rim of the sun had just appeared above the horizon when the voice of Mission Control came over the loudspeaker to start the final countdown. On the launchpad, the shuttle looked like a huge moth caught against the towering silos of its fuel tank and two booster rockets. At T-minus 7 seconds, the three shuttle engines were started, their power forcing the shuttle system to sway slightly off-center. As it came

of exhaust becoming first pink, then gold, then white as they spiraled up into the sky in the sun's first rays.

After two minutes, already at a speed of 3,000 miles per hour, the two solid rocket boosters separated from the shuttle and fell toward the ocean, where they would be retrieved and brought back for refitting. The shuttle now appeared as a ball of fire shooting upward. After eight minutes, the shuttle, now out of sight, ejected its empty external fuel tank. At this point, the shuttle was at near-orbital altitude and used its own smaller engines to give it the final boost into orbit. In less than nine minutes, the shuttle was in orbit 230 miles above the Earth, traveling 17,600 miles an hour.

It is hard to describe being at a shuttle launch, for it has little in common with watching a launch on television. I was overwhelmed by the danger, the power, and the beauty of it. When the voice of Mission Control approached T-minus 1 second, it felt as though my heart was stopping, and I couldn't breathe. Then, as the shuttle lifted off so gracefully, rising higher and higher in the dawn light, my whole body seemed to lift with it. As the ball of fire disappeared in the sky, it seemed impossible that human beings could be inside. After it was out of sight, I realized there were tears running down my face, and, looking around, there were tears on many faces. There was a communal feeling of having witnessed a secular miracle. And Jeff Ashby's bell had become part of that miracle.

The bell is one naval tradition that has been extended to space. Another is the tradition of having the ship's captain enter a personal note in the ship's log at the New Year as the clock rolls over. When the first crew of the Space Station celebrated the New Year, it happened to be the first year of the millennium. Commander Bill Shepherd made the following entry as a tribute to the Space Station Alpha (the formal name of the ISS), the new millennium, and the new world of space.

SHIP'S LOG 0000 01 JAN 2001

We sail onboard space station "Alpha"
Orbiting high above Earth, still in night
Traveling our destined journey
Beyond realm of sea voyage or flight.

A first New Year is upon us
Eight strikes on the bell now as one
The globe spins below on its motion
Counting the last thousand years done.

15 midnights to this night in orbit
A clockwork not of earthly pace
Our day with different meaning now
In this, a new age and place.

We move with a speed and time
Past that which human hands can tell
Computers programmed like boxes
Where only thoughts' shadows dwell.

"Central post" our ship's bridge aboard
Screens dancing shapes in pale glow
We guide her course by electronic pulse
In figures no compass could show.

Our panels set as sails to the Sun
With wake not ever seen but there
Only gyros feel the silent tugs
Wisps, swirls of such ocean rare.

On this ship's deck sits no helm now
Rudder, sheet, and rig long since gone
But here still—a pull to go places
Beyond lines where sky meets the dawn.

Though star trackers make Altair and Vega
Same as mariners eyed long ago
We are still as wayfinders of knowledge
Seeking new things that mankind shall know.

We commend to crews that will follow
Merit of the good ship we sail
Let Sun shine strong on Alpha's wings
A symbol, and bright star we long hail.

My interest became more the interest of the cultural historian, fascinated with the stories bells have to tell about people, places, cultures, and history.

A collection of English wedding bells with their stately handles that look like steeples.

AFTERWORD

As I read over these stories, I imagine Nannie marveling that not only have we gone into space and landed men on the moon, but there is a small, lovely bell that rings on the International Space Station as it circles the Earth sixteen times a day. So much had changed in the almost 100 years since she started out on her trip around the world. What would she think of the Internet or virtual reality? Or having the world of books at her fingertips on a Kindle? Or chatting with her grandchildren on Zoom? The changes have been amazing.

I also imagine Nannie being surprised—and pleased—that her adventures and the bells she collected became the beginnings of my own journeys and the stories that came out of them. Although I didn't circle the world as she did, I did go halfway around. And we both traveled

Author at the Temple of the Golden Pavilion in Kyoto.

by ship, Nannie on a Dollar Steamship Liner and me on a Hanjin freighter or container ship. Although many years apart, we both experienced the majesty of crossing the Pacific Ocean, with its vast emptiness and sweeping sunsets. When I looked out over that endless water, I often thought of her and wondered if she loved it as much as I did.

Nannie's interest in bells was mainly that of a collector. All through her life she was an insatiable collector of many things in addition to bells, such as buttons, postcards, old books, and semi-precious stones, although bells seemed to be the interest that she sustained the longest. My interest became more the interest of the cultural historian, fascinated with the stories bells have to tell about people, places, cultures, and history. I am still awed by the Zeng bells, their immense size and complex music, and by the power of the Tibetan bell to encompass so much of the sacred world

(BELOW): One of the Dollar Steamship Liners like the ones Nannie took on her trips. (BOTTOM PAGE): Hanjin container ship like the one the author took to China and back.

of Buddhism. I miss the peace of the temples of Kyoto and the days I spent there and the spiritual beauty of Iona. Change ringing, the carillon, and zvon continue to fascinate me, and I go to hear their music whenever I can, while I read in my daily newspapers about the debates over returning the Benin bronzes to Nigeria and the growing world of space tourism. On the Fourth of July, I look online to see what is happening at the Liberty Bell Pavilion in Philadelphia, and on September 21, I remember the Peace Bell will be rung that day at the United Nations, just a few blocks away from where I live. The bell stories continue to touch my life more than I ever expected. I wonder if that was true for Nannie, too; when she gave her talks to women's groups, was she drawn back into the memories of her travels and the bells she collected?

I also wonder if Nannie would have shared my fondness for my favorite bell poem, Friedrich Schiller's "Song of the Bell." I think she would have. She loved music, loved listening to the carillon concerts in the market square in Bruges and attending the opera at La Scala. Schiller's deeply humanistic poem traces how the hopes and sorrows and the dreams and failures of life can be imagined through the different stages of founding a bell. Each stage—making the mold, melting the metal, pouring it into the mold, letting it cool, and then breaking it out to release the new bell—risks failure, just as each stage of a person's life or the life of a nation risks failure. Writing not long after the excesses of the French Revolution, Schiller was all too aware what the ambitions and degenerations of men can do to their own lives and to the lives of their country. Even when warned, people did not always heed the better way. At the end, though, Schiller is hopeful, and, in the poem, when the new bell is broken out of the mold, it is whole and gleaming, ready to be lifted from the earth into the air to sing with joy. He writes:

Now with strength the rope is lending,
Raise the bell from out the ground,
In the atmosphere ascending,
Let it seek the realms of Sound!
Heave it, heave it, raise!
Now it moves, it sways!
Joy to us may it betoken,
Peace, the first sound by it spoken.

The song of the bell is many things through history, but, for Schiller, it becomes the song of peace, a lovely epilogue for this book of bell stories.

Fanciful flint glass bells, with coordinated handles and clappers, are thought to have been made in the Baccarat factories in France in the nineteenth century.

ACKNOWLEDGMENTS

A project that is created over twenty years requires sustained support. For me, that support came from three special people. The first is my sister, Wynanda Rosenberger, whose enthusiasm and curiosity about bells matched my own and who continually cheered me on, while searching out new bells for me to explore.

The second is my lifelong friend, journalist Patricia Nyhan, who picked me up when I lagged and, with a gentle voice, tried to steer me around some of the pitfalls of writing. I didn't always take her advice, but she was invariably right. The third is novelist/playwright James Magruder, who read the earliest draft of the book and encouraged me to continue. He also generously shared his contacts in the publishing world that led me to a loosely allied group of independent editors where I found my own editor and, from there, my designer and publisher. Without him, these linkages would not have happened.

William Boggess, my editor, took the first step by helping me shape the book, sharpening its focus and helping me balance the historical and cultural information with my personal experiences. Dinah Dunn then brought her brilliant design firm Indelible Editions to the book, becoming my valued agent and collaborator. I am deeply indebted to her.

Andrea Duarte of Indelible Editions deserves the greatest applause for her wonderful design of the book, transforming the photos and text into a visual delight. Thomas Singer contributed the lovely photographs of my own bells for the book, while Avram Dumitrescu created the book's fine illustrations.

Girl Friday Books took on publishing *Bells* under the leadership of Kristin Mehus-Roe. GFB provided me with a wonderfully creative team led by Leah Jenness and including Katie Meyers, Micah Schmidt, Paul Barrett, and Bethany Davis. Always courteous in including me in the decision-making, they did a remarkable job of publishing and marketing the book.

The other people who were most important to the book were the people who shared my journeys. In Japan, my guide and interpreter Kiyoji Tsuji introduced me to the life of Buddhist temples and the majesty of Buddhist temple bells. In Norway, Terje Tretnes took me to visit Sami reindeer herding families and helped me gain insight into Sami culture. In London, Mark Regan and the ringers of St. Mary-le-Bow shared their change ringing rehearsal with me and their love of bell ringing.

On Iona, I was helped by talks with Veni Vounastsou, Jose Brace, and Gilbert Mullen of the Iona Community, particularly Gilbert, who took me up to see the Iona monastery bell. At the Bok Tower Carillon in Florida, I was privileged to hear the magical music of carillonneur Geert D'hollander and to hear about his many experiences with carillons. And astronaut Jeff Ashby generously discussed his own fascinating life as an astronaut and the story of how he helped bring a bell to the International Space Station.

Other important conversations took place at home. The story of the bells of Benin was enhanced by early conversations with Benin scholar Joseph Nevadomsky, while Father James L. Foy contributed his knowledge of Irish bells for the story about Iona. Insight for the two stories about Buddhism came from my cousin Anne ten-Bensel, a Zen Buddhist, and my daughter Sarah Whitehead, a Tibetan Buddhist. There were also friends who generously accompanied me on some of my shorter bell trips; Katharine Blakeslee to the B & O Railroad Museum in Baltimore, Jane Milotich to Carmel Mission in California, and Diane Welling to the Circus World Museum in Wisconsin, where the ringmaster climbed up onto the bell wagon and played the bells for us. And I am indebted to the many institutions and individuals who granted me the rights to use their photos and quotations, such as NASA, the British Museum, Byodo-in Temple, and Parks Canada. Their contributions greatly enriched the book.

I am also grateful to the American Bell Association, the international association of bell collectors, for introducing me to the wide world of bells and to my friends in the Metropolitan New York Chapter of the association; Mary Levins, Joe Peknik, and the late Al Trinidad, among others. Joe was a curator of musical instruments for the Metropolitan Museum of Art at the time and often arranged for us to have our meetings there, a rare privilege. And I am particularly grateful to Bruce and Jane Clayton, both longtime leaders of the American Bell Association, who graciously read the manuscript with an eye toward vetting the technical bell information.

Finally, I owe a deep, personal dept of thanks to my mother, Jaan Walther, who read many of the early stories with the acute editorial eye of a former English and Latin teacher. She did not live to see the completion of the book, but I believe she would have been pleased that the family bells have taken on a new life. I also owe thanks to Gwen and David Hayes, distant Melville cousins, who brought Nannie's memoir and letters together in a single document that allowed me to follow her travels as she collected her bells. And I owe thanks to my brother Charles Walther for the extensive research he has done on the genealogy of our family, which gave me the context for Nannie's life. Finally, I thank my great-grandmother Nannie Melville, who was the origin and catalyst for the book.

ATTRIBUTIONS

OPENING

ILLUSTRATIONS

Page 3 Antique bronze bell courtesy of Ana Prego/Shutterstock.com.

Page 4 Bell tower courtesy of nadtochiy/Shutterstock.com.

Page 6 Temple bells courtesy of WovenSouls Cultural Images/Alamy Stock Photo.

QUOTATION

Page 5 The Great Bell Chant, courtesy of Thich Nhat Hanh, Plum Village, https://plum.village.org/library/chants/the-great-bell-chant.

INTRODUCTION

ILLUSTRATIONS

Page 9 "Emmanuel," courtesy of agefotostock/Alamy Stock Photo.

Page 10 Nannie as a young woman, courtesy of author.

Pages 12–13 The Dutch bells, courtesy of author, photo by Thomas Singer.

Page 14 Nannie in later life, courtesy of author.

Page 15 Mandarin hat button bells, courtesy of author, photo by Thomas Singer.

Page 17 Author in Kyoto, courtesy of author.

THE HISTORY AND CULTURE OF BELLS

ILLUSTRATIONS

Page 20 Ancient Chinese chimes, courtesy of Aizhong Wang/Alamy Stock Photo.

Page 23 Nao bell, courtesy of agefotostock/Alamy Stock Photo.

Page 24 Hoko-ji Temple bell, courtesy of Kiyoji Tsuji.

Page 26 Mission bells, San Juan Capistrano, courtesy of Richard Wong/Alamy Stock Photo.

Page 28 Taoist bells with Immortal handles, courtesy of author, photo by Thomas Singer.

Page 30 Meissen table bell, courtesy of author, photo by Thomas Singer.

Page 32 Mental Health Bell, courtesy of Mental Health America.

BELLS AND THEIR MUSIC

ILLUSTRATIONS

Page 34 Russian Orthodox bell, courtesy of Kusmina Svetlana/Dreamtime.com.

Page 35 Illustration of partials of bell, courtesy of Avram Dumitrescu.

Page 36 King David playing the chimes, courtesy of Lebrecht Music Arts/Alamy Stock Photo.

Page 37 Handbell ringers, courtesy of Chronicle/Alamy Stock Photo.

Page 38 English wedding bell, courtesy of author, photo by Thomas Singer.

Page 39 Meissen flower bell, courtesy of author, photo by Thomas Singer.

Page 41 Illustration of bell mold, courtesy of Avram Dumitrescu.

Page 42 Making the core, Rincker Bell Foundry, courtesy of dpa picture alliance/Alamy Stock Photo.

Page 43 Pour of molten metal, courtesy of Cultura Creative (RF)/Alamy Stock Photo.

Page 45 Bell Founder's Window, courtesy of Bridgeman Images.

JOURNEY TO CHINA: THE ZENG BELLS

ILLUSTRATIONS

Page 48 Zeng bells, courtesy of Ian Littlewood/Alamy Stock Photo.

Pages 52–53 Zeng bells, courtesy of Ian Littlewood/Alamy Stock Photo.

Page 55 Individual Zeng bell, courtesy of Imaginechina Limited/Alamy Stock Photo.

Page 57 Food vessel, courtesy of Heritage Image Partnership Ltd./Alamy Stock Photo.

Page 58 Wine vessel, courtesy of agefotostock/Alamy Stock Photo.

Page 60 Hubei Song and Dance Ensemble, courtesy of author.

QUOTATIONS

Page 61 "Song of Peace" (from "Symphony for Heaven, Earth, Mankind") by Tan Dun, courtesy of ©1997 by G. Schirmer, Inc.

THE BUDDHA IS CALLING: THE TEMPLE BELLS OF KYOTO

ILLUSTRATIONS

Page 62 Kiyoji Tsuji with Manpuku-ji Temple bell, courtesy of author.

Page 64 Sanmon gate, Tofuku-ji Temple, courtesy of Kiyoji Tsuji.

Page 65 Dry stone garden, Tofuku-ji Temple, courtesy of author.

Page 66 Bell tower, Hoko-ji Temple, courtesy of Kiyoji Tsuji.

Page 67 Eikan-do Temple bell, courtesy of Tibor Bognar/Alamy Stock Photo.

Pages 68–69 Ringing Chion-in Temple bell, courtesy of Robert Harding, www.images.robertharding.com.

Page 72 Phoenix Hall, Byodo-in Temple, courtesy of © Byodo-in Temple.

Page 73 Byodo-in Temple bell, courtesy of © Byodo-in Temple.

Page 74 Temple of the Golden Pavilion, courtesy of author.

Page 75 The Ojikicho bell, courtesy of Gakuro/Wikimedia Commons.

QUOTATIONS

Page 67 Beatrice Suzuki, *Buddhist Temples of Kyoto and Kamakura*, p. 47, courtesy of Equinox Publishing Ltd.

Page 75 Beatrice Suzuki, *Buddhist Temples of Kyoto and Kamakura*, p. 57, courtesy of Equinox Publishing Ltd.

RINGING THE MANDALA: BUDDHISM IN TIBET

ILLUSTRATIONS

Page 76 Bell and scepter, courtesy of author, photo by Thomas Singer.

Page 78 Vajra scepter, courtesy of author, photo by Thomas Singer.

Page 79 Hindu lotus bell, courtesy of author, photo by Thomas Singer.

Page 81 Hindu Nandi bell, courtesy of author, photo by Thomas Singer.

Page 83 Mandala, courtesy of Dennis Cox/Alamy Stock Photo.

Page 84 Base of Tibetan bell, courtesy of author, photo by Thomas Singer.

Page 85 Handle of Tibetan bell, courtesy of author, photo by Thomas Singer.

Page 86 Bell mandala, courtesy of author, photo by Thomas Singer.

Page 89 Bell on side, courtesy of author, photo by Thomas Singer.

QUOTATIONS

Page 77 Vessantara, *The Vajra and the Bell*, p. 56, courtesy of Windhorse Publications.

TURNING ART INTO POWER: THE BELLS OF BENIN

ILLUSTRATIONS

Page 90 Benin pyramid bell, courtesy of © The Trustees of the British Museum.

Page 92 Bird of prophecy plaque, courtesy of © The Trustees of the British Museum.

Page 95 Warrior plaque, courtesy of Adam Eastland/Alamy Stock Photo.

Page 96 Pyramid bell, courtesy of © The Trustees of the British Museum.

Page 97 Bell on warrior, courtesy of © The Eugene and Margaret McDermott Art Fund, Inc. Bridgeman Images.

Page 98 Pyramid bell, courtesy of © The Trustees of the British Museum.

Page 99 Oba head, courtesy of G. Dagli Orti/ De Agostini Picture Library/Bridgeman Images.

Page 102 British soldiers: courtesy of Pictures from History/Bridgeman Images.

QUOTATIONS

Page 91 Paula Ben-Amos, *Art, Innovation, and Politics*, p. 4, courtesy of Paula Ben-Amos.

Page 94 Paula Ben-Amos, *Art, Innovation and Politics*, p. 130, courtesy of Paula Ben-Amos.

Page 94 Paula Ben-Amos and Arnold Rubin, editors, *The Art of Politics; The Politics of Art*, Ben-Amos, Introduction, p. 14, courtesy of Paula Ben-Amos.

VISITING IONA: SCOTLAND'S "SACRED ISLE"

ILLUSTRATIONS

Page 106 Iona Abbey on the Isle of Iona courtesy of Silky/Shutterstock.com.

Page 110 Early bell, courtesy of Some Wonderful Old Things/Alamy Stock Photo.

Page 114 St. Patrick's bell shrine, courtesy of © Bridgeman Images.

Page 117 Illustration of bell shapes, courtesy of Avram Dumitrescu.

Page 118 Pelican bell, courtesy of author, photo by Thomas Singer.

Page 120 Abbey cloister, courtesy of author.

Page 121 Abbey bell, courtesy of author.

CALLING THE CHANGES: ST. MARY-LE-BOW

ILLUSTRATIONS

Page 122 St. Mary-le-Bow bell tower, courtesy of Bjanka Kadic/Alamy Stock Photo.

Page 124 Change Ringers, St. Mary's Church, Rotherhithe, London, courtesy of Jeff Gilbert/Alamy Stock Photo.

Page 129 Bow ringers with spider, courtesy of author.

Page 131 St. Mary-le-Bow steeple, courtesy of Neil Holmes/Bridgeman Images.

Page 132 War damage, courtesy of Commissioner of the City of London Police/ Bridgeman Images.

CREATING AN ICON: BIG BEN

ILLUSTRATIONS

Page 134 Elizabeth Tower, courtesy of Kovalenkov Petr/Dreamtime.com.

Pages 136–137 Houses of Parliament, courtesy of Annilein/Dreamtime.com.

Page 139 Bells in tower, courtesy of Look and Learn/Peter Jackson Collection/Bridgeman Images.

Page 140 Clock works, courtesy of Look and Learn/Peter Jackson Collection/Bridgeman Images.

Page 141 Big Ben, Houses of Parliament, courtesy of Eric Flamant/Dreamtime.com.

Page 143 Illustration of "Westminster Quarters," courtesy of Avram Dumitrescu.

Page 144 Clock face, Houses of Parliament, courtesy of Chris Dorney/Alamy Stock Photo.

PLAYING THE CARILLON: THE "SINGING TOWERS"

ILLUSTRATIONS

QUOTATION

REMEMBERING: THE BELLS OF WAR AND PEACE

ILLUSTRATIONS

RINGING THE ZVON: THE BELLS OF RUSSIA

ILLUSTRATIONS

FOLLOWING THE REINDEER: ARCTIC NORWAY

ILLUSTRATIONS

QUOTATIONS

Page 193 Nils Gaup and Knut Walle, Brask and Morgan, Aboriginal Voices: Amerindian, Inuit, and Sami Theater, p. 78, courtesy of Nils Gaup.

Page 206 Sami Legend, Video at Sampi Center, Karasjok, Norway, 2001, courtesy of author.

WITNESS TO HISTORY: THE LIBERTY BELL

ILLUSTRATIONS

Page 210 Liberty Bell, courtesy of © Cuboimages/Bridgeman Images.

Page 212 American postage stamp courtesy of Tamer Adel Soliman/Shutterstock.com.

Page 213 View of Independence Hall in Philadelphia in 1752 courtesy of Everett Collection/shutterstock.com.

Page 215 Paul Revere statue courtesy of Diego Grandi/Shutterstock.com.

Page 217 Signing the Declaration of Independence courtesy of Voinakh/Shutterstock.com.

Page 221 Women's Liberty Bell, courtesy of Universal History Archive/UIG/Bridgeman Images.

AMERICA'S BELLS: TRAINS, CABLE CARS, AND CIRCUS WAGONS

ILLUSTRATIONS

Page 222 Classic railroad bell, courtesy of radev/istockphoto.com.

Page 224 Trains at Promontory Point, courtesy of REUTERS/Alamy Stock Photo.

Page 225 "Best Friend of Charleston," courtesy of Science History Images/Alamy Stock Photo.

Page 226 Engine #119, courtesy of Rick Pisio/RWP Photography/Alamy Stock Photo.

Page 229 San Francisco cable car, courtesy of Paula Solloway/Alamy Stock Photo.

Page 228 Cable car bell, courtesy of author.

Page 231 Ringling Brothers bell wagon, courtesy of Circus World Museum.

Page 232 Player's seat, courtesy of author.

BELLS BENEATH THE SEA: THE *FITZGERALD* AND THE *EREBUS*

ILLUSTRATIONS

Page 234 The restored *Fitzgerald* bell, courtesy of Danita Delimont/Alamy Stock Photo.

Page 236 The *Edmund Fitzgerald*, courtesy of Great Lakes Shipwreck Historical Society/Bob Campbell photo.

Page 238 Map of Lake Superior, illustration courtesy of Avram Dumitrescu.

Page 240 Ship on seabed, courtesy of Great Lakes Shipwreck Historical Society/artwork by David Conklin.

Page 241 Bringing up the bell, courtesy of the Great Lakes Shipwreck Historical Society/Al Kamuda photo.

Page 243 Sketch of *Erebus* and *Terror*, courtesy of Pictures from History/Bridgeman Images.

Page 244 Map of Arctic, illustration courtesy of Avram Dumitrescu.

Page 246 First view of *Erebus* with side scanner, courtesy of Parks Canada, NU-WET-Erebus 2014-031.

Page 247 Bell found on Erebus deck, courtesy of Parks Canada, NU-WET-Erebus 2014-031.

Page 248 *Erebus* bell after it was brought up, courtesy of Parks Canada, NU-WET-Research 2014-004.

QUOTATIONS

Page 236 Gordon Lightfoot, "The Wreck of the Edmund Fitzgerald." Words and Music by GORDON LIGHTFOOT © 1976. (Renewed) W C Music CORP. Used by Permission of ALFRED MUSIC.

Page 249 Stan Rogers, "Northwest Passage," courtesy of Stan Rogers Fogarty's Cove Music, 1981.

BELLS IN SPACE: THE INTERNATIONAL SPACE STATION

ILLUSTRATIONS

Page 250 International Space Station, courtesy of © NASA/Novapix/Bridgeman Images.
Page 252 International Space Station Bell, courtesy of NASA.
Page 254 *Zayra* and *Unity* Modules, courtesy of © NASA/Novapix/Bridgeman Images.
Page 255 Astronaut Jeff Ashby, courtesy of NASA.
Page 257 Commanders Bill Shepherd and Brent Jett with bell, courtesy of NASA.
Page 259 Space shuttle launch, courtesy of Everett Collection/Shutterstock.com.

QUOTATIONS

Page 256 courtesy of NASA.
Page 258 courtesy of NASA.
Page 261 courtesy of NASA.

AFTERWORD

ILLUSTRATIONS

Page 262 English wedding bells, courtesy of author, photo by Thomas Singer.
Page 263 Author at the Temple of the Golden Pavilion, courtesy of author.
Page 264 Dollar Steamship Liner, courtesy of History and Art Collection/Alamy Stock Photo.
Page 264 Hanjin container ship, courtesy of Mark Sayer/Alamy Stock Photo.

ACKNOWLEDGEMENTS

ILLUSTRATIONS

Page 266 French Flint Glass bells, courtesy of author, photo by Thomas Singer.
Page 269 Handmade Portuguese sheep bells, courtesy of Cro Magnon/Alamy Stock Photos.

ATTRIBUTIONS

ILLUSTRATIONS

Page 270 Greek bells at sunset, courtesy of Leonid Katsyka/Dreamtime.com.

ABOUT THE AUTHOR

ILLUSTRATIONS

Page 288 Author at Great Bell Museum in Beijing, courtesy of author.

SUGGESTED READING

THE HISTORY AND CULTURE OF BELLS

BOOKS

Price, Percival. *Bells and Man.* Oxford: Oxford University Press, 1983.

Springer, L. Elsinore. *The Collector's Book of Bells.* New York: Crown Publishers, Inc., 1972.

Springer, L. Elsinore. *That Vanishing Sound.* New York: Crown Publishers, Inc., 1976.

NEWSPAPERS AND MAGAZINES

Greenfeld, Karl Taro. "Blind to Failure," *Time,* June 18, 2001.

The New York Times, May 21, 2020, coverage of Twin Tower ceremony.

BELLS AND THEIR MUSIC

BOOKS

Elphick, George. *The Craft of the Bellfounder.* Chichester: Phillimore & Co., 1988.

Jennings, Trevor S. *Bellfounding.* Buckinghamshire: Shire Publications, 1988.

Milsom, Michael J. *Bells & Bellfounding.* CreateSpace, 2017.

Westcott, Wendell. *Bells and Their Music.* New York: G. P. Putnam's Sons, 1970.

JOURNEY TO CHINA: THE ZENG BELLS

BOOKS

Falkenhausen, Lothar von. *Chinese Society in the Age of Confucius (1000–250 BC): The Archaeological Evidence.* Los Angeles: Colsen Institute of Archaeology, 2006.

Falkenhausen, Lothar von. *Suspended Music: Chime-Bells in the Culture of Bronze Age China.* Berkeley: University of California Press, 1993.

Lawton, Thomas, editor. *New Perspectives on Chu Culture During the Eastern Zhou Period.* Washington, DC: Arthur M. Sackler Gallery, Smithsonian Institution, 1991.

Ninghua, Mei and Xincheng, Tao, compilers-in-chief. *Ancient Bells.* Series of the Gems of Beijing Cultural Relics, Beijing: Beijing Publishing House, 1999.

Smith, Caron and Yu, Sung. *Ringing Thunder: Tomb Treasures from Ancient China.* San Diego: San Diego Museum of Art, 1999.

So, Jenny F. *Eastern Zhou Bronzes from the Arthur M. Sackler Collection,* Volume 3. New York: Abrams, 1995.

So, Jenny F. *Music in the Age of Confucius.* Washington, DC: Freer Gallery of Art and Arthur M. Sackler Gallery, Smithsonian Institution, 2000.

RECORDINGS AND VIDEOS

Behring Global Education Foundation, "Bianzhong of Marquis Yi: Traditional Chinese Bells," YouTube, 2017.

Dun, Tan. *Symphony 1997.* Jas Hennesey & Co., 1997.

The Hubei Song and Dance Ensemble, *The Imperial Bells of China,* Concert at the Cathedral of St. John the Divine in New York City, 1989.

THE BUDDHA IS CALLING: THE TEMPLE BELLS OF KYOTO

BOOKS AND ARTICLES

Bechert, Heinz and Gombrich, Richard, editors. *The World of Buddhism: Buddhist Monks and Nuns in Society and Culture.* London: Thames and Hudson Ltd., 1984.

Byodoin Temple. "Hoshokan Byodoin Museum Catalogue." Japan, 2014.

Hiroshi, Sugiyama. *Bonsho (Temple Bell). The Art of Japan* 12, Issue no. 355, The Agency of Culture, Tokyo National Museum, Kyoto National Museum, Nara National Museum, December 15, 1995.

Murata Manufacturing Company. "The Ohjikicho Temple Bell," *The Japanese Craftsman.* www.murata.com.

Richie, Donald and Georges, Alexandre. *The Temples of Kyoto.* Rutland, Vermont, and Tokyo, Japan: Charles E. Tuttle Company, 1995.

Suzuki, Beatrice Lane. *Buddhist Temples of Kyoto and Kamakura, Eastern Buddhist Voices,* Volume 4. Bristol, Connecticut: Equinox Publishing Ltd, 2013.

Suzuki, Shunryu. *Zen Mind, Beginner's Mind.* Boulder, Colorado: Shambhala, 2011.

Tomoshige, Tatsuko. "In Search of Bells: A Musical Pilgrimage." American Bell Association, *The Bell Tower,* July–August, 1995.

Unno, Taitetsu. *River of Fire, River of Water: An Introduction to the Pure Land Tradition of Shin Buddhism.* New York: Doubleday, 1998.

RINGING THE MANDALA: BUDDHISM IN TIBET

BOOKS

Bechard, Heinz, and Gombrich, Richard. *The World of Buddhism.* London: Thames and Hudson, 1984.

Beer, Robert. *Handbook of Tibetan Buddhist Symbols.* Boston: Shambhala Publications, 2003.

Laird, Thomas. *The Story of Tibet: Conversations with the Dalai Lama.* New York: Grove Press, 2006.

Leidy, Denise Patry, and Thurman, Robert. *Mandala: The Architecture of Enlightenment.* New York: Asia Society, 1998.

Powers, John. *A Concise Introduction to Tibetan Buddhism.* Ithaca, New York: Snow Lion Publications, 2008.

Rice, John Henry and Durham, Jeffrey S. *Awaken: A Tibetan Buddhist Journey Toward Enlightenment.* New Haven: Yale University Press, 2020.

Snellgrove, David, and Richardson, Hugh. *A Cultural History of Tibet.* Boston: Shambhala Publications 1995.

Vessantara. *Meeting the Buddhas: A Guide to Buddhas, Bodhisattvas, and Tantric Deities.* Birmingham: Windhorse Publications, 1993.

Vessantara. *The Vajra and the Bell.* Birmingham: Windhorse Publications, 2001.

TURNING ART INTO POWER: THE BELLS OF BENIN

BOOKS AND ARTICLES

Ben-Amos, Paula. *Art, Innovation, and Politics in Eighteenth-Century Benin.* Bloomington, Indiana: Indiana University Press, 1999.

Ben-Amos, Paula, and Arnold Rubin, editors. *The Art of Power, The Power of Art: Studies in Benin Iconography.* Los Angeles: Museum of Cultural History, University of California at Los Angeles, 1983.

Curnow, Kathy. "The Art of Fasting: Benin's Ague Ceremony," *African Arts,* Volume XXX, Number 4, Autumn, 1997.

Freyer, Bryna. *Royal Benin Art: In the Collection of the National Museum of African Art.* Washington, DC: Smithsonian Institution Press, 1987.

Marshall, Alex, "Imagining a New Home for the Benin Bronzes," *The New York Times,* November 14, 2020.

The Metropolitan Museum of Art. *Art and Oracle: African Art and Rituals of Divination.* New York: Metropolitan Museum of Art, 2000.

Neaher, Nancy C. "Nigerian Bronze Bells." *African Arts,* Volume XII, Number 3, May, 1979.

Nevadomsky, Joseph. "Contemporary Art and Artists in Benin City." *African Arts,* Volume XXX, Number 4, Autumn, 1997.

Nevadomsky, Joseph. "Studies in Benin Art and Material Culture, 1897–1997." *African Arts,* Volume XXX, Number 3, Summer, 1997.

Plankensteiner, Barbara, editor. *Benin Kings and Rituals: Court Arts from Nigeria.* Ghent, Belgium: Snoeck Publishers, 2007.

Collections in the National Museum of African Art, Washington, DC, the Metropolitan Museum of Art, New York, and the British Museum, London.

VISITING IONA: SCOTLAND'S "SACRED ISLE"

BOOKS AND ARTICLES

Adamnan. *Life of Saint Columba.* William Reeves, editor. Reprinted from the *Historians of Scotland,* Edmonston and Douglas, 1874.

Bitel, Lisa M. *Isle of the Saints: Monastic Settlement and Christian Community in Early Ireland.* Ithaca, New York: Cornell University Press, 1990.

Bourke, Cormac. "Early Irish Hand-Bells." *Journal of the Royal Society of Antiquaries of Ireland,* Vol. 110, Dublin: Elo Press Ltd., 1980.

Lehane, Brendan, *Early Celtic Christianity,* London: Constable and Company Ltd, 1994.

Low, Mary. *Celtic Christianity and Nature: Early Irish and Hebridean Traditions.* Edinburgh: Edinburgh University Press, 1996.

MacArthur, E. Mairi. *Columba's Island: Iona from Past to Present.* Edinburgh: Edinburgh University Press, 1995.

MacLeod, Fiona. *The Isle of Dreams.* Portland, Maine: Thomas B. Mosher, 1905.

McNamara, Martin. "Celtic Scriptures: Text and Commentary." *An Introduction to Celtic Christianity,* James P. Mackey, editor, Edinburgh: T&T Clark, 1989.

McNeill, F. Marian. *An Iona Anthology.* Glasgow: The Iona Community, 1947.

Royal Commission on the Ancient and Historical Monuments of Scotland, Volume 4. *Iona.* 1982.

Ryan, John, S. J. *Irish Monasticism: Origins and Development.* Dublin: Four Courts Press, 2nd edition reprint, 1992.

CALLING THE CHANGES: ST. MARY-LE-BOW

BOOKS AND ARTICLES: ST. MARY-LE-BOW

Cobb, Charles. *London City Churches.* New York: Holmes & Meier Publishers, Inc., revised edition, 1977.

Jeffery, Paul. *The City Churches of Sir Christopher Wren.* London: The Hambledon Press, 1996.

McCulloch, Joseph. *The Pictoral History of St. Mary-le-Bow: The Church of Bow Bells.* London: Pitkin Pride of Britain Books, 1964.

Regan, Mark. "Gordon Selfridge and the 1933 Restoration of Bow Bells." *The Ringing World,* No. 4469/70, December 20/27, 1996.

Regan, Mark. "A Short History of the Bells of St. Mary le Bow." Pamphlet, 1997.

Royal Commission on the Historical Monuments of England. *The City of London Churches, A Pictoral Rediscovery.* London: Collins & Brown Ltd., 1998. (Photographs by Derek Kendall).

BOOKS: CHANGE RINGING

Camp, John. *Bell Ringing: Chimes, Carillons, Handbells: The World of the Bell and the Ringer.* New York: A. S. Barnes and Company, 1974.

Camp, John. *In Praise of Bells: The Folklore and Traditions of British Bells.* London: Robert Hall, 1988.

Cook, William. *The Society of College Youths 1937–1987.* London: The Ancient Society of College Youths, 1987.

Hatch, Eric. *The Little Book of Bells.* New York: Hawthorn Books, Inc., 1964.

Ingram, Tom. *Bells in England.* London: David & Charles Publishers, 1954.

Wilson, Wilfrid G. *Change Ringing: The Art and Science of Change Ringing on Church and Hand Bells.* London: Faber and Faber, 1965.

CREATING AN ICON: BIG BEN

BOOKS

Houses of Parliament. *Big Ben and the Elizabeth Tower.* House of Lords and House of Commons, 2012.

McDonald, Peter. *Big Ben: The Bell, the Clock and the Tower.* Phoenix Mill, Gloucestershire: Sutton Publishing Ltd., 2004.

McKay, Chris. *Big Ben: The Great Clock and the Bells at the Palace of Westminster.* Oxford: Oxford University Press, 2010.

Westcott, Wendell. *Bells and Their Music.* New York: G. P. Putnam's Sons, 1970.

PLAYING THE CARILLON: THE "SINGING TOWERS"

BOOKS AND ARTICLES

Barnes, Ronald. "The North American Carillon Movement: The Instrument, Its Players and Its Music." *Bulletin of the Guild of Carillonneurs in North America,* Vol. XXXVI, January, 1987.

De Turk, William. "William Gorham Rice and the North American Carillon Movement." *Bulletin of the Guild of Carillonneurs of North America,* Vol. XXXIX, 1990.

Gouwens, John. *Campanology: A Publication of the North American Carillon School.* North American Carillon School, 2013.

Johnston, Jill. *England's Child: The Carillon and the Casting of Big Bells.* San Francisco: Cadmus Editions, 2008.

Keldermans, Karel and Linda. *Carillon: The Evolution of a Concert Instrument in North America.* Springfield, Illinois: Springfield Park District, 1996.

Lehr, André. *The Art of the Carillon in the Low Countries.* Tielt, Belgium: Lanoo Printers and Publishers, 1991.

Price, Frank Percival. *The Carillon.* London: Oxford University Press, 1933.

Rice, William Gorham. *The Carillon in Literature.* New York: John Lane Company, Press of Eaton & Gettinger, 1915.

Rice, William Gorham. *Carillons of Belgium and Holland.* New York: John Lane Company, 1914.

Rombouts, Luc. *Singing Bronze: A History of Carillon Music.* Leuven, Belgium: Leuven University Press, 2014.

Smith, Margaret. *The Edward Bok Legacy: A History of Bok Tower Gardens.* Lake Wales, Florida: The Bok Tower Gardens Foundation, Inc., 2002.

Swagger, Brian. *A History of the Carillon: Its Origins, Development, and Evolution as a Musical Instrument.* Doctoral Dissertation, Indiana University, 1993.

REMEMBERING: THE BELLS OF WAR AND PEACE

BOOKS AND ARTICLES

Clements, Brian, Teague, Alexandra, and Rader, Dean. *Bullets into Bells.* Boston: Beacon Press, 2017.

Elliott, Joan. "War and Peace." *The Bell Tower,* January–February, 2015.

Freeman, Kirrily. "The Bells, Too, Are Fighting: The Fate of European Church Bells in the Second World War." *Canadian Journal of History,* December, 2008.

Price, Percival. *Campanology, Europe 1945–1947: A Report on the Condition of Carillons on the Continent of Europe as a Result of the Recent War.* Ann Arbor, Michigan: University of Michigan Press, 1948.

Thorne, Stephen J. "The Seizing of Europe's Bells." *Legion: Canada's Military History Magazine,* November 21, 2018.

RINGING THE ZVON: THE BELLS OF RUSSIA

BOOKS

Billington, James H. *The Icon and the Axe: An Interpretive History of Russian Culture.* New York: Vintage Books, 1970.

Clendenin, Daniel B. *Eastern Orthodox Christianity: A Western Perspective.* Grand Rapids, Michigan: Baker Academic, Second Edition, 2003.

Herrin, Judith. *Byzantium: The Surprising Life of a Medieval Empire.* Princeton, New Jersey: Princeton University Press, 2007.

McGuckin, John Anthony. *The Eastern Orthodox Church, A New History.* New Haven: Yale University Press, 2020.

Williams, Edward V. *The Bells of Russia: History and Technology.* Princeton, New Jersey: Princeton University Press, 1985.

WEBSITE ARTICLES

Blagovest Bells (www.russianbells.com):

- "A Brief History of Russian Bells." Fr. Roman Lukianov.

- "Overview of the Origin and History of Russian Bell-Founding." John Burnett.

- "Ring Like the Masters of Old!" Blagovest Bells.

- "The Typikon of the Russian Orthodox Church."

- "Zvons." (Listing of oral recordings of Russian bell ringing).

The Return. Harvard University and St. Daniel Monastery (www.danilovbells.com):

- "Historic Bells." Pylyaev, M. I.

- "On Bell Ringing in Russia." S. V. Smolensky.

- "The Phenomenon of Russian Church Bell Ringing." Hierodeacon Roman.

- "The Ruination of Church Bells in 1920–1930." V. R. Kozlov.

- "Russian Art of Bell-Ringing." A. S. Yareshko.

FOLLOWING THE REINDEER: ARCTIC NORWAY

BOOKS AND ARTICLES

Benko, Jessica. "Sami: The People Who Walk with Reindeer." *National Geographic Magazine,* November 2011.

Bjorklund, Ivar. *Sami—Becoming a Nation.* Tromso: Tromso University Museum, 2000.

Brask, Per and Morgan, William. *Aboriginal Voices: Amerindian, Inuit, and Sami Theater.* Baltimore: The Johns Hopkins University Press, 1992.

Gaski, Harold, editor. *In the Shadow of the Midnight Sun: Contemporary Sami Prose and Poetry.* Karasjok: Davvi Girji o.s., 1996.

Gaski, Harald, editor. *Sami Culture in a New Era: The Norwegian Sami Experience.* Karasjok: Davvi Girji o.s., 1997.

Haetta, Odd Mathis. *The Ancient Religion and Folk-Beliefs of the Sami.* Alta: Alta Museum, 1994.

Haetta, Odd Mathis. *The Sami; an Indigenous People of the Arctic.* Karasjok: Davvi Girji, 1996.

Howarth, David. *We Die Alone.* North Salem, New York: The Adventure Library, 1996.

Lehtola, Veli-Pekka. *The Sami People: Traditions in Transition.* Fairbanks, Alaska: University of Alaska Press, Revised Second Edition, 2004.

Manker, Ernst and Tryckare, Tre. *People of Eight Seasons.* New York: Crescent Books, 1972.

Paine, Robert. *Herds of the Tundra: A Portrait of Saami Reindeer Pastoralism.* Washington, DC: Smithsonian Institution Press, 1994.

Pelto, Pertti J. *The Snowmobile Revolution: Technology and Societal Change in the Arctic.* Menlo Park, California: Cummings Publishing Company, 1973.

WITNESS TO HISTORY: THE LIBERTY BELL

BOOKS

The Bell Tower Supplement. *The Liberty Bell: Symbol of Freedom.* American Bell Association, May–June 1991 (reprinted from "The Story of the Liberty Bell Since 1751" by

Paul Ditzel, *The American Legion Magazine*, December 1968).

Boland, Michael Charles. *Ring in the Jubilee: The Epic of America's Liberty Bell.* Riverside, Connecticut: The Chatham Press, Inc., 1973.

Nash, Gary B. *The Liberty Bell.* New Haven, Connecticut: Yale University Press, 2010.

Sands, Robert W. and Bartlett, Alexander B. *Independence Hall and the Liberty Bell.* Charleston, South Carolina: Arcadia Publishing, 2012.

Springer, L. Elsinore. *That Vanishing Sound.* New York: Crown Publishers, Inc., 1976.

Vile, John R. *The Liberty Bell and Its Legacy.* Santa Barbara, California: ABC-CLIO, 2020.

AMERICA'S BELLS: TRAINS, CABLE CARS, AND CIRCUS WAGONS

BOOKS AND ARTICLES

Clauss, Francis J. *Cable Cars Past and Present.* Menlo Park, California: Briarcliff Press, 1982.

Dahlinger, Fred. "The Ringling Bros. Bell Wagon," *Bandwagon.* November–December, 1984.

Fox, C. P. *Horse Drawn Wagon Collection at the Circus World Museum.* Milwaukee, Wisconsin: The Great Circus Parade, Inc., 1994.

Goeppinger, Neil. *Large Bells of America.* Sarasota, Florida: Suncoast Digital Press, Inc., 2016.

Hubbard, Freeman H. "Romance of Locomotive Bells." *Railroad Magazine,* March 1949, Reprinted in American Bell Association, Bell Tower, July–August, 2009.

Laubscher, Rick. *On Track: A Field Guide to San Francisco's Historic Streetcars and Cable Cars.* Market Street Railway, 2014.

Wolmar, Christian. *The Great Railroad Revolution: The History of Trains in America.* New York: Public Affairs, 2012.

Yenne, Bill, editor. *The Romance & Folklore of North America's Railroads.* New York: Smithmark Publishers, 1995.

BELLS BENEATH THE SEA: THE *FITZGERALD* AND THE *EREBUS*

BOOKS AND ARTICLES: THE *EDMUND FITZGERALD*

Barry, James P. *Ships of the Great Lakes.* Holt, Michigan: Thunder Bay Press, First Edition, 1973, Second Edition, 1996.

Bishop, Hugh E. *The Night the Fitz Went Down.* Duluth, Minnesota: Lake Superior Port Cities, Inc., 2000.

Farnquist, Thomas. "Requiem for the Edmund Fitzgerald." *National Geographic Magazine,* Washington DC, January 1976.

Lee, Robert E. *Edmund Fitzgerald 1957–1975.* Detroit, Michigan: Great Lakes Maritime Institute, Dossin Great Lakes Museum, 1997.

MacInnis, Joseph. *Fitzgerald's Storm: The Wreck of the Edmund Fitzgerald.* Holt, Michigan: Thunder Bay Press, 1998.

Schumacher, Michael. *The Trial of the Edmund Fitzgerald.* Minneapolis: University of Minnesota Press, 2019.

Stonehouse, Frederick. *The Wreck of the Edmund Fitzgerald.* AuTrain, Michigan: Avery Color Studies, First Edition, 1977.

Wede, Karl. *The Ship's Bell: Its History and Romance.* New York: South Street Seaport Museum, 1972.

BOOKS: THE *EREBUS*

Beattie, Owen and Geiger, John. *Frozen in Time: The Fate of the Franklin Expedition.* Vancouver: Greystone Books, 2014.

Canadian Geographic. *A Franklin Find! The Real Inside Story of How Erebus was Discovered.* Special Collector's Edition, December, 2014.

Cookman, Scott. *Ice Blink: The Tragic Fate of Sir John Franklin's Lost Polar Expedition.* New York: John Wiley & Sons, Inc., 2000.

Lambert, Andrew. *Franklin: Tragic Hero of Polar Navigation.* London: Faber and Faber, 2009.

Palin, Michael. *Erebus.* Vancouver: Greystone Books, 2019.

Savours, Ann. *The Search for the North West Passage.* New York: St. Martin's Press, 1999.

Watson, Paul. *Ice Ghosts: The Epic Hunt for the Lost Franklin Expedition.* New York: W. W. Norton & Company, 2017.

Woodman, David. *Unraveling the Franklin Mystery: Inuit Testimony.* Montreal: McGill-Queen's University Press, 1991.

BELLS IN SPACE: THE INTERNATIONAL SPACE STATION

BOOKS

Bell, Jim. *The Interstellar Age.* New York: Dutton, 2015.

Bizony, Piers. *Island in the Sky: Building the International Space Station.* London: Aurum Press Ltd., 1996.

Burrows, William E. *The Infinite Journey: Eyewitness Accounts of NASA and the Age of Space.* New York: Discovery Books/Random House, 2000.

Burrows, William E. *This New Ocean: The Story of the First Space Age.* New York: The Modern Library, 1998.

Dean, Margaret Lazarus. *Leaving Orbit: Notes from the Last Days of American Spaceflight.* Minneapolis: Graywolf Press, 2015.

Holden, Henry M. *The Coolest Job in the Universe: Working Aboard the International Space Station.* Berkeley Heights, New Jersey: Enslow Publishers, Inc., 2013.

Impey, Chris. *Beyond: Our Future in Space.* New York: W. W. Norton & Company, 2015.

Launius, Roger D. *NASA: A History of The U.S. Civil Space Program.* Malabar, Florida: Krieger Publishing Company, 1994.

Launius, Roger D. and McCurdy, Howard E. *Robots in Space: Technology, Evolution, and Interplanetary Travel.* Baltimore: Johns Hopkins University Press, 2008.

Launius, Roger D. and Ulrich, Bertram. *NASA and the Exploration of Space.* New York: Stewart, Tabori & Chang, 1998.

NASA. *Reference Guide to the International Space Station: Assembly Compete Edition.* Washington, DC: NASA, 2010.

Nespoli, Paolo and Miller, Roland. *Interior Space: A Visual Exploration of the International Space Station.* Italy, Damiani, 2020.

Wells, H. G. *The War of the Worlds.* "The Life of H. G. Wells," introduction by James Gunn, New York: Tom Doherty Associates Inc., 1988.

INDEX

ABOUT THE AUTHOR

JAAN WHITEHEAD has been researching and collecting bells for more than twenty-five years. Originally an economist, she earned her doctorate in political theory from Princeton University and taught for a number of years at Georgetown University. More recently, she has been working in the theater world and is the coeditor of *The Art of Governance: Boards in the Performing Arts* and the author of essays on art and culture. She lives in New York City.

The author at the Great Bell Museum in Beijing.